CURING STUDENT UNDERACHIEVEMENT

Clinical Practice for School Leaders

Philip Esbrandt and Bruce Hayes

Published in partnership with the
American Association of School Administrators

ROWMAN & LITTLEFIELD EDUCATION
A division of

ROWMAN & LITTLEFIELD PUBLISHERS, INC.
Lanham • New York • Toronto • Plymouth, UK

Published in partnership with the American Association of School Administrators

Published by Rowman & Littlefield Education
A division of Rowman & Littlefield Publishers, Inc.
A wholly owned subsidary of The Rowman & Littlefield Publishing Group, Inc.
4501 Forbes Boulevard, Suite 200, Lanham, Maryland 20706
http://www.rowmaneducation.com

Estover Road, Plymouth PL6 7PY, United Kingdom

Copyright © 2012 by Philip Esbrandt and Bruce Hayes

British Library Cataloguing in Publication Information Available

Library of Congress Cataloging-in-Publication Data

Esbrandt, Philip.
 Curing student underachievement : clinical practice for school leaders / Philip Esbrandt and Bruce Hayes.
 p. cm.
 ISBN 978-1-61048-536-4 (cloth : alk. paper) — ISBN 978-1-61048-537-1 (pbk. : alk. paper) — ISBN 978-1-61048-538-8 (electronic)
 1. Underachievement. 2. Academic achievement. 3. Education—Research. 4. School improvement programs. 5. Educational change. 6. Educational planning. 7. Educational leadership. 8. School management and organization. I. Hayes, Bruce. II. Title.
 LC4661.E75 2012
 371.2'8—dc23   2011027169

∞™ The paper used in this publication meets the minimum requirements of American National Standard for Information Sciences—Permanence of Paper for Printed Library Materials, ANSI/NISO Z39.48-1992.

Printed in the United States of America

TABLE OF CONTENTS

PREFACE

We, the authors, have a combined experience as educators of nearly eighty years. During that time with our students and our colleagues, we have experienced the greatest highs and the deepest lows, celebrated successes and mourned failures, planned to achieve lofty goals, and struggled to solve the incessant problems inherent in organizations. Throughout it all, we have never lost faith in the efforts of dedicated students, parents, teachers, and administrators to improve organizational performance and increase student achievement. We have learned from and been encouraged by the work of all of those individuals, and we have been blessed by the opportunity to learn from them. We have also struggled to identify and eliminate those forces that, by default or otherwise, have opposed those efforts. Where progress has been made, we have sought to share it and have it shared with us.

We are aware that a sharing among educational professionals occurs in district consortia, in professional associations, at conferences, and in many less-formal settings. What has been missing in these settings is a commonly applied systematic approach to learning about what works in education to produce better results, a common protocol to identify problems and to produce potential solutions, a peer review that analyzes the results attained in light of the strategies used under the conditions present, and a wider sharing of this information in a ready-to-use format. We offer in this book the beginning steps and the framework by which, we believe, the forces that support higher performance and increased student achievement can be identified and reinforced, and by which the forces that inhibit and reduce the realization of that potential can be eliminated. In these efforts, we believe, education can, like other fields before it, realize its potential as a profession.

ACKNOWLEDGMENTS

We are thankful for the many colleagues who have worked so hard to point education in this direction. We are indebted to those in other professions who have taken risks to learn about and identify what works, and we appreciate their willingness to share their successes and setbacks. Our students have been our greatest teachers, and our teachers, administrators, and parents have inspired us to learn by encouraging us to teach. To all of them we offer our gratitude. This book would not have been possible without the support and hard work of Tom Koerner, Lindsey Schauer, and Lynda Phung of Rowman and Littlefield and Kitty Porterfield of AASA.

Phil Esbrandt and Bruce Hayes

I owe a great deal to the countless people in my life that have challenged and inspired me. My teachers, students, their parents, fellow educators, board members, and others who have always expected improved opportunities within and better results from schools have taught me to never be satisfied.

I am especially indebted to my partner in this book. Phil has given me the opportunity to explore how to really make a difference in schools and to enjoy intellectual collegiality at the highest level. My parents, who always knew I would be a teacher, taught me the power of expectation and unconditional support. My sons, Greg and Geoff, showed me what it means to refuse to accept less than what is possible. I learned from them more than from anyone else how to grow and achieve in spite of how schools operate. My wife, Christine, kept my feet on the ground, my head forward, my heart ever hopeful, and picked me up when no one else had the courage to stand with me. To all of them, I owe thanks greater than I can express.

Bruce Hayes

God and my wife, Gloria Jean, haven't given up on us yet!

Whom does one acknowledge for a career that has provided challenges, learning, disappointment, and enjoyment? Whom does one acknowledge for the friendships, camaraderie, and love that have sustained one throughout that career? And whom does one acknowledge for inspiring the thoughts and devotion over many years to create new thinking in order to transform education and possibly other professions as well? This book is intended to transform educator thinking and practice for the benefit of all students. The design to support that transformation is applicable to many other professions that organize people and resources to achieve desired outcomes. An understanding of current practice, accomplishments, and views of potential desired futures is required. Who better to acknowledge than the persons who raise expectations of a much greater future through the ultimate transformation that provides permanent joy.

Phil Esbrandt

Curing Student Underachievement: Clinical Practice for School Leaders
Authors: Phil Esbrandt and Bruce Hayes

Book Errata Sheet

For aspiring and practicing leaders, it is recommended that you examine chapters 11-14 before starting the book from the beginning. In this way you will become acquainted with the expectations for performance improvement managed within the organization and the leadership roles emphasized by the authors.

Page 24—number 14, first paragraph should read:

Student Behavior and Performance Data: *All the quantifiable data and qualifiable information about individual students and student groups, collected and organized to enhance understanding of present behavior and performance, and used to improve organization and personal practices. These data are compared with the results obtained in similar and best-performing districts and schools and are used to establish the baseline upon which improvements and progress will be measured.*

Page 114—end of chart, divide the total score by 10, not five.
Page 114—last paragraph, divide the total score by "ten."

INTRODUCTION

Clinical Practice in Education

No shortage exists in the number of critics and defenders of schools and educators. The public debate for three decades has focused on test results and the nation's weakening competitive position compared to other countries. Yet, talented educators strive every day to encourage, guide, incite, and mentor students to improve performance and to develop the knowledge and skills needed to thrive in the twenty-first century. Educational practices have improved. Still, educators struggle to find answers to the most daunting problems, particularly low student achievement.

Reformers have implemented hundreds of different strategies and programs designed to improve performance but have not achieved consistent results. Success with a particular strategy in one place has not ensured similar results from the same strategy when used somewhere else. Entire libraries are filled with research studies related to school and student performance that fail to agree on a clear path to performance improvement.

Adopting the strategies that are reported to be successful elsewhere is not enough. Solutions need to be developed that are focused specifically on the discovery of the real underlying causes of problems. Can such steps be taken in education? For the last century and a half, medicine has developed processes, protocols, standards of practice, assessments, and treatments that range from the needs of one unique individual to those of epidemic proportion.

This book introduces educators to the fundamental processes of clinical practice in medicine and shows how clinical practice methods have been adapted for use in solving educational problems. Implications for new practice are examined, descriptions of clinical practice in districts and schools are provided, and many varied strategies are presented to illustrate the best use of clinical practice in grades prekindergarten through twelve.

A school board member was overheard to say, "We don't want to be like physicians who may not get the correct prescription and treatment until the third or fourth try. In education we want it done correctly the first time, every time." Well, it's not possible to be right the first time, every time. It is unrealistic to expect that any single program or practice will correct complex organizational and individual learning problems, and get it right the first time, every time. Unfortunately, in many districts and schools, it hasn't always been possible to get it right even after four or five tries.

Clinical practice offers the promise to education now that it did to medicine many years ago. The gradual improvement in medical practice that required more than a century to accomplish can be accelerated in education through adoption of an existing clinical practice design. Clinical practice is not a "one shot" reform but a process that organizes and guides the use of performance data, identifies the root causes of problems, and contributes to the selection, implementation, and monitoring of the best remedies.

The protocols of clinical practice that are the foundation of the training and practice of physicians have significantly improved our health and quality of life. The fundamental medical processes of diagnosis, prescription, and prognosis can be applied to educational problem solving. Specific protocols can be easily learned and implemented in daily practice to uncover real root causes, treat them effectively, and record and share successful strategies across the profession of education.

ADAPTING CLINICAL PRACTICE FOR EDUCATION

The field of education is in the same stage of development as was medicine over a century ago, with numerous unproven remedies for nonspecific maladies. The diagnostic expertise of most educators at the beginning of the twenty-first century is much like that of the physicians of the nineteenth century whose remedies varied from the use of antiseptics to the sale of snake oil. Like most nineteenth-century physicians, educators lack the evidence and experience necessary to understand which of the many available remedies has the greatest promise for success in each situation.

What is lacking in education is a comprehensive diagnostic approach that can identify problems individually as symptoms and collectively as syndromes, and treat them with appropriate interventions. Through daily practice and discovery of what works and what doesn't, through analysis of problems and data derived from interventions, and by subjecting case studies to the scrutiny of colleagues, educators will come to recognize symptoms related to specific problems and common syndromes, and ultimately learn more about the "real" root causes of underperformance and failure.

Medicine is not a perfect science, and physicians make mistakes. But modern medicine provides an important model that has a great deal to offer the field of education. According to the Harris Poll #61,[1] physicians are the most trusted professionals in the United States. Most people are familiar and comfortable with the routines, processes, and protocols used by physicians and, consequently, trust the judgments that are developed as a result.

Clinical practice has earned the trust of patients because highly trained physicians use standardized protocols in the collection, analysis, and application of data that pertain to vital signs of individual health. At the same time, new and ever-improving interventions have been designed, implemented, monitored, assessed, and reported for the benefit of all medical practitioners and shared through ongoing education, publication, and practice. With apologies to the medical profession for errors of over-simplification and in adaptation, a similar clinical model, utilized in the diagnosis, prescription, and prognosis of the underlying impediments in education is now available to generate trust among educators, families, and the public.

ART AND SCIENCE IN PROBLEM SOLVING

It was discovered early in the development of medical science that even when the cause of a disease was unknown, it might still be treated successfully, one symptom at a time. That is, even if rabies was incurable, by treating every symptom that presented itself, the disease, in rare cases, might be survived. In most cases, the patient died anyway, but each case increased the collective knowledge of medicine.

Ultimately, continued study of the disease and documentation of its symptoms and effects led to the discovery of its cause. Educators have spent most of their time and resource treating symptoms but have lacked the protocols and processes needed to discover true, underlying causes, and then to treat them appropriately.

In medicine, problem solving requires a consideration of patient-health history and a careful and thorough physical examination. Diagnostic studies may be done, but the availability and results of such tests, even those that point to clear conclusions, do not eliminate the need for careful observation, examination, and study of the patient within the context of the larger population and health trends.

Information and data collected from the history, physical examination, and diagnostic studies are analyzed to eliminate false leads, identify occasional abnormalities that are not related to the problem, and discover the root cause. If needed, specialist opinion and analysis is sought to verify a proposed diagnosis and prescription. This evidence-based effort ensures that patients derive the full benefit of their physician's scientific knowledge and enhances the formation of a diagnosis.[2]

Even as the science of medicine continually improves, the art of medicine remains crucial because the newest science and technologies do not always cut through the maze of confusing symptoms, conflicting physical signs, and laboratory data to reveal the critical clues that guide the best solution. The most appropriate treatment under these circumstances does not automatically emerge from test results but from judgment acquired through the application of talent, training, and solid practice.[3]

INTRODUCING DIAGNOSIS, PRESCRIPTION, AND PROGNOSIS

The modern medical protocols used in diagnosis, prescription, and prognosis can be used to guide educators. The identification of strengths, weaknesses, and needs of districts and schools that impact student achievement (diagnosis); a selection of appropriate interventions and remedies (prescription); and an accurate prediction of milestones leading to outcomes (prognosis) can quickly become the daily arsenal of education diagnosticians.

These protocols promote a systematic collection and sharing of remedies and interventions that are documented to improve board, district, school, teacher, and student performance, and lead to better decision making that guides districts and schools toward greater accountability and performance improvement.

For the last fifty years, diagnostics has been incorporated into the identification of the learning needs of individual students. Special education mandates have required that students be identified as exceptional when their abilities and/or performance differ significantly from an accepted normal range across a variety of measures. There has been significant success in dealing with learning differences and the needs of special students.

At the same time, however, the establishment of specific data-driven criteria has created an overreliance on testing, a loss of flexibility in selection of programs and services, a creation of a distinct and separate class of students, and a significant increase in the costs of education. Attempts to adopt diagnostics in regular education, including individual learning plans for students, have had even more mixed results.

Too often, the model selected for individualizing student instruction has been the one used in special education. A physician would not treat a less-than-healthy person with the same prescription used by a healthy person to maintain health without first discovering the nature, cause, and consequences of abnormal vital signs. To ignore vital signs invalidates the training and experience of the physician.

In truth, education's lack of diagnostic practice exemplifies the notion of benign neglect, and reflects Voltaire's observation, "The art of medicine consists in amusing the patient while nature cures the disease."[4] It is the combination of art and science in medicine that leads the physician to select the most appropriate course of action in the treatment of illness; and it is the developing art and science of diagnostics in education that identifies more appropriate and applicable remedies for failure of schools.

That combination of art and science is captured in *The Merck Manual*, one of the most important references used by physicians in the diagnostic process since 1899. The manual compiled, for the first time, the most important symptoms of physical disorder, organized by anatomic predilection, etiological relationship, and specialized therapy. It brought consistency to diagnoses; validity to the treatments prescribed, reliability to the outcomes of improved health and longevity, and fundamentally changed the design of medical education.[5]

Education needs its own equivalent to *The Merck Manual*.

MOVING BEYOND COMPLIANCE

Performance-improvement processes in schools and school districts are not as firmly established as the processes and structures that have evolved to meet compliance responsibilities. While student test scores and performance improvement have been concerns for over three decades, compliance requirements have evolved for over a century. Compliance requirements will not be cast aside to make room for new designs and performance-changing processes.

Performance improvement is a major link to improved student achievement, and many educational leader and teacher behaviors have been researched and placed into designs for job descriptions, evaluation procedures, and professional development programs. Yet, the expectations for improved performance have not been met by a majority of schools because their efforts to improve are incorporated into the compliance model without appropriate modifications.

This book provides the methodology to build performance-improvement practices into school and district operations without taking the place of compliance requirements and not being squeezed out by them, either. After substantial research into the performance-improvement practices of several professions, we selected the medical model of health improvement as the beginning source to build a model for performance improvement in education.

Each of the chapters is introduced by paragraphs that include the performance-improvement clinical-practice concepts for educators and those from medicine that are covered in the chapter. Beginning with chapter 2, there are two or more strategies designed for team use in schools and districts to help participants understand the concepts covered and how to use them to solve local problems.

A MODEST PROPOSAL

When the population of Ireland was facing one of its persistent famines in the eighteenth century, there was a great debate in the chambers of the British Parliament regarding what, if anything, should be done. As in so many cases past and present, the crisis generated a lot of talk but no real solution. Always ready to poke and provoke his contemporaries, Jonathon Swift made a "Modest"[6] proposal to solve the financial, social, political, and moral concerns, both spoken and unspoken, of the members of Parliament.

Swift proposed that the children of Ireland be sold as meat to the nobility at the age of one, thus relieving their parents of the burden of raising them, providing income to the poor, providing a new source of food, and reducing the population of the needy. His proposal was not modest, it was shocking.

While we do not propose that educational problems be solved by eating the nation's young, we would like to bring the same level of attention and action to the challenges faced today in districts and schools. Unlike the facetiousness of Swift's proposal, however, we are very serious about ours.

The clinical practice model (CPM) provides a framework for learning about what is effective in a variety of teaching and learning environments. Plans and actions that produce progress can now be documented and utilized in formulating new, more effective prescriptions that move districts, schools, and students closer to desired performance levels. The profession of education can produce and report, through clinical practice, a body of experience within a reliable framework that contributes to educator growth and higher student achievement.

This is our modest proposal.

1

THE CLINICAL PRACTICE CYCLE
FOR PERFORMANCE IMPROVEMENT

Educators do not use a common problem-solving process, supported by a common vocabulary, to organize the discussion about district, school, staff, and student performance. This chapter provides an introduction to the medical clinical cycle that is applicable to problem solving and decision making in education.

There is trust in the judgment of the family doctor. The physician listens to what the patient has to say, collects other important health information, identifies the cause of the problem, and prescribes treatment to make the patient feel better. Regardless of their individual personalities, faith in physicians' medical training and in the clinical process breeds confidence in their professional reasoning.

Modern clinical practice has evolved over the last 150 years and has been used in medicine to treat illnesses ranging from the common cold to HIV, cancer, and the plague. There is a tradition of thorough training, guided experience, and measured results that builds confidence in its use to solve a very wide variety of medical problems. As a result of individual experiences with medical treatment, most people have developed some understanding of and trust in the clinical process. The same processes and protocols that build confidence in the clinical model in medicine can be adapted for education.

In searching for a better way to uncover and treat the real causes of underperformance in education, problem-solving strategies used in many different fields, including engineering, law, the military, business, architecture, finance, and intervention psychology, to name only a few, have been explored. Ultimately, the clinical practice model has been selected here because of its foundation in training, clear protocols, records of precision and success, and the fact that most educators are familiar and comfortable with the process.

The clinical practice model (CPM) for education incorporates the same planning and decision-making protocols as medicine, organized in four consecutive phases identified as "Discovery"; "Solution Scenario"; "Implementation"; and "Assessment and Revision." Each of these phases is described briefly below and then examined in greater depth through a review of the entire clinical cycle.

PHASE I: DISCOVERY

Discovery begins with the awareness of a problem and the willingness to explore all of its causes. Research and analysis of performance data identify current district and school performance levels and discover the strengths, needs, and improvement opportunities involving students, employees, and the organization. The results of a thorough discovery are the identification of potential root causes of poor performance so that remedies can succeed.

PHASE II: SOLUTION SCENARIO

During this phase multiple, practical, and appropriate solutions are defined. They are discussed and weighed as parts of a general diagnosis that includes possible solutions to the problem. Clinical efforts include collection and analysis of data from many sources, including student behavior and performance measures, diagnostic inventories and tests, observations of staff behavior and performance, and records and observations of meetings among employees and among other district and school stakeholders.

Additional data are collected from interviews of teachers, administrators, students, parents, and other stakeholders, and the ongoing dialogue about trends, needs, and priorities. A deeper analysis of all available data results in an outline of key potential solutions. The solution scenario phase concludes with the design and presentation of a diagnosis, prescription(s), and prognosis that comprise the major components of an implementation and improvement plan.

PHASE III: IMPLEMENTATION

Planned interventions and strategies are implemented during this phase to solve the identified problem. In districts that are using the model for the first time, this phase begins with preparation and training of selected stakeholders, especially formal leaders, teachers, students, and parents that will be involved in the implementation efforts.

Prescriptions and prognoses are detailed and milestones are established to help monitor action and measure progress. This phase generates greater stakeholder involvement; educates appropriate stakeholders through workshops and coaching activities; records any new accomplishments; reports on measured progress and new discoveries; and provides a basis to monitor and assess the success of the selected prescriptive strategies.

PHASE IV: ASSESSMENT AND REVISION

All work is work in progress. Too often problem solving in schools is considered completed once a potential solution has been implemented. Problem solving in clinical practice goes well beyond implementing remedies. It includes measuring the impact and determining the value of the prescription, and considering modification or replacement of the prescription to improve treatment. The major goals in this phase include a review of milestones reached, measurements recorded, and progress reported. The results are reported to colleagues and used to determine if any other steps can be taken to obtain better results.

Assessment and revision efforts are keys to continuous improvement. New discoveries develop from the analysis of results. The analysis includes a comparison of the expected outcomes with actual results, and includes forecasts of new levels of success with modified or new prescriptions. Each succeeding attempt to continue the existing prescription or to implement a new one should produce further improvements.

THE CLINICAL PRACTICE CYCLE FOR IMPROVED PERFORMANCE HEALTH

The clinical cycle begins with an understanding that there is some level of dissatisfaction. Ultimately, there will be no beginning and no end to the cycle since the processes of diagnosis, prescription, prognosis, and assessment and revision are ongoing in the improvement of performance. Discussion of a problem must begin with the awareness of an existing concern.

The model is represented here as the face of an analog clock and the cycle begins at one o'clock. Like the hours on the face of the clock, there are twelve distinct and successive activities among the four phases in the cycle. Each of these activities must be taken in order; none can be ignored. Of course, it is always appropriate to go back to a previous step if more information is needed or to better prepare to proceed further.

The activities, phases, and effectiveness of the clinical cycle can be understood as a visit to a physician by a patient that is not feeling well (underperformance). Even when not ill, people are encouraged to go to the doctor's office for "checkups" to maintain their health and prevent serious problems from occurring in the first place (preventive health). Some also consult with their physician to improve good health, or like an athlete, adopt strategies that will optimize their performance (optimization).

Everyone understands that there are times when he or she will not feel well. That condition may be temporary—brought on by a lack of proper rest, a reaction to bad food, sprained muscles, or any number of other factors that result in discomfort, or worse. Discomfort may also be the result of disease, infection, or some other condition that will lead to further problems, even death, if proper medical attention is not provided. If the discomfort continues beyond a few days, most people seek the advice and treatment of a physician.

There is trust and hope that a well-trained physician will give a precise diagnosis, a reasonable prescription, a positive prognosis, and the result will be a return to full health. If the individual is fortunate, the medical treatment may cure the ailment and even improve the state of health because the treatment cured other underlying conditions that the person had become used to and ignored.

DISCOVERY—ONE TO THREE O'CLOCK

Districts and schools deserve the same benefit of treatment that is provided to patients by the best physicians. Figure 1.1 graphically represents the clinical cycle in education. The hours in the clock represent each of the progressive steps in the cycle. The hours do not represent that each step in the cycle requires the same amount of time but simply that each follows the protocol in a specific order.

The cycle begins in the physician's office with "Awareness" at one o'clock, which represents the understanding that the individual is not well. The physician will at two o'clock "Gather Data" from the patient that will serve as clues to determine the reasons for concern. By asking about patient condition, recent activities, and similar conditions experienced by other members of the family, as well as other related questions, the physician compares and contrasts circumstances among patients she has seen.

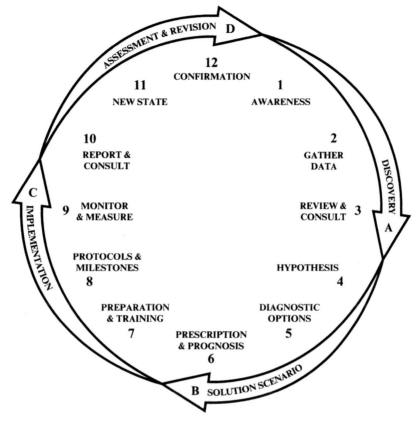

Figure 1.1   Clinical Practice Cycle

She will examine vital signs; observe the patient and look for indications of disease, infection, or disorder. The physician will "Review and Consult" with the patient at three o'clock about her observations. The patient's description of discomfort is coupled with the physician's trained and experienced interpretation of patient health history and vital signs.

SOLUTION SCENARIO—FOUR TO SIX O'CLOCK

The physician at four o'clock will look for syndromes, identifiable collections of symptoms, in order to form "Hypotheses" that will explain all of the evident vital signs, health and family history, and description of discomfort, taking into account her knowledge of viral and bacterial agents known to be present and viable in the community. By using all of this data, the physician will begin to organize a thoughtful consideration of the cause of the patient's condition in order to complete the hypothesis.

The doctor will share all of the likely and possible explanations for the patient's condition and what can be done to treat the problem at five o'clock. The "Diagnostic Options" are developed and represent the accumulated experience of the physician that can be used to discover a probable cause of the discomfort. Only when there is a reasonable and sound diagnosis can the physician (or the district or the school) proceed to a treatment that can be predicted to succeed.

This expertise is critical. Food poisoning should not be confused with appendicitis, pneumonia should not be mistaken for tuberculosis, and leukemia should not be misunderstood as anemia. The number of trials needed to build diagnostic accuracy is more than one doctor can experience. Physicians share their experience and knowledge with colleagues so that consistency and accuracy in diagnosis are improved throughout the profession.

"Prescriptions and Prognoses" are formed next, at six o'clock, and represent the treatments or interventions that can be applied to the diagnosed problem with a reasonably predictable result, called a prognosis. Every diagnosis has a number of potential prescriptions, each of which carries a number of different prognoses. No single treatment may be applied without completion of this step.

No clinically trained physician will select a treatment, however, until additional options are considered. The knowledge and research of the physician are used, in consultation with the patient, to select the most appropriate prescription. The pairing of both of these factors, the disorder and patient characteristics, is essential. Some treatments can cure the disease at the risk of death in one patient, while the same treatments may be insufficient to cure the ailments in other patients.

The physician describes the treatment and its possible side effects; she provides a prognosis for progression of the illness and recovery, the time required for treatment and other reactions, and experiences the patient will likely encounter during treatment. The physician reviews the costs of treatment with the patient, especially if new expensive prescriptions are recommended.

Together, "Discovery" and "Solution Scenario" lead to a viable diagnosis and prescription. When a district and school are viewed as the patient, it is important to consider the impact of the prescription and prognosis on both the organization and individual stakeholders. This balanced view is as critical to school and district leaders as it is to the physician's consideration of the implications of a prescription on all of the patient's organs as well as on the family and larger population.

IMPLEMENTATION—SEVEN TO TEN O'CLOCK

At seven o'clock, the physician provides "Preparation and Training" to the patient to facilitate recovery. Expectations for self-administration of medicine, ongoing therapeutic and rehabilitation exercises at home, and recording of vital signs are only a few of the instructions that a physician may provide. The physician and patient need to engage in an honest dialogue in which the doctor will explain that the first prescription, and every one after the first, must be considered preliminary and conditional until the patient has fully recovered.

After the physician "Prepares and Trains" the patient at seven o'clock, the patient, if not incapacitated and under hospitalization, is given the responsibility to implement the prescription and most of the recovery program. In the eight o'clock position, "Protocols and Milestones" are described by the physician so that the patient can monitor progress and compare the physician's prognosis with the patient's actual experience. Even if the patient does not require close supervision, the doctor instructs the patient in how to administer treatment, how to adhere to the regimen of care, and to report regularly to the physician regarding all consequences, no matter how positive, negative, large, or small.

Understanding the prognosis and the self-monitoring of progress prepares the patient to "Monitor and Measure" progress, represented at nine o'clock, through ongoing consultation and team work with the doctor. While the prognosis provides a reasonable assurance of recovery, the patient and treatment must be monitored for adverse reactions or lack of improvement.

If the recovery process fails to meet expectations (prognosis), the patient should "Report and Consult," at ten o'clock, with the doctor about progress concerns. For most patients, the recommended dosage and time frame are followed; patient recovery occurs according to schedule; and the patient establishes reasonable behaviors that maintain health over time. However, when recovery is slow, nonexistent with a recurrence of former symptoms, or new symptoms arise, the patient and physician reexamine the conditions and the reasons that led to the first prescription.

ASSESSMENT AND REVISION—ELEVEN TO ONE O'CLOCK

Most patients, as well as most districts and schools, abandon intervention processes before entering this phase. Even slight improvement leads many patients or school districts to discontinue the prescription before health has been fully restored. Many individuals possess a collection of partially filled bottles of old prescriptions in their medicine cabinet. If full recovery has not been achieved and results fall below expectation, it should be evident that medication levels, development of new behaviors, or treatment was not sufficient.

The original prescription and prognosis must be reevaluated by the physician in view of the progress and response of the patient. At eleven o'clock, a description of the "New State" or the current level of patient health provides the patient and physician with an understanding of the new level of health achieved through the first guided treatment, whether that level of health has improved or has deteriorated.

New information gathered by the consulting physician often results in changes to the treatment regimen, including a possible change in the dosage and strength of the medication originally prescribed. "Confirmation" at twelve o'clock provides the critical information to determine if a revised prescription and prognosis are needed. The patient may think that he can provide the confirmation by phone; nonetheless, physicians usually want to see the patient in a clinical setting for a follow-up examination to confirm the appropriateness of the initial prescription or the need to change the prescription, or maybe form a new diagnosis.

New levels of "Awareness" at one o'clock bring the patient full cycle, hopefully with more sensitivity to conditions that may have been previously unaddressed, and therefore, may require another cycle of improvement. Districts and schools should not approach performance improvement any differently from the cycle followed above. The typical educational intervention generally focuses on selecting and implementing treatment and little else.

The ultimate failure of most interventions in districts and schools lies primarily in the failure to

- accurately diagnose the real root cause of the problem;
- complete the full cycle of treatment;
- monitor progress continually;
- re-prescribe and provide new and more precise prognoses; and
- describe accurately the "New State" through a measurement and reporting of progress and changes that result from the treatment.

It is important to remember that dealing with the health of underperforming districts and schools is not like dealing with the common cold, where the fatigue and discomfort will be gone in a week with reasonable care. Underperformance must be considered a serious, "life threatening" condition that requires careful treatment and monitoring.

Only after the prescription has been administered and results observed can the treatment be more fully understood and appreciated for its effectiveness. District and school leaders have not received training comparable to that received by physicians and are not aware when interventions are incomplete, nor do they understand when performance health has reached a desirable level. District and school efforts to implement new programs and services are rarely monitored, and measures of effectiveness are not established in planning.

Even in those rare instances where measurements are taken, modifications are not considered that might make the intervention even more effective. Instead, educators tend to move on to other problems and do not consider how the organization has changed as a result of previous interventions. In cases where adverse reactions are noted, there is a tendency to abandon interventions early instead of adjusting them; and, programs, services, or processes that have promise for positive impact are discontinued.

The clinical cycle appears simple and straightforward. Educators understand its principles and that performance-improvement processes benefit from its application. The cycle serves as the model for the development of a precise diagnosis, the delivery of a reasonable prescription, the realization of a positive prognosis, and the creation of healthy district and school organizations that supports the fulfillment of student potential. The clinical cycle unites and focuses the energies and available resources of the organization to implement real continuous improvement.

THE GUIDED IMPLEMENTATION PHASE MINI-CYCLE (GIPMC)

After completing the full clinical cycle for the first time, additional improvement occurs through repetition of the critical steps in the cycle. Beginning with the second cycle, a mini-version of the cycle is introduced during the "Assessment and Revision" phase to take full advantage of the steps at nine through one o'clock. Through this mini-cycle, a new understanding of the relationship between the problem and the prescription develops to produce new and better results. Thus, there is a constant repetition of the clinical cycle in microcosm. "Discovery," "Solution Scenario," "Implementation," and "Assessment and Revision" phases are repeated two or more times following the first assessment and revision phase to move health and performance to even higher levels.

It is during these repeated mini-cycles that treatments are customized and new knowledge is acquired about the system (district, school, classroom, employees, students, etc.), about the quality of the intervention, the precision of the prognosis, and the direct and indirect consequences of the intervention. These cycles need to be repeated during treatment until full health is restored, a program of health maintenance is developed, or new treatment regimens are recommended.

The same sequence of mini-cycle implementation is needed to push performance levels in schools and districts past the level at which most are stuck. Graphically, the guided implementation phase mini-cycle is integrated into the larger clinical cycle in figure 1.2.

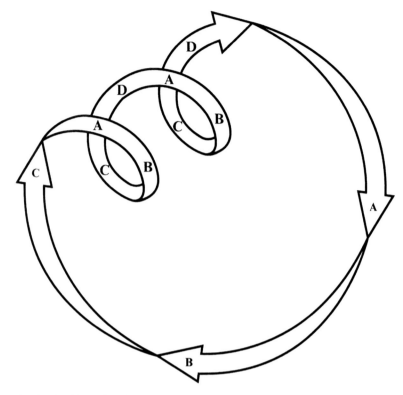

Figure 1.2   Clinical Practice Cycle with GIPMC

Steps A (Discovery), B (Solution Scenario), C (Implementation), and D (Assessment and Revision) in the mini-cycle are the repeated steps that occur in the entire clinical cycle. Since the physician, consultant, or team that is responsible for health or performance improvement has collected the basic background information and data about what will likely improve performance, a complete background workup is unlikely to be needed in a mini-cycle. While the diagram in figure 1.2 has two mini-cycles in it, any number of mini-cycles may be needed to achieve the desired results.

With new knowledge of the reaction of the patient or the organization to the first prescription whose implementation was monitored and whose results were measured and reported already, it becomes easier to determine how a modified prescription will produce improvements. In effect, the first and larger "Assessment and Revision" phase is followed by repeating all four phases—a process that refines and improves treatment.

In medicine, when a particular illness or disease fails to respond to a variety of treatments provided by a number of different physicians, the best diagnosticians start again from the beginning of the clinical cycle, collecting a new history, new examination, and diagnostic test results, to view the problem from a totally new perspective.[1] When schools and districts deal with intractable problems, a completely new workup with consultation of inside and outside diagnosticians may be most helpful to develop a more successful prescription.

EXPLORING THE CLINICAL PRACTICE MODEL

Each of the following twelve chapters will explore each of the twelve steps in the clinical cycle in greater detail. Part of that exploration will include strategies to use in training leaders and team members and provide practice in applying the elements of the clinical practice model in districts and schools. The CPM is a collaborative and professional experience, and all readers are invited to share observations, findings, and discoveries to facilitate the development of educational diagnosticians

UNDERSTANDING THE ANATOMY AND PHYSIOLOGY OF DISTRICTS AND SCHOOLS

Performance improvement begins with an awareness of current performance levels and what contributed to their existence. Understanding the organization, its parts, and how the parts impact one another produces the foundation for future problem-solving success. This chapter introduces the critical performance categories or surface and internal activities that have enormous impact on district, school, staff, and student performance.

> *Clinical Cycle Step 1—Awareness: The patient realizes that she is not in good health. Perhaps there is sudden discomfort and incapacity or there is recognition of a slow deterioration in health that has left the patient less capable of pursuing her preferred lifestyle and activities. In either case, she has been unable to successfully resolve the condition through her own efforts. The advice of a physician is sought.*

Feeling ill is a source of great discomfort and uncertainty. It is often difficult to explain exactly what is wrong, but the feeling persists that everything is not as it should be. The aches, coughing, upset stomach, and the more acute pain of a physical problem cannot be ignored, but people often hesitate to see a doctor. Things may get better if left to run their course. Sometimes they do, and sometimes the delay in seeking treatment can literally be the difference between life and death.

It is really no different in districts and schools. Educators understand when performance is not as healthy as it might or should be, despite the fact that everyone is doing the best they can. Leaders are so busy taking care of every crisis that erupts that there is little time to plan how to improve the larger state of performance.

Most are anxious to do something about less-than-perfect "performance health," but what is the real problem? Where do educators go for help? Most are left to wonder if they are suffering the same problem they have heard and read about in the journals, or if the problem is unique to their school, district, and collection of stakeholders.

Often, awareness of problems in schools is treated just like awareness of problems with personal health. Leaders wait to see if the problem takes care of itself. If it doesn't, decisions are made to treat the problem with "off-the-shelf" remedies. If self-treatment is unsuccessful, professional guidance is sought as long as costs cause less suffering than the course of the illness. Sometimes the problem may disappear if the staff can just get through the end of the year. The clinical practice model (CPM) provides insights needed to more clearly understand and respond to the awareness that performance needs to be improved.

TRADITIONAL HIERARCHY: THE SKELETON

If administrators and teachers are to become diagnosticians, they must first understand the anatomy, framework, and systems that make up districts and schools. The organization of districts and schools is very traditional and is re-inforced by certification and other legal requirements. For clinical practice to be successful in education, efforts to improve performance must go beyond the traditional to deeper views of the organization, like those internal views of the human body that contribute to successful medical diagnosis and treatment.

More-sophisticated and less-invasive medical technologies reveal details about internal systems and their interactions that make more-effective treatment possible. Similarly, clinical practice in education offers views of district and school structures, and adult and student interactions beyond formal roles and responsibilities, to uncover unseen activities that impact performance and student achievement.

School and district functions (SDF) are the individual jobs, roles, and functions used to organize the work of people in each district and school, often found in job descriptions and organization charts. There are nearly two hundred SDF that have been identified by districts and schools that have been engaged in the CPM, but experience suggests that there are about thirty-five to fifty identified core functions. Identifying the specific SDF in a district or school is the first step to constructing an improved understanding of anatomy needed to use the CPM.

It is not the number of school and district functions that matter but the ways that people are organized and interact that make a difference in results. Ultimately, however, the SDF are only a skeletal representation of how the district and school assign and accomplish work. In traditional organization charts, each role and function of the organization is depicted as a single box, and is connected by lines to other boxes to show reporting relationships and shared responsibilities.

These position boxes both define and limit the responsibility and authority of the individuals in each box. The roles and functions in school districts have been adopted from the early industrial and manufacturing model and used for many decades. These designs tend to separate and isolate individuals within the organization as shown in a typical "organization chart," in figure 2.1.

It has been assumed that organization charts provide clear distinctions among roles, establish clearer organization patterns, and promote efficient supervision, planning, evaluation, and the control of resources. This may have been true in a time period of little change, but the complexity of problems that cut across individual roles and the need for team work makes such an assumption obsolete.

The growth of specialties has resulted in an increasing separation and segregation of job responsibilities. Positions grouped around similar responsibilities have become "Towers of Expertise"[1] that are natural outgrowths of the way districts and schools are organized. Increasing mandates, rules, and department of education requirements for specialized training and certification have created unintended barriers that separate and isolate employees who should be working together.

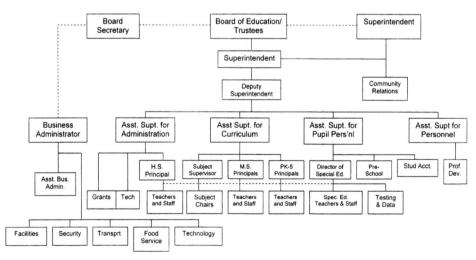

Figure 2.1   Generic School District Organization Chart

For educational problem solving, the study of SDF is analogous to the medical student's beginning study of anatomy. Without an understanding of the underlying framework of the human body, it would be impossible, and meaningless, to explore the other dimensions of medicine, including pharmacology, surgery, or therapy. Educators need to understand how the organizations in which they work are put together if they hope to get to the root causes of problems and select appropriate remedies.

At a workshop we conducted for new superintendents, strategies were explored for improving organization performance. When asked to describe improvement strategies, none of the participants considered reorganization as a viable option. All participants assumed that the organization structure they headed was a given, something that should not change unless forced to because of budgetary reductions, for example. As a result, most district and school structures become rigid and defy change.

WHITE SPACE AMONG THE ORGANIZATION BOXES

Individuals isolate themselves and are isolated within the boxes that define and position their formal roles and responsibilities. The boxes are easily explained, understood, and defended. To improve performance, however, there needs to be more than improved efforts in each box; there needs to be increased work effort and improved work quality between and among the boxes.

Even when every individual performs his or her own responsibilities well, the overall district and school performance can still be disappointing because individuals do not understand how their work is affected by and, in turn, how their own work affects everyone else in the organization, especially in the most distant boxes. Too often the "white space" between the boxes on the organization chart is simply considered "not my job."

Educators should think about and utilize the white space between and among the boxes. Within the white space are the shared responsibilities and common goals that unite and organize the work of many individuals with different job duties. Every individual needs to understand the extent to which the success of his or her own work is dependent upon and impacts others. Today, collaboration and cooperation are required for performance improvement.

To use a medical analogy again, anatomy provides the structure, but the organism moves only through the coordinated efforts of all parts. Each bone and muscle works in concert with other muscles and bones in ways each simply could not work by itself. And one of the great glories of the human body is its ability to nearly instantaneously respond to new challenges in ways not consciously dictated or planned before. Shouldn't this also be a goal of activity in districts and schools? (See Strategy One at the end of the chapter to practice application of this concept.)

This view of the organization takes work activities out of the neat boxes defined by organization charts, job roles, and job descriptions. Hierarchy is reduced in importance, and cooperation within the white spaces becomes more obvious and meaningful. The transition in thinking about improving performance in districts and schools beyond the skeleton of roles and functions (teachers, professional development, curriculum, students, and testing) is not necessarily an easy one. It is a challenge that must willingly be undertaken if educators hope to fundamentally improve their capacity to solve the problems that inhibit improved performance and higher student achievement.

Teams and team work are concepts with which many professionals believe they are familiar, but few have participated in work groups that are truly teams. Teams in the clinical practice model are not just groups of people brought together by a supervisor to delegate work. Clinical practice teams are comprised of collegial individuals who share specific responsibility and, consequently, hold each other accountable for improved results.

CONSTRUCTING A NEW ANATOMY AND PHYSIOLOGY

The traditional organization chart, supported by written job descriptions, represents only the first dimension of the district and school organization. The understanding that individual work extends beyond the specific roles of the box improves the potential impact of each individual and empowers teams to perform in ways individuals cannot. (See Strategy Two.)

ADDING ORGAN SYSTEMS TO THE SKELETON: CRITICAL PERFORMANCE CATEGORIES (CPC)

When physician knowledge was limited to use of the five senses and treatments for internal ailments were limited to trial-and-error administrations of plant extracts and bloodletting, recovery rates of patients were discouraging. Additional knowledge of anatomy and physiology of internal systems and their interactions dramatically improved recovery rates. Likewise, working in only one dimension of specific roles and responsibilities in districts and schools ignores the depth and breadth of interaction needed to plan and implement real improvements.

Defining and delegating responsibilities among carefully selected people, no matter how talented they are as individuals, is not enough to improve performance across the entire organization. Like the medical systems of the body—pulmonary, digestive, and nervous systems, for example—district and school organizations are served by the development and collection of knowledge contained in seventeen critical performance categories (CPC) that connect with each other and every SDF to unify and give purpose to the roles and responsibilities of the skeleton.

When considered as a whole, the seventeen critical performance categories provide the basis for improvement plans that produce high levels of satisfaction, increased performance health, and improved student achievement. Each of the seventeen CPC is based in the research of education and other fields related to performance improvement. The CPC are taken from the most promising results in fields of study, several of which have traditionally not been thought to be a part of the field of education.

The SDF define minimum roles and expectations, but the CPC determine the level of performance quality in the work accomplished beyond mere role functions. The recent Marzano, Waters, and McNulty mega-analyses[2] of leadership practices of principals and superintendents and their impact on student achievement are examples of two fields of study among the seventeen CPC that impact SDF and how the SDF are expected to perform.

The seventeen CPC are related to the work of every function, like "Customer Focus," "Team Work," and "Leadership," for example. Each of the CPC relates to and is found within the responsibilities of each of the SDF, and when the CPC are understood and applied correctly, they focus energy and resource on interventions that improve performance. The seventeen CPC are:

1. Alignment of Work Processes,
2. Business/Financial Acumen,
3. Customer (Stakeholder) Focus,
4. District and School-Wide Culture,
5. Effective and Integrated Governance,
6. Human Resource Excellence,
7. Information, Measurement, and Reporting,
8. Leadership,
9. Planning and Planned Change,
10. Professional Learning and Instruction,
11. Programs and Services That Accelerate Learning,
12. Staff, Student, and Family Interactions,
13. Structures That Nurture Improvement,

14. Student Behavior and Performance Data,
15. Team Work and Problem Solving,
16. Technology That Supports Programs, Personnel, and Students, and
17. Universal Acceptance of Expectations.

CPC Origins

These seventeen CPC have appeared as pieces throughout educational practice and in research but have not previously been organized as a whole. This new concept for organizing performance-improvement practice has evolved from experiences within the quality movement, from formal and informal training experiences of teachers, principals, and superintendents, from a wide variety of performance-improvement activities within districts and schools, and from research of performance-improvement practices in other fields, including business, medicine, and the military.

The seventeen CPC are the responsibility of every individual engaged in the work of the organization. Implementation of CPC concepts establishes higher levels of understanding, trust, and capability within all stakeholder groups, as well as greater success for selected prescriptions.

CPC Definitions and Descriptions

The definitions and descriptions of the critical performance categories (CPC) are presented in alphabetical order and do not reflect any priority among them. Depending on the specific circumstances in a district or school, any one or more CPC may be more essential than others.

The seventeen CPC have been defined to draw attention to their ongoing influence on district and school performance. In each category, only a title and brief definition and description have been included. It should be evident that the CPC complement one another and add significantly to the performance-improvement knowledge of individuals in every SDF position.

1. Alignment of Work Processes: *Precise adjustments made to district and/or school structures, work processes, and efforts that improve performance to increase student achievement and counteract ineffective processes and efforts that hinder attainment of desired results.*
   Alignment of goals, action plans, stakeholder involvement, and resources among work groups reduce overlapping responsibilities during implementation of improvement strategies. As new results are achieved, follow-up alignment activities increase the likelihood of continuing

success. A lack of alignment causes time-consuming conflicts and less-satisfactory results.

2. Business/Financial Acumen: *The knowledge and skill needed to guide the financial support of district and school operations, provide support for performance improvement activities, meet performance goals, and shape the management and control of funds for protecting the public's investment in the educational enterprise.*

   Protecting the assets of the district and schools is essential for better performance outcomes. This process cannot be confined to business offices and line administrators because such restrictions create suspicion, especially when resource allocations are reduced. Developing trust among stakeholders can take substantial time; and yet, trust is needed to make cost-effective decision making everyone's business. Districts and schools need the commitment of all stakeholders to use resources efficiently in planning and decision making.

3. Customer (Stakeholder) Focus: *The philosophical and operational expectation that employees will focus their attention and efforts on the needs of students and other customers of the district and schools.*

   The concept of customer focus is believed by many educators to be a concern exclusively of the private sector. However, customer focus in education insures that programs and services are implemented in the best interests of the student instead of the "other way around" where students fit within existing school designs and programs. In problem solving and performance improvement, the customers of district and schools are students, their parents, and staff members. However, in many situations, there are additional customers outside this traditional group.

4. District and School-Wide Culture: *The collective attitude, values, and actions that nurture the organization and its stakeholders as they learn, interact, and perform the challenging tasks necessary to meet and exceed expectations and to attain optimum performance.*

   All student, employee, and other stakeholder behaviors reflect the organization's culture that shapes all future accomplishments. The foundation of the culture is the belief system that comes from leaders and is carried throughout the organization by employees and students. The culture rests in ethical behaviors that are based in doing the right things in the right way. Culture, like the organizational structures, must not be taken for granted; a positive culture must be projected through actions based upon the beliefs by which the district and school want to be known.

5. Effective and Integrated Governance: *The distribution, delegation, and use of the authority legally invested in the board of education, directors,*

or trustees and integrated through district- and school-level structures and positions to accomplish desired district and school performance results.

This CPC has three basic components that all need to be in place in order to accomplish improved performance. The *first* requires the fulfillment of board roles that control and direct the making of administrative policy. The *second* requires that the board approve and oversee the establishment of the organization structures and positions to meet compliance obligations and achieve expectations. The *third* component requires that the board oversee and evaluate the superintendent/CSA's work to obtain desired student performance results. The work of every individual is related to the work of the board through this CPC.

6. Human Resource Excellence: *Every employee will perform in a superior fashion and surpass performance expectations. District and school policies and procedures that govern the selection, training, supervision, and evaluation of employees, along with recognizing, rewarding, and compensating exemplary performance, should all focus on preparing and sustaining every employee for success at the highest performance levels.*

   Human resource excellence is a complex concept based on a relatively simple expectation—the best available performers are sought to work in districts and schools. Yet, for many reasons the candidate pool or the selection process does not always provide the level of quality desired or that students deserve. Conditions change frequently and employees need to continually learn new skill sets. These concerns can be addressed by implementing practices that upgrade the competence and performance quality of all staff members.

7. Information, Measurement, and Reporting: *An operating system designed to maintain, update, and distribute the organization's lifeblood of information and data about district, schools, and students to continually focus the attention of employees, students, and other stakeholders on the level, meaning, and characteristics of current performance in order to design and sustain efforts to establish new levels of success.*

   Blood is an appropriate metaphor for usable information in this CPC. Blood carries oxygen and nutrients to sustain cellular, organ, and system function of all physical and mental activities. Blood also carries white cells to fight infection, immunities to prevent reinfection, and enzymes that help optimize performance. Districts and schools need to distribute similar nutrients to sustain themselves and to conduct the many activities that comprise the complex educational enterprise.

8. Leadership: *The purposeful day-to-day activities planned and accomplished by employees who have responsibility for the organization, or any*

part of it, to produce desired outcomes; these employees have authority to drive the organization to higher performance levels, and they are willing to be held accountable for the results achieved.

The primary role of leadership in districts and schools is similar to that of the brain and the nervous system in managing human body functions. The brain is the organ that coordinates all functions, often by responding to a variety of external and internal stimuli. The brain has enormous capability for conscious and unconscious control of the body's health.

The brain is the organ responsible for organizing thought and planning processes that support decision making and action. Likewise, leadership is responsible for organizing and supervising the collective action of others to improve performance health. When leadership behaviors are modeled and used appropriately, teachers and students accept responsibility for helping the organization perform more successfully over time. As more employees learn to lead, new levels of commitment and capacity become available to address more-difficult circumstances.

The human mind, without conscious thought, is capable of making corrective and adaptive decisions in response to threats to well-being. In a similar way, leaders help others and the organization become adaptive and responsive to circumstances and conditions that influence performance outcomes. Like the human brain, leaders help stakeholders adapt consciously and unconsciously to the impediments to learning and school success.

9. Planning and Planned Change: *Authorized processes used by individuals and groups to think about, organize, and implement strategies to create better ways to achieve optimum results for the district, schools, and students.* The purpose of planning is to identify and initiate practices that will move current practice and performance levels to preferred levels in the future. Every employee, committee, and team is expected to carry out effective planning with confidence gained through training and practice. Charting a course, adjusting direction, learning from experience, recording what has been experienced, and measuring the progress of the voyage are all essential exercises in improving outcomes. Each major step is guided by protocols used by all stakeholders to build consistent practice that improves performance in the district, school, and classroom.

10. Professional Learning and Instruction: *The lifelong process of acquiring and using the knowledge, skills, and attitudes needed to be an outstanding district and school employee with the intent of becoming a better resource and communicator, and teacher and leader of students and adults. Em-*

ployees have responsibility to define performance expectations and offer programs and services that support the development of knowledge and skills for on-the-job success.

One of the formal characteristics of a profession is the availability and use of a body of specialized knowledge transmitted through intensive academic preparation. As specialized knowledge expands and is changed by ongoing study, research, and experience, more effective ways to meet the needs of patients and clients are created. This growth is under the control of the professional.

Improving instructional and leadership skills of all teaching and administrative personnel is a major component within this CPC. For most of the training in the clinical practice model, it is recommended that parents, students, board members, and other stakeholders be included to prepare them for participation in performance-improvement activities.

11. Programs and Services That Accelerate Learning: *The system of programs and services that is planned, designed, implemented, evaluated, and upgraded to increase student knowledge, understanding, and skills. These programs and services represent the district and school's commitment to the success of all students. At least annually, the system is assessed to determine if all students are prepared to meet current and future academic goals. Discrepancies between the performance goals sought and the results obtained establish the basis for ongoing diagnosis and modified prescriptions.*

    This CPC supports connecting a student's present and future performance through the programs and services that support effective and efficient achievement of learning goals and content standards. The combination of programs and services constructs a "cognitive bridge" that supports a student's move from simple memorization to true understanding with the ability to express and use knowledge in new applications.

12. Staff, Student, and Family Interactions: *All the personal and interpersonal behaviors and communications that support the fulfillment of the legal and professional obligations of a district and school; provide direction, resource, and energy to improve performance; facilitate and guide students through learning activities; and make working together enjoyable and beneficial.*

    Interactions among key stakeholders are significant indicators and measures of the district and school climate as well as the level of trust needed for successful problem solving. Among stakeholder groups, the focus always should be on two goals: 1) increase student academic success levels, and 2) improve performance health of the organization.

In reality, increased student success follows improvements in the performance of the organization. The organization shapes adults' and students' interactions, behaviors, and attitudes that lead students to more effective self-discipline, greater awareness of themselves and the world to which they will contribute, and higher achievement. The quality of interactions among stakeholders contributes to both major goals.

13. Structures That Nurture Improvement: *Offices, departments, and committees that are authorized to resolve legal, regulatory, and policy obligations; and councils and teams that have responsibility to improve organizational performance and increase student achievement.*
Districts and schools authorize the formal and informal structures that maintain performance health and guide energies and resources for improvement. Administrators and teachers manage improvement efforts with a variety of stakeholders; and monitor, measure, and report progress. Work groups, councils, and teams are the primary vehicles of performance improvement, and their success depends on the support received by the hierarchical, formal structures that exist in every district and school.

14. Student Behavior and Performance Data: *All the quantifiable data and qualifiable information about individual students and student groups, collected and organized to enhance understanding of present behavior and performance, and used to improve organization and personal practices are compared with the results obtained in similar and best-performing districts and schools and used to establish the baseline upon which improvements and progress will be measured.*
By using data available under each CPC, it becomes possible for every SDF position to have an impact on student achievement. It becomes an expectation that every employee will contribute to student success, and strategies can be established for every employee to make successful contributions to the district's two primary goals.

15. Team Work and Problem Solving: *A team is a learning and problem-solving group with specific responsibilities to resolve issues of purpose and understanding; conflicts of philosophy, values, and opinion; relationships and alignment of processes to complete tasks; to improve operational performance health; and/or to increase student achievement.*
Historically, the description of a team was "two or more draft animals harnessed together to the same vehicle or implement."[3] The yoke and harness provided the means for the driver to control the animals to pull together. Today, we look to human teams to pull together just as powerfully; yet, without a yoke and harness for control.

The work of teams, today, is harnessed by common purposes, goals, training, and practice, with periodic reviews to provide feedback to improve team performance. As in sports, teams with poor attitudes, symptoms of "me-ism," narrowly defined roles, and an unwillingness to accept responsibility for performance that is less than best, do not match up well against teams driven by collective excellence and a sacrifice of individual benefits for those that benefit the team.

16. Technology That Supports Programs, Personnel, and Students: *Computer hardware, software, communications systems, and related technologies that support school and district efforts to accomplish work tasks; communicate with and among stakeholders; help board members, staff members, students, and parents assess current performance levels; and support the establishment, implementation, and monitoring of prescriptions to close the gap between current and expected performance levels.*

    Technology organized to support programs, personnel, and students, provide district, schools, personnel, and students with the information that supports improvement. Efforts ranging from developing lesson plans to the much more complex activities of a district-level performance-improvement coordinating council and anything in between are supported by local technology.

17. Universal Acceptance of Expectations: *Clear and comprehensive expectations are developed, deployed among stakeholder groups, accepted as appropriate and legitimate, used to improve organizational performance, and guide the improvement of student behavior and achievement.*

    Improved performance requires organizations to identify legitimate expectations for administrators, teachers, students, and other stakeholders; use strategies to gain support for them; and eliminate confusion. Shortcomings and weaknesses need to be shared with stakeholders for discussion and to obtain their commitment for better performance. Expectations are powerful influences on decisions and behaviors.

    Expectations should never be confused with exhortations that dictate and demand greater performance without any clear definition of outcomes and processes to achieve those outcomes. Exhortations are often intended to impress others with the strength, vehemence, or rhetoric used to deliver them. Expectations, on the other hand, are clear, precise indications of performance and behavior that are challenging but both achievable and reasonable. Expectations are expressed in the prognoses developed with prescriptions. District and schools need to use protocols and processes through which new expectations can be met.

MAPPING THE INTERNAL ORGANS OF DISTRICTS AND SCHOOLS

School and district functions (SDF) represent the skeleton and connective tissue of the organization and, as a result, provide only a very limited opportunity to implement successful strategies. The walls of the "towers of expertise" and the largely underutilized "white space" among positions in the organization severely limit improvement efforts.

It is too easy for individuals to remain within their roles and not contribute to organization performance improvement. The physical systems, comprised of the critical performance categories (CPC), provide a counterpoint to the SDF. The seventeen performance categories cut across all functions and, for the first time, demonstrate how to tie together the work of individuals. Together the two dimensions offer an entirely new view of the organization and the work of people within it. (See Strategy Three.)

The intersection of each function in the framework (skeleton) with each unifying performance area in the physical system produces a two dimensional map. This map can be used to identify the collection of behaviors, expectations, attitudes, and outcomes that reveals the "real" work of the organization more clearly and allows precise planning and action.

The physical map of the surface of the "body" of the organization is displayed in figure 2.2. Any number of SDF in the first dimension can be listed in the left hand column; and up to seventeen of the CPC or performance expectations can be listed across the top, thereby providing an intersection of each SDF and CPC.

The preliminary examination of that physical "body" surface and the internal organs provides the opportunity to analyze and understand performance health as the interrelationships among specific roles and the expectations for performance quality. The first symptoms of illness are often physical manifestations found or felt on the surface; yet, only a deeper examination of the performance health in the CPC leads to an understanding of what performance behaviors are or are not occurring inside the organization.

The seventeen critical performance categories (CPC), when considered in conjunction with the traditional school and district functions (SDF), provide at their intersections the best opportunities for accurate problem identification and successful intervention. Without the conscious use of the CPC by all stakeholders, districts and schools are very unlikely to attain the integrated organization, group, and individual efforts that support every child reaching her or his optimum level of performance.

Examination of the interactions mapped on the matrix produces a better understanding of the anatomy and physiology of a school and district and of

Surface Map: Interactions of SDF and CPC							
	CPC 1	CPC 2	CPC 3	CPC 4	CPC 5	CPC 6	ETC.
SDF 1							
SDF 2							
SDF 3							
SDF 4							
SDF 5							
SDF 6							
SDF 7							
SDF 8							
SDF 9							
SDF 10							
ETC.							

Figure 2.2 Surface Map of SDF and CPC

the underlying causes of distress. There has been a strong tendency to focus solely on "how and/or where do we start to improve performance and who is responsible?" Minimally, a much stronger list of questions can be generated and answered to promote performance health through clinical practice:

1. What kind of treatments should be considered?
2. Where does the treatment begin?
3. Will we have stakeholder cooperation?
4. What level of personal and organizational commitment will be needed to turn around this negative condition?
5. What capacity currently exists to implement and monitor treatment?
6. What capacity is needed in the future?

Clinical practice strategies are used to gather the information and data to answer the above questions and to take advantage of the interrelatedness of many of the systems and subsystems in and around schools and students. Taken together, data gathered about schools and their students combine to suggest several possible courses of action to turn around performance health.

Each of the actions can be implemented individually or in coordination with others in ways that negate the notion that there is only one place or way to begin.

The CPM offers protocols that help establish the cooperative efforts on the surface among the SDF in the first dimension, linked to the underlying systems of influence on performance among the CPC in dimension two.

As the inner workings of schools and districts are explored and employees become more familiar with the connections among the SDF and the CPC, they can understand how behaviors and activities influence performance health. This exploration is more like an ultrasound examination of living multiple and connected organs and is less like a medical dissection of a cadaver.

The next chapter begins to explore the mapping of the critical SDF/CPC intersections where interventions make a real difference. The specific behaviors in those intersections that promote and inhibit performance will be identified and the "vital signs" of performance health will be defined and monitored.

CHAPTER 2 STRATEGIES

Strategy One: Understanding Anatomy and "White Space"

To help individuals and teams better understand school anatomy, engage them in the development of a "White Space Map." Using an organization chart from your district or school, have the team members plot the lines that connect the work of individuals. These "triangles," "squares," and other shapes represent the interrelationships that need to be recognized if larger problems are going to be solved and performance improved. (See figure 2.3.)

Start by examining the roles of teams within these shapes and move to the less formal interactions that are needed to deliver programs and solve problems.

Strategy Two: Reorganize the Boxes

To help leaders and team members better understand the anatomy of schools and districts, design a new organization. Literally, cut all of the existing boxes out of your organization chart. Ask the team to reorganize the boxes and consider new reporting and cooperative relationships. Where it is helpful, relabel boxes and eliminate or create new ones. The object is not to eliminate people but to better organize the formal structure. Think about the design of the roles; put people in those roles later.

When the team thinks they have an improved organization, go back to Strategy One and draw the formal and informal connections through the white spaces and see where and how the organization is improved. What additional changes could help improve the organization design further?

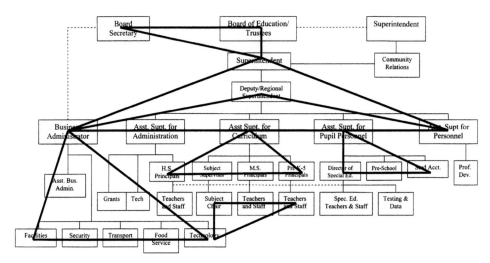

Figure 2.3   Organization Chart and "Improvement Planning Team Triangles"

Teams that go through this exercise are better able to see beyond the boxes and think more broadly about how roles and people can interact in improved ways.

Strategy Three: CPC Worksheet

In order to encourage educators to think about the CPC and the importance of each to improving performance and achievement, use the CPC Worksheet in figure 2.4. Simply, the worksheet lists each of the seventeen CPC and asks each individual (or team) to respond to:

1. In your experience, what issues related to each CPC promote higher performance in this school or district, and
2. In your experience, what issues related to each CPC inhibit higher performance in this school or district?

Critical Performance Categories	Issues that Promote this CPC	Issues that Inhibit this CPC
Alignment of Work Processes		
Business/Financial Acumen		
Customer Focus		
District & School-Wide Culture		
Effective and Integrated Governance		
Human Resource Excellence		
Information, Measurement, & Reporting		
Leadership		
Planning and Planned Change		
Professional Learning and Instruction		
Programs and Services that Accelerate Learning		
Staff, Student, and Family Interactions		
Structures that Nurture Improvement		
Student Behavior and Performance Data		
Team Work and Problem Solving		
Technology that Supports Program, Personnel, and Students		
Universal Acceptance of Expectations		

Figure 2.4   CPC Worksheet

3

RESEARCH IS EVERYONE'S RESPONSIBILITY AND IT STARTS WITH DATA

Solutions to problems can be no more effective than the reliability of the data and information collected to support the performance-improvement process. This chapter explores the type of data that should be collected and how they can be displayed and used to construct an understanding of problems.

Clinical Cycle Step 2—Gather Data/Information: The doctor asks the patient to complete a comprehensive medical history, including past problems and health concerns and the reasons for the patient's visit. The physician reviews the history with the patient and asks questions to gather critical information not included by the patient.

The patient understands that a visit to the physician is just the beginning of a fact-finding journey. The doctor reviews the file of past health history and asks questions to bring all information up-to-date. It is important that treatment decisions about the present discomfort be based in the context of a complete understanding of the history of the patient's health.

Educators tend to be less thorough in solving problems in districts and schools. The focus is on the immediacy of the problem and the availability of resources. Clinical practice provides a more-complete view of the problem and leads to a more-effective solution. The foundation for this framework rests on a complete understanding of background data.

DISTRICT AND SCHOOL HEALTH TRENDS

The multiple pieces of a performance-health history database are available already within every district and school, most within the many reports filed with state and federal departments of education and agencies connected with public schools. The data available describe the community, its residents, and students, the district's finances, its workforce, and more. The point of developing a performance-health database is to ensure that administrators and teachers understand past performance levels and issues, the environment in which current problems exist, and to ensure that diagnoses and prescriptions to improve performance are developed in the context of the health history of the district and school.

District, school, and employee performance-health issues are connected directly and indirectly to student achievement. Data and information that describe district, school, and classroom practices and the connections to student performance and behavior are found within general background information, as well as the specific data within the SDF and CPC introduced in the last chapter.

Data and information for educator problem solving can be organized into ten general categories, as listed below. Nine include the data used primarily in reports, but also exist in unorganized formats that describe, but do not analyze, work performed. Trends in expenditures for programs and services, instructional strategies used by teachers, effectiveness of professional-development programs, strategies used to engage parents, and many other practices are needed to understand the impact of current practice and expenditures on student performance.

The tenth data package, community and family health trends, can be partially constructed from U.S. census data. However, it has been fully developed by The Annie E. Casey Foundation and has significance for both community agencies and school districts. On the foundation's website (www.aecf.org), the KIDS COUNT Data Center provides useful local community and family information that increases the awareness of educators and improves their ability to solve student learning problems.

Together, these ten packages provide comprehensive trend data and information that provide a context for effective analysis of problems:

- district budgetary and financial;
- curricular and cocurricular programs;
- district/school office, organization, and leadership;
- employee characteristics, preparation, and performance;
- partnerships and outside services;
- school-level services and supports for students and staff members;

- stakeholder group and engagement;
- student proficiency rates and trends within each AYP group;
- student behavior and attendance; and
- community and family health trends (Annie E. Casey Foundation).

Collection, organization, and analysis of school district, school, employee, student, and other data are integral parts of the discovery process. This comprehensive collection of information forms the basis for initial review and allows project teams to assess trends that influence and help predict behaviors and performance of adults and students alike. (See Strategy Four at the end of the chapter.)

Obvious areas for study include trends in student behavior, achievement, and activities; teacher preparation, performance, and contributions; district and school finance, spending, and resource allocations; and community development, housing, and economic stability. Less obvious, but equally important, areas of study include trends in policy development; problem identification and resolution; planning and assessment of change; contract development and management; litigation; organization and modification of processes; students in postgraduate activity; and many others.

The data collected need to be compared with districts and schools having similar socioeconomic, cultural, and community characteristics, as well as with districts and schools that are "best performing" in the region and nation. Many state departments of education provide in-state data comparisons based on the socioeconomic levels of the community and families, so that differences among schools in the same district can be considered, and performance in these schools can be compared with performance of similar schools in other districts.

OTHER SOURCES OF DATA

Stakeholder satisfaction and perceptions related to outcomes provide a wealth of information for problem-solving efforts. A survey developed to measure stakeholder satisfaction and perceptions, the District and School Performance Health Diagnostic Inventory (DSPHDI), provides substantial information for analysis. The responses of stakeholders to the DSPHDI are organized by the seventeen CPC and are used to determine strengths and improvement needs. The initial perceptions can be used as a baseline to track changes over time.

Other diagnostic inventories exist to gather feedback regarding current school and district performance. Inventories that assess the performance of leadership, board, staff, and students provide invaluable information.[1] Self and 360-degree assessment results (asking the person in the role as well as others that work with that role for feedback) can be kept confidential, but when leaders are open to share feedback about their own performance, other stakeholders are more likely to participate honestly in the process. Specific training to interpret and use this data is not difficult and is strongly recommended.

Trends and patterns in perceptions reported by different groups of stakeholders provide significant insight into the root causes of persistent problems. Within each stakeholder group, responses should be examined and questions asked to find out what are perceived to be the critical issues. (See Strategy Five.)

In addition to inventories, discovery-phase interviews help to fill in the gaps left in incomplete data records. Both formal and informal interviews with individuals and focus groups provide the opportunity to pursue background information in greater detail and to explore connections that might not be as obvious when looking at a written record.

MULTIPLE USES OF THE SDF/CPC MATRIX

In the last chapter, the two dimensional matrix that visually represents the interconnections among all SDF and CPC was introduced in figure 2.2. Placing the SDF on the vertical or y-axis and the CPC on the horizontal or x-axis makes it possible to illustrate the powerful insights that can be generated from the interaction of the two dimensions. New understanding is generated about how districts, schools, and other organizations actually operate; and which interventions have the greatest likelihood of success among which roles and performance categories.

Each of the boxes on the matrix identifies the intersection of one school and district function and one critical performance category. Even a blank matrix illustrates the fact that every SDF has a relationship to every CPC. No individual, office, or department can argue that the work for which they are responsible is not related to "Customer Focus," "Staff, Student, and Parent Interactions," or "Student Behavior and Performance Data," for example. No matter how distant such a relationship may appear, every work effort in every office, department, classroom, or other place has an expanded impact on performance through one or more of the seventeen CPC.

Only when every individual and group accepts the responsibility to carry out the purposes of every CPC can real accountability be established and performance improvements accelerate. Ultimately, administrators, teachers, other employees, and students attain greater levels of accomplishment as they develop deeper understanding about and use CPC.

These matrices are comparable to maps of various body systems often seen hung on the wall of the doctor's examination room. The matrix can be used to illustrate in which of the intersections there is organizational capacity, needs, critical issues, or improvement opportunities. The matrix serves as an instrument to collect, analyze, and display data related to the work of the organization and all of its parts. This can be accomplished by placing symbols or by shadings in the intersecting box in which specific conditions exist.

Following is a key that can be used for identifying the level of priority among activities taking place in the intersection.

Once a matrix representing the district and school is created, there are a number of important ways to use the matrix to record information. As team members become familiar with the form of the matrix, it becomes a highly adaptable format to record and display perceptions, behaviors, interactions, outcomes, and any other recording of observations at any intersection of SDF and CPC.

---

1. *No Indication of a Critical Issue*: ☐ Documentation shows low levels of concern and a comfort level with this intersection. These intersections will be monitored and considered for future intervention if needed.

2. *Indication of a First Level Critical Issue*: ▒ Documentation shows levels of concern in two or more investigated areas that if not addressed will prevent some future success. While these intersections have potential for successful intervention, they are a low priority that will not be immediately addressed, but will be monitored.

3. *Indication of a Second Level Critical Issue*: ▒ Documentation shows strong levels of concern among several areas of investigation that indicate either opportunities for or obstacles to further success. These intersections have greater potential for successful intervention, and they are a level of priority high enough to be considered a secondary priority for action.

4. *Indication of a Third Level Critical Issue*: ▓ Documentation shows strong levels of concern among most areas of investigation that indicate either significant opportunities for or obstacles to further success. These intersections have significant potential for successful intervention, and they are a high priority considered for immediate action.

5. *Indication of a Fourth Level Critical Issue*: ■ Documentation shows strong levels of concern among all areas of investigation that indicate either significant opportunities for or obstacles to further success that require immediate attention. These are the first intersections to be considered in planning action to improve performance.

A segment of a performance-improvement opportunity matrix is provided in figure 3.1 as an example of the two-dimensional mapping of performance concerns, called critical issues, at the intersection of CPCs and district and school functions. Usually the critical issues in the third and fourth levels are examined and weighed together in the development of the prescription.

DESCRIPTION OF THE MATRIX

The segment of the performance-improvement opportunity matrix in figure 3.1 is taken from work in a small district that was plagued by the long-term in-

School Functions	Critical Performance Categories								
	A Align WP	B B&F Acumen	C Custmr Focus	D D-W Culture	E Eff&Int Gov	F HRE	G Info, Ms, Rpt Sys	H Leader-ship	I Plng&Pl Change
1. Bd/CSA									
2. Business Office									
A. Acctg.									
B. Bdgting									
C. Payroll									
D. Purchsing									
3. CSA Teams									
A. Leadership Team									
B. ASAs									
C. BA Bd									
D. ASAs, CSA									
E. HR									
F. Pup Persnl									
G. BA, Sects									
H. Bldg, Tech									
4. Certificated Staff									
A. Instruction									
B. Prof. Develop									
C. Planning									
5. Child Study Team									
6. Co-Curricular									
7. Communications									
8. Comm. Relations									
9. Curriculum									

Intervention Priority Scale

1. Not a priority at this time
2. Low level priority
3. Mid level priority
4. High level priority
5. Highest level priority

Figure 3.1   Partial SDF x CPC Matrix

ability to improve its performance. While everyone wanted to improve student achievement, there was great reluctance to uncover the real underlying causes of poor performance. This district adopted one "silver bullet" reform after another without any real understanding of the appropriateness or fit with existing programs, personnel, and students.

Then, the board began to turn over district leaders trying to find the perfect background and experience— a "silver bullet" by a different name. Through the analysis of student performance and behavior data, interviews, and observation, the critical intersections of SDF and CPC related to planning for change were easy to identify. Considering specific SDF and deciding how each related to the most problematic CPC helped the leadership team understand where resources could be applied with the greatest potential for improvement.

The SDF in italics in figure 3.1 represent the specific offices of a newly organized leadership team for this small district. The individual members of the team recognized that in order to lead the changes that were necessary for improved performance, they needed training in planning and implementing change processes, supervising staff during times of transition, and leadership behaviors that could establish, promote, and maintain increased responsibility and accountability among all stakeholders. They learned that their efforts shouldn't be limited to finding appropriate solutions, but to finding how to implement them successfully as well.

Each of the intersections on the matrix afforded the opportunity to identify and consider very specific behaviors, programs, and relationships that can be observed, measured, and related to improving performance. When these behaviors, programs, and relationships were translated into specific indicators, they became the equivalent of the vital signs measured by physicians to determine the relative health of the individual, and they helped determine the intervention strategies likely to be most effective in improving performance.

As critical as the issues of planning and planned change (level three) were in this school, improved leadership behaviors (level four) were needed even more to carry out responsibilities for planning needed changes. The need for improved leadership behaviors was the most critical concern, and leaders were eager to accept coaching to produce the greatest positive change in the shortest amount of time.

An analysis and discussion among administrators and consultants found meaning within the matrix and produced a better understanding of the district's recent history prior to the appointment of this leadership team. The team considered its options for improvement and organized a prescription it thought would improve performance and gain the confidence of a demoralized staff.

There was no attempt to identify any individual members of the leadership team or SDF office as a "problem," but instead to focus on where the opportunities for positive change existed, and what efforts could be made by each administrator, with the help of her or his coach, to contribute to the plan. The matrix served to focus research, discussion, and planning; and it provided the basis for the district to engage more stakeholders in planning improvements beyond its leaders.

The leadership team invited broader and more open participation by teachers and other stakeholders. Leaders modeled learning activities and acknowledged their own needs, a risky undertaking in an environment that encouraged self-preservation. Teachers, especially those who had previously been content to remain within their classroom, exhibited a new willingness to invest more energy and time in planning and implementing changes, including making revisions to student-discipline procedures, parent communication, and activities designed to align programs across subjects and grades.

Through the course of the project, the matrix changed a few times. At the end of the engagement, the leadership team expressed a higher level of confidence in its own capacities, and the faculty and other staff members recognized that their work life had improved. Problems they confronted continually for two years without success had diminished, and they expressed satisfaction in the professional growth they experienced that would be applied in new circumstances.

A full matrix taken from the work of another district is presented in figure 3.2. This matrix shows the full array of coded boxes for a school with strong leadership that had struggled to find strategies to improve student achievement. The strategies identified after analyzing the matrix included the creation of structures and teams within and across grade levels to align curriculum, organize and analyze performance data, and plan strategies to monitor and measure student performance more frequently during the year to ensure that curriculum content standards and instructional objectives were being met.

SIMPLIFYING THE MATRIX: THE ROLL-UP

When the matrix is coded with numbers, symbols, or colors, its appearance may be overwhelming, but in most cases, less than one-quarter of potential intersections are identified as immediate priorities (levels three and four). In order to more easily see relationships and reduce the size of the matrix, the SDF and CPC that are not important to the analysis can be removed in what is called a "roll-up." Figure 3.3 is the roll-up from figure 3.2. Later, the roll-up will be used to develop "clusters" of intersections that are related so that the clinical concepts of symptoms and syndromes can be introduced to diagnosis and prescriptions.

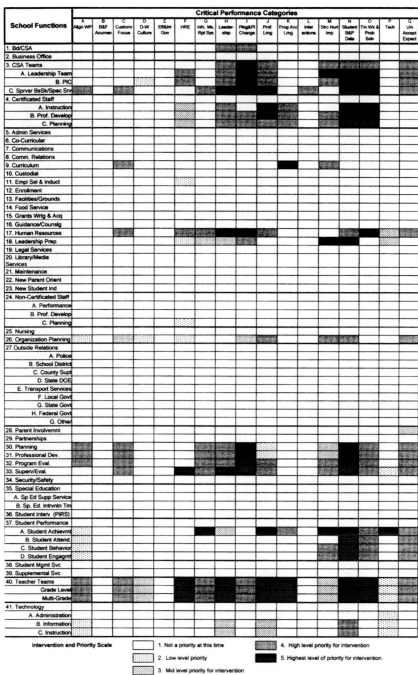

Figure 3.2   Trapper Hill Academy Functions (SDF) x Critical Performance Categories (CPC) Matrix: Critical Issues and Functions for Interventions and Performance Improvements

School Functions		Critical Performance Categories															
	A Align WP	B B&F Acumen	C Customr Focus	D D-W Culture	E Eff&Int Gov	F HRE	G Info, Ms, Rpt Sys	H Leader-ship	I Plng&Pl Change	J Prof. Lrng	K Prog Acc Lrng	L Inter actions	M Strc Nurt Imp	N Student B&P Data	O Tm Wk & Prob Solv	P Tech	Q Uni Accept Expect
1. Bd/CSA																	
3. CSA Teams																	
A. Leadership Team																	
B. PIC																	
C. Sprvsr BasSk/Spec Serv																	
4. Cert. Staff A. Instruction																	
B. Prof. Develop																	
C. Planning																	
9. Curriculum																	
17. Human Resources																	
18. Leadership Prep.																	
24. C. Planning																	
26. Organization Planning																	
28. Parent Involvemnt																	
30. Planning																	
31. Professional Dev.																	
32. Program Eval.																	
33. Superv/Eval.																	
37. Stud Prf A. Achievmt																	
B. Student Attend.																	
C. Student Behavior																	
D. Student Engagmt																	
40. Teacher Teams																	
Grade Level																	
Multi-Grade																	
41.Tech A. Administration																	
B. Information																	
C. Instruction																	

Intervention and Priority Scale

1. Not a priority at this time
2. Low level priority
3. Mid level priority for intervention
4. High level priority for intervention
5. Highest level of priority for intervention.

Note: Applying remedies to the most critical priority intersections will create the greatest progress in the shortest amount of time. The diagnosis, prescription, and prognosis should address at least the high level and highest level priorities.

Figure 3.3 Trapper Hill Academy Functions (SDF) x Critical Performance Categories (CPC) Matrix: Critical Issues "Roll-Up"

It is important for teams to practice using the matrix before progressing to an examination of what takes place at the intersections of the SDF and CPC. (See Strategy Six.) Several uses of the matrix are introduced in this strategy. Teams can record the location of improvement in the recent past and where new capacities have been formed. Or, the same matrix can be used to identify critical issues, opportunities for performance improvement, and the intervention priorities that would cause additional performance improvement.

MAPPING THE ANATOMY

For all of the added understanding that the combination of the skeleton and the physical systems provides, we are still only cartographers, mapmakers. Knowledge of the interactions of the SDF and the CPC reveals new information about the organization's anatomy and physiology in rather simple ways for solving problems. Still, the doctor and patient do not fully understand ongoing interactions "inside the organization." The surface and some of the surrounding tissue have been mapped, but its depths have not been fully explored.

People, and the organizations in which they work, need information about activities and behaviors deep within the organization in order to understand and shorten the connecting pathways between current performance levels and more desirable outcomes. The model of clinical practice is expanded further in the next few chapters to establish those pathways through the exploration of the third and fourth dimensions of organizational life.

CHAPTER 3 STRATEGIES

Strategy Four: Data Notebooks

The task of gathering and organizing historic and trend data can seem overwhelming, especially when so little time is available to take on new responsibilities. Gather and organize as much pertinent data as possible and engage a team to create a resource that employees own and can use to improve problem solving processes and results.

Give each of the team members a list of the ten categories and request copies of all data they have related to each. Prepare a large notebook (either paper or electronic) for each category of data and simply amass all of the available data. Once the data have been collected, give one or more notebooks to team members and ask them to organize the data with a table of contents to reflect that organization. The data should be kept in their original form, as they were produced, to save time. Later, you might consider how data reports can be improved.

Assignment of team members to organize each category presents some interesting possibilities. It is sometimes best to give the notebook for organization to the person already most familiar with the data (e.g., ask the business administrator to organize the financial data). On the other hand, it is often helpful to give each notebook to another team member familiar with but not directly responsible for the data maintenance. Many teams prefer two members of different responsibilities to share the organizing task. Ask the curriculum director to organize financial data, the business administrator to organize the student performance data, and so forth.

At the next meeting of the team, ask members to present and summarize their efforts to better organize the data. As the team begins to more regularly use the data, organization will improve, but most importantly, each notebook is available for reference, and each notebook has team member experts in its organization.

Strategy Five: Analyze Stakeholder Perceptions

Using any appropriate survey or inventory, measure and graph the perceptions reported by different stakeholder groups and develop possible explanations for the differences in perception that each group has regarding district and school performance. (Figure 3.4 identifies the perceptions held by stakeholder groups about the quality of team work and problem solving in the district.)

1. Which stakeholder group perception of team work and problem-solving effectiveness is lowest? Speculate why.
2. Which stakeholder group perception of team work and problem-solving effectiveness is highest? Speculate why.
3. Which stakeholder groups express perceptions of team work and problem-solving effectiveness most different from each other? Speculate why.
4. Which stakeholder groups express perceptions of team work and problem-solving effectiveness most like each other? Speculate why.

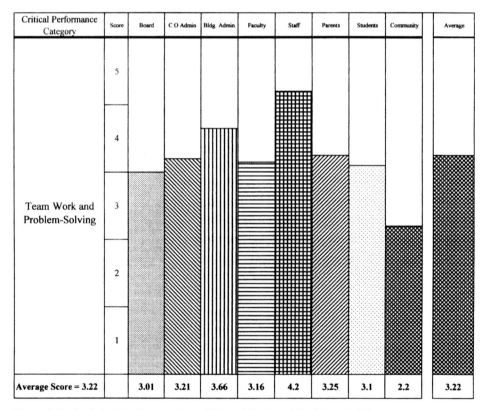

Critical Performance Category	Score	Board	C O Admin.	Bldg. Admin.	Faculty	Staff	Parents	Students	Community		Average
Team Work and Problem-Solving	5 4 3 2 1										
Average Score = 3.22		3.01	3.21	3.66	3.16	4.2	3.25	3.1	2.2		3.22

Figure 3.4   Stakeholder Perceptions of Team Work and Problem Solving

5. If steps were taken to improve the perceptions of any one group, how would the perceptions of other groups be affected? Why and how?

Strategy Six: Multiple Matrix Maps

A blank matrix is provided in figure 3.5. There are a variety of ways that the matrix can be used to map discovery data. Make copies of figure 3.5 or create your own matrix. Fill in the appropriate SDF in the left-hand column of the matrix and try each of the following exercises. Involve the team.

Opportunities: Place an "X" in any intersection where the opportunity for improvement is obvious. When you look at the completed map, do these opportunities cluster around specific SDF? Do they cluster around any specific CPC?

Critical Issues: Review the trend data contained in the data notebooks. Place a check in each intersection that can be identified in the data as critical for improvement. Using a gray scale, a "yellow to orange to red to black" color scale, or some other scheme, color each box progressively darker for increased numbers of checks. What are the patterns?

Improvement: Place a checkmark in each intersection where performance has improved in the last three years. Are these intersections still viable sites for improvement? Which other intersections are most influenced by those improved sites? How can the interactions found in those intersections be used to improve other interactions?

It is also possible to use a light-green–to–dark-green scale to record the amount of improvement that has taken place at any intersection over a selected period of time.

Intervention Priorities: Color code or mark the intersections that you believe provide the best opportunities for successful intervention. You can code different intersections for intervention with different resources, strategies, or programs.

Increased Capacity: Use a blue scale to map increased capacity over time. Develop your own color scales for different kinds of matrices.

School Functions	Critical Performance Categories																
	A Algn WP	B B&F Acumen	C Customr Focus	D D-W Culture	E Eff&Int Gov	F HRE	G Info. Ms. Rpt Sys	H Leader-ship	I Ptng&PI Change	J Prof. Lrng	K Prog Acc Lrng	L Inter actions	M Strc Nurt Imp	N Student B&P Data	O Tm Wrk & Prob Solv	P Tech	Q Uni Accept Expect
1. Bd/CSA																	
2. Business Office																	
3. Leadership Team																	
4. Certificated Staff																	
A. Instruction																	
B. Prof. Develop																	
C. Planning																	
5. Admin Services																	
6. Co-Curricular																	
7. Communications																	
8. Comm. Relations																	
9. Curriculum																	
10. Custodial																	
11. Empl Sel & Induct																	
12. Enrollment																	
13. Facilities/Grounds																	
14. Food Service																	
15. Grants Wrtg & Acq																	
16. Guidance/Counslg																	
17. Human Resources																	
18. Leadership Prep.																	
19. Legal Services																	
20. Library/Media Svcs																	
21. Maintenance																	
22. New Parent Orient																	
23. New Student Ind																	
24. Non-Certificated Staff																	
A. Performance																	
B. Prof. Develop																	
C. Planning																	
25. Nursing																	
26. Organization Planning																	
27. Outside Relations																	
A. Police																	
B. School District																	
C. County Supt																	
D. State DOE																	
E. Transport Services																	
F. Local Govt																	
G. State Govt																	
H. Federal Govt																	
G. Other																	
28. Parent Involvemnt																	
29. Partnerships																	
30. Planning																	
31. Professional Dev.																	
32. Program Eval.																	
33. Superv/Eval.																	
34. Security/Safety																	
35. Special Education																	
A. Sp Ed Supp Service																	
B. Sp. Ed. Intrvntn Tm																	
36. Student Interv (PIRS)																	
37. Student Performance																	
A. Student Achievmt																	
B. Student Attend.																	
C. Student Behavior																	
D. Student Engagmt																	
38. Student Mgmt Svc																	
39. Supplemental Svc																	
40. Teacher Teams																	
Grade Level																	
Multi-Grade																	
41. Technology																	
A. Administration																	
B. Information																	
C. Instruction																	

Intervention and Priority Scale

1. Not a priority at this time
2. Low level priority
3. Mid level priority for intervention
4. High level priority for intervention
5. Highest level of priority for intervention.

Note: Applying remedies to the most critical priority intersections will create the greatest progress in the shortest amount of time.

The diagnosis, prescription, and prognosis should address at least the red (high level) and black (highest level) priorities.

Figure 3.5 School District Functions (SDF) x Critical Performance Categories (CPC) Matrix: Critical Issues and Functions for Interventions and Performance Improvements

4

IDENTIFYING THE VITAL SIGNS
OF PERFORMANCE HEALTH

Education diagnosticians need to consider and share data in relatively simple form about the organization's organ systems, behavior and activities of employees and students, and the results of diagnostic instruments. Vital signs provide a communication and diagnostic format for physicians, and vital-sign performance indicators (VSPI) provide a similar benefit to educators. This chapter looks briefly at the development of VSPI and introduces the topic of ethics for educators engaged in clinical practice for performance improvement.

Clinical Cycle Step 3—Review and Consult: The doctor reviews with the patient pertinent points in the patient's medical history, asks clarifying questions, and places the patient's present state in the context of medical trends and conditions present in the larger community. Vital signs of current health are collected, compared with past readings, and analyzed to uncover direction for further investigation. The doctor discusses with the patient issues to be explored further and the best and the worst scenarios are outlined as a context for that exploration.

VITAL-SIGN PERFORMANCE INDICATORS (VSPI)

The physician updates health-related information since the last visit before beginning the physical examination, which includes the measurement and recording of vital signs, measures of the body's basic physical functioning. Respiration, heart rate, temperature, blood pressure, and other measures are taken to make sure the patient's vital signs are within expected ranges. If any measures fall outside of the expected range, they may show an exacerbation of an existing condition or the first signs of another problem.

In the clinical practice model, vital-sign performance indicators (VSPI) are measures of behaviors that relate to performance in schools. VSPI are used to illuminate the behaviors that should be the targets of change, whether they are the behaviors of individuals or groups. Performance improvement requires changes in behavior.

The objective of Clinical Cycle Step 3 must be to discover vital signs related to the attainment of goals and mission of the district and schools, and then to utilize the vital signs indicating underperformance to develop effective interventions. In short, most of the data gathered in the creation of the notebooks in Strategy Four (chapter 3) can be translated into VSPI. The authors have identified over six hundred different VSPI and have used a majority of them in work with schools.

Vital signs of healthy educational practice are measurable; their use leads to the diagnosis of specific causes of failure and can eventually be as powerful as medical vital signs are to the treatment of humans. They become the basis for designing educational prescriptions that overcome underperformance. Processes and instruments have been designed to identify normal ranges of healthy performance and to determine if the participating district and school vital signs lie outside the ranges deemed appropriate to success.

Vital signs possess different values under different circumstances. For example, an elevated heart rate, often a critical sign of distress, should be expected as normal for an athlete following exertion. Muscle pain can suggest certain diseases, but is a logical consequence of muscle development through weight training. Some vital signs that might indicate problems in one case are, in other cases, merely the expected by-products of healthy practice. Districts and schools engaged in change processes must expect elevated concern and increased activity and even some discomfort within some VSPI when seeking performance improvement.

Some vital signs are more specific than are others in assessing root causes of problems. An elevated temperature may not be especially meaningful to a physician until other vital signs are measured and grouped as a syndrome. It is the combination of this general vital-sign information along with more specific signs of blood antigen levels, skin rash, and breathing problems, for example, that lead to the identification of root causes of problems.

Individual VSPI can provide evidence of performance, including individual, group, and organizational efforts, and the performance of students. The vital signs can be found at the intersections of the SDF and the CPC. In other words, the VSPI occur as a result of the interactions among the roles and functions within the organization (SDF), the unifying performance categories (CPC) that drive the organization toward its goals, and stakeholder behaviors, attitudes, and perceptions that support or defy improvement efforts.

Just as physicians understand the relationship between physical exertion and increased breathing and heart rates, educators can learn more about complex relationships among the district office and schools, acceptable best practices, and stakeholder behaviors that connect with student achievement. For example, connections can be drawn among lesson plans developed by teachers (SDF), customer focus (CPC), and the achievement of students (stakeholders).

As measurements are taken to compare behaviors like these, educator confidence grows as the right remedy is selected to treat each problem. The ongoing and public call for schools to respond to the latest concern about youth behavior or underperformance does not have to result in educators jumping to treat the fever while the disease goes unchecked.

COMPOSITION OF VSPI

VSPI can be graphed and charted, just like physical vital signs, tracked over time, and compared with desired, even optimum, behaviors. At a glance, VSPI graphs describe current performance levels as well as any gaps between current performance and where performance ought to be for students, school, district, and/or board. The same VSPI used to prepare a prescription and prognosis can be used again later to measure and report progress. VSPI in any individual district or school are designed to help investigators in other districts and schools as well. Following are definitions and descriptions of VSPI concepts.

VSPI Norms and Scales—Norms and scales provide the ranges in which performance rates can be plotted and compared for the purpose of understanding current performance levels and diagnosing underlying causes of poor performance. VSPI are measured, reported, and compared with the performance levels of districts, schools, and students with similar characteristics and the highest performers. The first obligation in creating VSPI is to establish reasonable ranges within which healthy, successful schools and districts operate.

VSPI Reporting Templates—Templates are the bar-graph formats used in reports that provide displays of information in the form of VSPI. These formats enable accurate reporting and tracking of changes in performance and can be easily compared with measures from similar districts and with districts and schools with consistent performance health and those approaching optimized performance.

VSPI are presented sometimes using rubric scales to document and track performance levels, and as percentages, percentiles, numeric scores, or frequencies.

Stakeholders can assess performance by comparing present performance efforts and outcomes against past performance results, desired performance results, as well as the performance quality of other districts and schools. Appropriately designed and used VSPI concentrate discussion and the energies and interests of stakeholders on the problems and interventions that move the district, school, employee group, and students to higher and more desirable performance levels.

Individual vital signs provide a focused perspective on the performance health at the intersection of all three dimensions—SDF, CPC, and activities of stakeholders. Multiple VSPI or clusters of VSPI, described in the next chapter, provide a clearer picture of performance health at intersections, and guide a more-detailed analysis across different activities of specific stakeholders.

Determining which VSPI are most significant to the diagnosis and which should be used in the ongoing measurement of the prescription falls within the art of educational decision making.

With observation and practice, it becomes possible to determine which one or more VSPI are most critical to a problem and which intersections of the SDF and CPC are most significant intersections.

PRESENTATION OF INDIVIDUAL VSPI

Use of VSPI leads district and school stakeholders to decisions about what kinds of data need to be maintained in ongoing efforts to understand and influence performance. In Holland Valley High School (the name is fictitious, but the data are real), there were concerns about the overall achievement and attendance of students among certain subgroups. As in most schools, Holland Valley dealt with achievement and attendance issues as separate problems. A focus on performance improvement changes that approach.

The first step in a deeper analysis of student performance was the construction of a performance indicator that compared Holland Valley student attendance rates to students in high schools in the same district and in similar high schools elsewhere. A disparity became evident. Even more important, there was an even greater disparity when the attendance of students was compared with attendance of students in the highest performing high schools. After some research within the attendance data, it was easy to discover that the lack of progress in student achievement was strongly correlated to lower-than-expected student attendance.

Figure 4.1 presents one of five VSPI used to examine attendance and achievement patterns of students. The analysis of underachievement did not end until a clear understanding of the causes of troublesome attendance patterns led to the

VSPI: The average daily rate of attendance (ADA) at Holland Valley High School

Source: District and high school attendance data, interviews, analysis

Comparative Analysis: Holland Valley High School reports an average daily attendance of 87 percent. Similar high schools report an average daily attendance rate of 93-95 percent. Highest performing high schools report daily attendance rates of 95-98 percent, or higher.

Finding: Average daily attendance at Holland Valley High School is lower than in other high schools in the same district and lower than in similar and highest performing high schools.

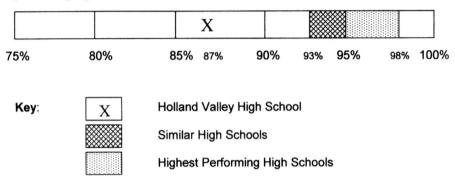

Key: X   Holland Valley High School

              Similar High Schools

              Highest Performing High Schools

Figure 4.1   Vital Sign Performance Indicator (VSPI)

home, school, and business communities working together to resolve a rather difficult problem. Ultimately, the prescription helped relieve concerns about attendance and led to higher achievement within the subgroup. (See Strategy Seven at the end of the chapter.)

The Holland Valley School District had approximately twenty thousand students coming from a large geographic area of several townships. This consolidated district became known as one of the region's most successful, and it received recognition for its effective leadership, programs, and successful high school and college graduates. Of the district's four high schools, Holland Valley, the most recently opened high school, had the lowest attendance and achievement rates.

The average daily rate of attendance scale has a range of 80 to 100 percent and a quick review revealed that Holland Valley High School (HVHS) had an attendance rate six percentage points below similar high schools and 8 percent below the best performers. As a result of this very basic comparison, district leadership disaggregated the student attendance data to more closely examine where the disparity in attendance rates was most significant.

This deeper analysis was important when other VSPI demonstrated different rates of achievement among subgroups of students who attended school less often. Attendance was discovered not to be the cause of underperformance, but an indicator of other behaviors that directly and indirectly related to lower academic achievement.

Upon further examination of VSPI that measured and compared standardized test data, HVSD leaders identified disturbing patterns. Decreasing minority student performance had gone largely unnoticed because this population had, to date, met basic proficiency requirements. Yet, declining scores were projected to fail to meet increasing AYP proficiency standards within a year. And, significant differences in student proficiency rates in both reading and mathematics were discovered between genders of African American students.

Examining one behavior outside the expected performance range resulted in identification of a symptom of the problem and led to the identification of other indicators that were more closely tied to the root causes of underperformance. (See Strategy Eight.)

This deeper examination produced information that led to the development of more promising interventions. Instead of treating the symptom of low attendance, the district and high school were able to address issues of gender and minority student attitude, expectation, and achievement when it was determined that both attendance and achievement were tied to patterns of employment and employment expectations in the community and family.

Like the physicians before, educators will learn to identify, measure, cluster, track, and monitor the specific appearances of vital-sign performance indicators in order to better understand and modify prescriptions and prognoses. Within the CPC of "Student Behavior and Performance Data," many more VSPI exist than in any of the other sixteen CPC. The potential combinations of student behavior and performance VSPI with the VSPI in one or more of the other CPC reflect the uniqueness of each school environment. VSPI define the unique circumstances that can lead to the selection of the most appropriate prescriptions.

Analysis of vital signs of underperformance in one location has been useful to the diagnosis of problems in other locations. A comparison of VSPI from multiple schools provides clues to approach similar problems in another school. However, the internal physiology and activities within the district and schools' depths are very different, requiring different prescriptions to reach the same performance goals. VSPI convey information about performance quality on the surface and among stakeholders within all three dimensions of organizational space. (See Strategy Nine.)

Ultimately, a cause of underperformance of African American students was found to be based on the community business and family expectations that minority females could miss school to work as substitutes in local health-care facilities. As was observed at Holland Valley High School, the in-depth review of vital signs led to improved understanding of connections among student attendance and achievement and the school, home, and community work environments.

Without confronting the underlying cause of attendance and achievement problems, the issue of low achievement could have grown later into political issues that would have disguised clues to the real root causes and further complicated intervention planning. VSPI are most helpful when they reveal performance activities in the interior, below the surface where the root causes of underperformance can be found, allowing school and district leaders to take appropriate action before problems become more complex.

SOLVING COMPLEX PROBLEMS

Serving a diverse group of students offers challenges as complex as those faced by physicians dealing with very serious medical conditions. Consider the patient that weighs 350 pounds at five foot ten inches tall, forty-five years of age, with a family history of heart trouble and diabetes. The patient has a glucose-tolerance reading of 350. His feet are badly swollen, infected, and there is potential for gangrene. Many of his vital signs are outside normal ranges.

This patient hasn't worked in six months, and all his previous jobs have been outdoors in construction. The patient has been a heavy drinker and, for many years, has maintained a "fast food" diet that could best be described as unbalanced. He has no family support network and lacks a formal medical plan. Where does the treatment of this patient begin? Will he cooperate in his treatment? What level of personal commitment will be needed to turn around this patient's condition?

Even though educators are not physicians, they understand that this patient's condition is not the result of a single cause, and the patient cannot be treated with a single remedy, even if another patient with similar symptoms has had success with it. It is essential to examine how the patient's different problems are interrelated, just as educators need to study the complex collection of symptoms in schools needing improvement.

The information gathered about a district, its schools, and students can suggest many different courses of action to improve the educational health of the school and student. Complications inherent in the case of the patient described above require the consultation of many specialists for opinions from their particular perspectives. A plan needs to be proposed to the patient so that treatment can begin as soon as possible. Adjustments to the initial plan should be expected based on the attitude and commitment of the patient.

The construction worker needs to see progress and improve his health habits in order to believe that future prospects will be better. Similarly, schools, administrators, teachers, students, parents, and other stakeholders involved in performance-improvement efforts need to see progress in order to sustain their commitment. Old habits, entrenched practices, minimal expectations, low standards, and traditions can discourage participants and limit their future involvement. Data and clinical practice reveal these symptoms of underperformance.

The review and analysis of documents contained in the data notebooks (chapter 3) support team-member efforts to understand the history, trends, and most-recent experience of stakeholders. This vitally important step precedes the acquisition of data related to current performance, behavior of adults, and behavior and achievement of students. These trend data need to be reviewed, summarized, and mapped on the matrix.

Plotting the critical issues at intersections of the SDF and the CPC on the matrix organizes the data in ways that uncovers the interrelationships among roles, categories of performance, and improved outcomes. The accumulation of data and other knowledge about the patient is not enough, however, to guide the selection of appropriate treatments.

THE ETHICS OF PRACTICE

The physician is not in charge of the patient, but is a peer with specialized knowledge that guides treatment of the patient. But, this knowledge needs to be used judiciously and not at the expense of important values. In some circumstances, treatments have implications for the patient, society, and even the treating physician. An increased emphasis on standardized test results, for example, has raised the specter of nefarious adult behaviors, such as cheating to increase student test scores rather than waiting for improved strategies to be effective. Ethics in education will need greater consideration, just as it has in medicine, politics, and business.

Data and expectations for the patient's recovery are not enough to guide the physician. Principles that have guided physicians for centuries are found in the Hippocratic Oath and in the growing field of medical ethics. Most medical texts and handbooks make reference to ethics and remind physicians how to proceed when faced with conflicting practices and interests.

For example, in the *Oxford American Handbook of Clinical Medicine*, the editor, John Flynn, M.D., explains that the aim of the physician is to "do good by promoting people's health."[1] Yet, this general guideline also includes four chief duties—not doing harm, doing good by positive action, respecting autonomy or respecting the person, and promoting justice.[2] Each of these four duties is further explained to guide physician decision making.

Horace Mann[3] and others have offered ethical guidelines for educational decision making. Most of these guidelines cover the scope of knowledge needed for the proper management of the classroom and school. The multitude of confidential data, complexity of issues, and the impact that decisions have among people and groups require ethical standards beyond those described by Horace Mann. Proposed here is a set of ethical guidelines for educator decision making to support this model of diagnostics.

These guidelines are not exhaustive, but they form the basis of ethical behavior for clinical practice in education. These guidelines serve to remind educators which basic human behaviors are needed to achieve progress while dealing with complex situations. The aim of using the CPM's ethical guidelines should be to improve the accuracy of decisions, to improve performance, and to guide the actions of all stakeholders.

These ethical guidelines should be used to resolve dilemmas over priorities, decisions, and actions.

1. Expect and foster nothing less than honesty, integrity, openness, optimism, confidence, and mutual support.
2. Commit to professional lifelong learning, including sharing learning with others.
3. Earn trust based on the belief in the value, contribution, and expected success of every student, employee, and stakeholder.
4. Take no action that causes harm to students, employees, other stakeholders, or previous accomplishments; and take action to prevent harm.
5. Establish an agenda for adults that commits time, energy, and resource to the success of students evidenced in ongoing conversations about student success.
6. Promote the work of teams at every level among all stakeholders to support improved performance.
7. Focus on high expectations for performance success by every student, teacher, and administrator.
8. Respond to disappointment and failure positively, without evidence of punitive action.
9. Demonstrate a willingness to take on the risks of leadership.
10. Empower students, colleagues, and other stakeholders who accept responsibility and accountability, and readily credit others for success.

Successful use of the CPM and the development of consistent, high-quality practice in districts and schools are dependent upon decision making consistent with the philosophy and principles included in these guidelines. As the CPM and ethical guidelines are used they will evolve, become embedded in the culture of the district and schools, be included in the education of professionals, and add immeasurably to the appropriate use of data in planning and decision making.

CHAPTER 4 STRATEGIES

Strategy Seven: Comparing Vital Signs

Figure 4.1 provides an example of a VSPI developed from data in the Holland Valley School District. Plot what you believe to be the performance of your own school or district on the above VSPI. How do you compare with Holland Valley High School, with similar schools, and with highest performing schools? What are the implications for planning improvement in your own district or school?

What changes in behavior are necessary to improve the measure of this VSPI? Is the average daily rate of attendance important to improved performance in your school or district? Why or why not?

Many more VSPI will be presented throughout this book. Build a comparative library of your own experience in each as a foundation for your own improvement manual.

Strategy Eight: Creating VSPI

Vital signs are the metrics that document specific behaviors related to performance. Many exist and any number remain to be documented. Use the form below to copy, create, or modify VSPI for your own use. After defining the VSPI and deciding the most closely associated CPC and SDF, select the appropriate scale to measure and record the VSPI. The first measure is a baseline to be used to compare measured changes over time.

Involve the team in generating, recording, and maintaining a library of VSPI.
VSPI:
Source:
Related SDF:
Related CPC:
Comparative Analysis:
Scale:
Key:
Baseline and Comparative Performance Measures:

Strategy Nine: Designing VSPI

Based on the information presented in figure 4.1, identify three other potential VSPI that address concerns about student attendance and/or achievement that can be assigned to teams for analysis in development of a diagnosis. What other data need to be obtained and graphed in order to better understand the basis of both the problem and the best possible solutions?

CLUSTERING VITAL SIGNS TO DETERMINE A COURSE OF ACTION

This chapter explores the meaning that is generated in a cluster of VSPI. When analyzed, VSPI clusters should push understanding beyond that which comes from a single VSPI or symptom to form a diagnosis. Multiple VSPI can be clustered to demonstrate connections among the critical performance categories needed for problem analysis. VSPI clusters are used to summarize levels of critical performance behaviors and lead to diagnostic options.

Clinical Cycle Step 4—Hypothesis Based on Observation and Evidence: The doctor weighs the importance and apparent significance of the described and observable symptoms to begin to narrow the range of possible explanations for the patient's illness. Based on past experience and knowledge specific to the subject patient, the physician establishes a possible line of investigation that can lead to a specific diagnosis. In the assessment and possible prescription, the physician may have to make judgments based on experience and expertise that stabilize the patient's condition before more-sophisticated tests and measurements can be made to investigate the underlying causes of the malady.

Physicians understand that a single vital sign outside of normal range means very little unless and until it is grouped with other indicators that focus the search for a more specific diagnosis. The presence of two or more vital signs outside the normal range will lead to the consideration of additional vital signs that, if also outside or bordering on abnormal, combine to point toward a particular malady or disease.

Likewise, a single vital-sign performance indicator (VSPI) in a district or school may lead to consideration of many possible explanations for poor performance. However, symptoms of poor student achievement, as indicated across several VSPI, can narrow considerations to those areas that are likely to have caused this failure.

Additionally, if the student group for which achievement data is reviewed also demonstrates higher rates of suspension, absenteeism, and/or tardiness, a substantial amount of data can be analyzed for a more precise search of root causes and the development of more-meaningful remedies. In the last chapter, we introduced individual VSPI. In this chapter, clustering VSPI for expanded views of the evidence are presented to uncover the root causes of problems.

VSPI CLUSTERS

Multiple VSPI that are related symptomatically and functionally to one another and to SDF and CPC to reveal the likely underlying causes of current performance are considered clusters. VSPI clusters are the education equivalent of syndromes used in medicine. A description of the VSPI cluster can include desired outcomes and the gap that exists between current performance and future preferred levels, thereby pinpointing areas for interventions.

Clusters of VSPI provide greater insight into current performance levels and operational relationships, and create reliability and validity in the determination of an accurate diagnosis and prescription. Improvements result from even small changes in behavior, perception, or understanding of those working in one or more of the VSPI in the cluster.

VSPI CLUSTERS AND DIAGNOSIS

It is inappropriate to prescribe the same remedy in every school that experiences low achievement without understanding the combination of circumstances that contributes to low performance. In education, as in medicine, one prescription does not fit all maladies nor can the same malady in different schools be effectively treated with the same prescription. How do we begin to understand what is different about each collection of signs and symptoms?

In figure 5.1, several different vital signs produce more information and generate more implications when they are clustered than when viewed separately. In the Holland Valley School District (HVSD) and the Holland Valley High School (HVHS), the challenge was to find out why student achievement at this one high school was so different from the levels existing at the other district high schools, and what might be preventing students from making better progress.

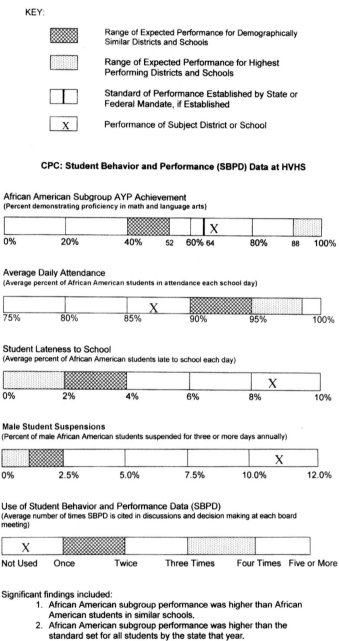

KEY:

Range of Expected Performance for Demographically Similar Districts and Schools

Range of Expected Performance for Highest Performing Districts and Schools

Standard of Performance Established by State or Federal Mandate, if Established

X   Performance of Subject District or School

CPC: Student Behavior and Performance (SBPD) Data at HVHS

African American Subgroup AYP Achievement
(Percent demonstrating proficiency in math and language arts)

| 0% | 20% | 40% | 52 | 60% 64 | 80% | 88 | 100% |

Average Daily Attendance
(Average percent of African American students in attendance each school day)

| 75% | 80% | 85% | 90% | 95% | 100% |

Student Lateness to School
(Average percent of African American students late to school each day)

| 0% | 2% | 4% | 6% | 8% | 10% |

Male Student Suspensions
(Percent of male African American students suspended for three or more days annually)

| 0% | 2.5% | 5.0% | 7.5% | 10.0% | 12.0% |

Use of Student Behavior and Performance Data (SBPD)
(Average number of times SBPD is cited in discussions and decision making at each board meeting)

| Not Used | Once | Twice | Three Times | Four Times | Five or More |

Significant findings included:
1. African American subgroup performance was higher than African American students in similar schools.
2. African American subgroup performance was higher than the standard set for all students by the state that year.
3. African American subgroup performance was substantially below that in the highest performing schools.
4. All of the remaining VSPI, average daily attendance, daily lateness to school, and male student suspensions indicated that HVHS students had behaviors that fell well outside the expected or normal ranges.
5. The HVSD Board of Education did not consider student behavior and performance data to make decisions at monthly meetings.

Figure 5.1   Clustering Vital Sign Performance Indicators (VSPI) for Diagnosis

Within the CPC of student behavior and performance data, there was special interest in the VSPI combination of African American subgroup AYP achievement data, average daily attendance, student lateness, male student suspensions, and administrator and board use of student behavior and performance data. This last VSPI was also viewed from the perspective of the CPCs of leadership and effective and integrated governance.

Preliminary examination included the development of a relevant history of the district and the organization of HVHS as a new high school ten years earlier. Additional data were obtained through interviews, diagnostic inventories, focus-group meetings, and discussion with key administrators, board members, teachers, staff members, parents, and student leaders.

Despite the many district, school, and student successes, attention was drawn to concerns in three major CPC: student behavior and performance data, team work and problem solving, and professional learning and instruction.

Among many VSPI examined, there were several that clearly required additional investigation. These VSPI, clustered in two CPC, were developed utilizing data provided by the district and school and compared to similar and best-performing districts and schools at that time. The VSPI graphic displays are similar to those presented earlier, but the coded keys that provide information to assist understanding and interpretation have differences.

The range of scores or performance rates in similar high schools and districts is found in the crosshatch area of the scale, and the range of scores or performance rates in the highest performing high schools and districts appears in the dotted area of the scale. The Holland Valley High School and School District performance rates are designated with an "X" and when a state standard existed, it is marked by a bold vertical line.

Typically, districts treat performance concerns evidenced in single VSPI as a symptom requiring a separate intervention. However, these cluster-data displays are the beginning steps in understanding and analyzing phenomena that cut across a wider array of behaviors. A deeper look discovered that there were, among African American students, substantial differences in achievement, attendance, and lateness when disaggregated by gender. The deeper analysis forced a more-careful examination of gender-related variables.

The search for answers provided some surprises. High rates of absence and tardiness were related to female work opportunities in the local health-care industry. Interviews revealed a family- and community-based business connection that had a direct impact on student attendance and tardiness, and an indirect impact on achievement. High-school girls had an opportunity to work as substitutes in care facilities and missed school during the week, and, if the older students worked afternoons or evenings, they missed school the next day or came to school late. Homework was often unfinished and study time among these students was greatly reduced.

Academic achievement had stagnated, and it was determined that this subgroup would not reach the next increase in AYP proficiency rates without improvements in all three areas of concern—attendance, tardiness, and achievement. The complicated solution to this problem involved generating understanding and obtaining the cooperation from employers in the local health-care industry, the parents of involved students, and the students themselves.

The first step in finding the most appropriate solution was taken by the school performance leadership team. Individually, some team members were aware of students working in these well paying jobs; however, none were aware of the significant number of students involved. There had not been any school effort to coordinate a plan to influence the behaviors of students involved in order to change performance outcomes.

The leadership team sought to determine how large the number of working students was by utilizing the trust existing among certain staff members and students. Every student identified was interviewed and assured that the information was confidential and not going to lead to suspensions or a loss of a job, and the collective body of information found would lead to a creative way to handle these concerns. The goal of these efforts was to prepare students for life beyond high school and these jobs.

A comprehensive effort was initiated to create short- and long-term plans that recognized the contributions of these students to the community and to organize efforts of family, students, employers, and school to correct a situation that was leaving these students academically underprepared. An agreement among all parties was reached, interventions were structured and implemented, and some students chose to work less frequently, although online courses and schedule adjustments were made for those that continued their busy working schedule.

Some improvements were documented by addressing this one issue. However, other problems identified during the discovery phase and related to district professional practice persisted. Some were related to the VSPI found in the CPC of team work and problem solving, and were the responsibility of the district office. Concerns were found among the cultural norms, specifically the formal and informal expectations and practices that influenced the levels of participation on teams by certificated employees, as shown in figure 5.2.

The indicators for team work and problem solving were well outside the expected ranges in all four VSPI and substantially below the range for school districts of similar size and socioeconomic makeup. While the VSPI identified critical issues in the CPC of team work and problem solving, they also directed

Team Responsibility
(Percent of teams responsible for implementing, monitoring, evaluating, and reporting results of improvement)

Average Faculty Participation on Teams
(Number of teams on which the average faculty member serves annually)

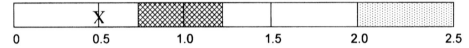

Percent of Faculty Participating on Teams
(Percent of faculty that have served on teams in the last year)

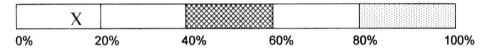

Adoption and Implementation of Team Recommendations
(Percent of team recommendations that are adopted and implemented by the district)

Significant findings included:

1. The school district had not utilized teams of staff members to design and implement plans for improved performance.
2. The amount of participation on teams by faculty members was low.
3. The percent of faculty that participated on teams in the last year was low.
4. The historical rate of adoption and implementation of team recommendations was low.

Figure 5.2   CPC: Team Work and Problem Solving

attention to the CPC of professional learning and instruction and district and school-wide culture.

Perceived low levels of trust among administrators and teachers had resulted in infrequent use of teams and low-participation rates of staff on teams. Team recommendations were not accepted for implementation by leadership and board, and teams that studied problems were not usually used in implementing solutions. Frequently there was a long delay between the work of the team studying a problem and recommending improvements, and the start up of a team to implement changes.

Importantly, the superintendent took responsibility for lack of responsiveness to previous team efforts and provided a new commitment to making team work attractive and influential. The board supported the superintendent's recommendations by committing resources to future implementation of team recommendations in a timely fashion. Further support was evident from the inclusion of training for effective team work in the formal professional-development program.

Workshops included training in roles and responsibilities of team leadership, membership, and team functioning. These added to the perceived value and importance of team work and team effectiveness. The changes included new structures and expectations to manage team and performance-improvement processes. Team success was expected, and it was supported in a variety of new ways.

In addition to increasing staff-member participation on teams, the district invited its staff members, long considered an untapped talent resource, to share their expertise and to help solve broader district and school problems. It was determined that staff members needed better performance-improvement and problem-solving skills, and a program was developed to prepare the best-performing faculty members to lead and teach others the skills needed.

The professional-development program was analyzed further to determine its relevance to:

- solving current and future problems,
- aligning content standards and instructional skills for implementing the curriculum,
- motivating and engaging students to improve behavior and achievement, and
- developing and applying clinical-practice skills to concerns identified in the CPC.

Within a short period of time staff members in the HVSD learned to look at problems in new ways. Data analyses led to the discovery of deeper meanings and connections to areas of investigation that were previously unexplored. The investigation of the cultural issues of trust in decision making and stakeholder involvement in performance-improvement processes led to a district commitment to have key stakeholders, especially teachers, as partners in improvement efforts. (See Strategy Ten at the end of the chapter.)

Entrenched organizational practices were examined carefully to determine if old habits had created roadblocks to more-productive behaviors that could connect board, district, school, student, and even family and community efforts. Involving parents and students in preparatory workshops built capacity needed to make partnerships across stakeholder groups a reality. The commitment to build on this new performance reality was reviewed by each team engaged in performance-improvement activities, and the leadership team required recent measurements of current performance before authorizing any team to proceed to next steps.

STUDY PROTOCOL FOR VSPI CLUSTERS: DEVELOPING DIAGNOSES

The clinical practice model is designed to make sure that often-overlooked data are collected, analyzed, and discussed along with the more-obvious data related to problems. In addition to asking questions that encouraged thinking and performing outside traditional roles and into the "white spaces" where people work together, it became necessary to expand the use of individual VSPI to VSPI clusters. VSPI clusters provide more-usable clues to develop diagnoses of the underlying causes of problems. (See Strategy Eleven.)

Effective educator diagnosticians organize data and look for patterns that help form a hypothesis of the root cause. The more precise the diagnosis, the more likely a design for the proper remedy will result. The following questions have been designed to be considered for every VSPI cluster to help select the best problem definition or diagnosis, and produce a potential prescription.

1. Are there perceived relationships among the VSPI in the cluster that suggest a common root cause or causes for the underperformance?
2. Are there perceived discrepancies among the VSPI in the cluster that contradict a common root cause or causes for the underperformance?
3. What other stakeholder groups need to analyze this cluster of VSPI, and how should they be involved?
4. What additional analysis needs to be made of the VSPI presented?
5. What additional VSPI need to be examined to better confirm or deny the identified root causes of the underperformance?
6. What diagnoses are suggested by the analysis and identification of causes?
7. Which potential diagnosis can be used to address the common and contradictory elements of the cluster?

8. How can the identified diagnosis be tested to determine its potential effectiveness in the treatment of the identified root cause of current performance?
9. What interventions (prescriptions) are suggested by the most precise of the diagnoses that can be implemented to improve performance across the cluster of VSPI?
10. What indications or outcomes, including counter-indications, are likely to be observed that will validate (or invalidate) the accuracy or appropriateness of the selected diagnosis and prescription?
11. To whom, how, and when will the results of the above analysis and study be reported?

As diagnosis and prescription protocols are followed more frequently, educators get further away from traditional problem-solving habits and come to rely increasingly on the more-precise use of evidence and meaning found in data. Also, educator diagnosticians experience professional growth and greater problem-solving success by analyzing VSPI and working together to design and implement solutions across and among the SDF and CPC.

CHAPTER 5 STRATEGIES

Strategy Ten: Develop a VSPI Cluster

Develop a VSPI graphic related to a student-achievement issue. Develop a potential cluster of VSPI related to this student-achievement issue. Determine the extent to which the cluster helps explain the cause of poor performance better than the student-achievement VSPI alone.

A VSPI cluster is not restricted to VSPI from only one CPC. It is often made up of VSPI from several CPC.

From your district and/or school, identify at least one issue related to student achievement in each of the following CPC:

- customer focus;
- leadership;
- alignment of programs;
- universal acceptance of expectations;
- team work and problem solving;
- staff, student, and family interactions.

To the extent possible, discover new VSPI in these CPC or replace some of the original VSPI in the cluster with others that better focus the issue.

Strategy Eleven: Critical Issue Priority Worksheets

Critical issues are too often defined by the existing patterns of problem solving and traditional ways of accomplishing role responsibilities. In other words, our definition of problems is determined by the solutions we already have.

The following questions are taken from "Critical Issue Priority Worksheets" used in training educators in the CPM. Answer each of the following questions related to the cluster of VSPI you developed in Strategy Ten to provide greater illumination of the underlying issues.

1. What is the existing capacity of the stakeholder group (administrators, teachers, board, staff, parents, students, etc.) to address this issue?
2. Which stakeholder groups will be *most* satisfied if this issue is successfully resolved?
3. Which stakeholder groups will be *least* satisfied if this issue is successfully resolved?
4. Will students and parents (teachers, staff, the community, etc.) cooperate in efforts to resolve this issue?
5. Which groups benefit because this issue has not been resolved?
6. Which groups will *gain* influence because this issue is resolved?
7. Which groups will *lose* influence because this issue is resolved?
8. What resources will be expended in resolution of the issue and at the expense of which existing programs or services?
9. Will those resources be available for use elsewhere if the issue remains unresolved?
10. Will a solution increase or decrease the commitment of other groups to problem solving?
11. What other issues will emerge if we try to resolve this one?
12. What positive and negative impact will resolution of this issue have on student achievement over the next three–five years?

DIAGNOSTIC OPTIONS FOR THE DISTRICT, SCHOOLS, EMPLOYEES, AND STUDENTS

Having diagnostic options is important to educators, but picking among them is not easy. The process of diagnosis is explored in this chapter using a diagnostic funnel to sift and analyze several layers of data to identify symptoms, possible syndromes, and root causes of problems that need solution to promote performance improvement.

> *Clinical Cycle Step 5—Diagnostic Options: The physician cannot yet be assured of a conclusive diagnosis because very different medical conditions can exhibit similar symptoms. The development of diagnostic options must be based on the studied collection and combination of symptoms related to the individual patient. Various diagnoses are hypothetically tested for comprehensiveness and appropriateness.*

DIAGNOSTICS IN EDUCATION

Diagnosis is a process based on a set of protocols that leads to an understanding of the relationships among the various symptoms and to the identification of the disease or infection, and sometimes its cause. When specific causes cannot be identified, the physician studies the collection of vital signs and symptoms to place the disease in the context of what is known, and in some rare cases even today, identifies a previously undocumented disease.

The diagnosis is intended to be specific enough to lead to a prescription for a course of effective treatment. Over time, collected and shared experience among physicians leads to ever-higher rates of diagnostic accuracy and effective interventions. Continued study of the disease and its remedy can ultimately lead to preventive strategies that protect the larger population from suffering the consequences of succumbing to the same illness.

Educators can benefit greatly from adoption of the processes used to make a diagnosis and prescription. They can improve the art of planning and performance improvement by raising the standards of professional practice and developing protocols to clearly and correctly identify the weaknesses, strengths, and needs of districts, schools, and students. As a result, the remedies that focus on improving student achievement will be more readily identified and applied.

Clinical physicians understand that study and discussion of their experiences and those of their colleagues sharpen their skills at diagnosis, prescription, and prognosis. Educational leaders and teachers need to be engaged in similar study and discussion. The intention to adapt diagnosis and prescription to educational performance improvement involves observing and analyzing the major influences on and characteristics of performance at every level—board, district, school, employees students, and other stakeholders.

A significant amount of current reform effort in education is based on the hope that a number of individual improvements, aimed at larger problems, will have a positive overall impact. Like the old game of "Battleship," reformers often shoot torpedoes at random coordinates until they hit something and then concentrate their efforts in that area.

Alignment of curriculum with standards and state tests, improvements in teacher preparation, instructional delivery, and supervision have a positive impact on performance. However, initial positive results rarely continue to increase over time in even the best schools and districts and fall far short of improving performance and increasing student achievement in schools and districts with greater needs. New strategies are needed.

PRE-DIAGNOSTIC ASSESSMENT

In most districts and schools, there is a strong tendency to focus solely on "how and where do we start and who is responsible?" That is too narrow a focus with which to begin a diagnosis. Having collected and initially analyzed past performance data and information about SDF, CPC, and VSPI, questions help focus the attention of investigators. (See Strategy Twelve at the end of the chapter.)

Effective leadership throughout a district or school is necessary to organize, design, coordinate, and implement strategies that influence student achievement. The beginning steps of this process are found in the pre-diagnostic assessment. The answers to the pre-diagnostic questions found in Strategy Twelve are only a beginning, and they alone are insufficient to facilitate improvement in districts and schools, especially in those that have a complex array of dysfunctional practices and weak performance. Pre-diagnostic assessment prepares participants in performance-improvement efforts for better diagnostic practice.

DIAGNOSIS

Effective diagnosis takes advantage of the many interrelated systems and subsystems in and around schools and students. Taken together and in parts, the data gathered about schools and their students combine to suggest many possible courses of action to turn around the performance health of the district, school, and students. Each of the actions can be implemented individually or in coordination with others in ways that provide multiple options.

The medical model of diagnosis is dependent on the collection and interpretation of vital-sign data and the development of a broad base of recorded experience. The educational model of diagnosis does the same. Abundant data related to the performance of students, staff members, other stakeholders, boards of education, school and district programs, and other activities already exist, but have not been organized and utilized productively.

The data provide a comprehensive description of organization- and student-performance health, but they are not used in ways that simplify and reduce the number of potential options that diagnosticians must consider. What determines or guides the choices of which data are significant and which data should be ignored? The steps taken to narrow the broad array of data and reduce the many potential solutions to those few that are most likely to work are found in the "diagnostic funnel."

THE DIAGNOSTIC FUNNEL

One way to visualize the protocols that produce a diagnosis and prescription is to follow steps through a large funnel, wide at the top and narrow at the bottom, with several levels of screens inside, as presented in figure 6.1. The beginning levels represent the collection, organization, and analysis of data and information that covers the past performance of the board, district, school, students, and stakeholders. Protocols are followed to collect, organize, and evaluate these data and information. Once there is a secure hypothesis formed about the ailment, the diagnostician(s) select among potential options.

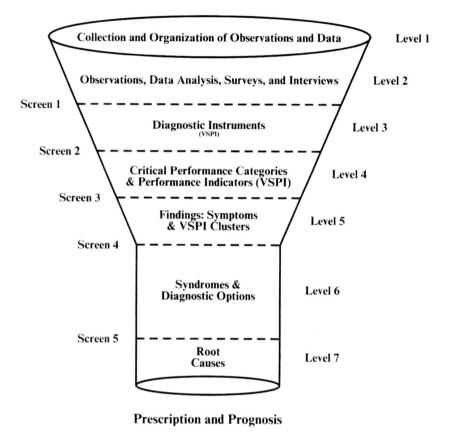

Figure 6.1   The Diagnostic Funnel

The major purposes for using the funnel are to understand the critical issues affecting performance and how they are related to one another, and to discover the root causes of underperformance. When there is insufficient data or experience to identify root causes, the symptoms may be treated in clusters and the responses monitored to see if there is any improvement. After treating each of the related symptoms individually, it may still be possible to identify the root cause.

The following steps, in succession, represent the levels of the diagnostic funnel and the screens through which the data are sifted to discover ever-more focused and specific clues to the underlying causes of underperformance.

First Level: Collection and Organization of Observations and Data

A wealth of data exists within the data notebooks developed in Strategy Four of chapter 3. Regularly updating the notebooks fills the first level of the diagnostic funnel in preparation for new diagnoses. First level "sifting" focuses on general questions that begin to identify the data that will be helpful in defining the problem. These questions help to refine the data that will be used in subsequent levels of screening and sifting. (See Strategy Thirteen.)

Second Level: Observations, Data Analysis, Surveys, and Interviews

Surveys of staff and stakeholders related to satisfaction, goal setting and accomplishment, program evaluation, and a variety of other issues and topics should be administered, analyzed, and reported regularly. The more regularly feedback is solicited, reported, and incorporated into planning, the more honest and useful the responses and the greater the trust and willingness of stakeholders to share important information and invest in change processes.

When surveys identify areas of concern, more-specific information can be obtained in focused individual and group interviews. Stakeholders invited to meet and explore potential problems and concerns provide important insights not always evident to leaders, and an important positive side effect of these discussions is that stakeholders learn to trust those who listen to them. Sharing concerns with those impacted by both the problem and the solution builds a base of support for successful change. (See Strategy Fourteen.)

Third Level: Diagnostic Instruments

The District and School Performance Health Diagnostic Inventory (DSPHDI) was developed to gather feedback from any number of different stakeholder groups on behaviors and outcomes related to all seventeen CPC. Strategy Five in chapter 3 presents a graphic representation of stakeholder responses to the CPC of "Team Work and Problem Solving." The DSPHDI and some other diagnostic inventories focus on levels of commitment and capacity among major stakeholder groups for performance improvement. The perceptions of stakeholders reported on these inventories provide invaluable evidence of the existence and specific characteristics of problems. The extent to which the data notebooks supports or opposes the reported perceptions of stakeholders is important in defining the true nature of the problem. (See Strategy Fifteen.)

Fourth Level: Critical Performance Categories and Performance Indicators

The disparities between documented information and stakeholder perceptions provide invaluable input at this level regarding specific characteristics of problems that are often ignored. Administrative and staff discussions are essential to develop an understanding of what has been examined. At this point, the SDF and CPC matrices are very useful to produce clarification and the identification of multiple potential problems. Once the question, "What caused that set of responses?" is asked, the investigation moves into activities and behaviors not usually considered.

By sifting evidence through the SDF and CPC matrices and by using the worksheet introduced in Strategy Three in chapter 2, behaviors inhibiting performance health can be examined further. These two exercises provide a deeper consideration of observations gleaned from the surveys at level two and the diagnostic inventories at level three. Investigators now can see more clearly the relationships among the SDF, CPC, and the behaviors and activities taking place and reported as VSPI. (See Strategy Sixteen.)

Fifth Level: Findings: Symptoms and VSPI Clusters

Too often, problem identification begins and ends with symptoms. As a result, most solutions are designed to treat the manifestations but not the root cause of problems. An analogous situation in medicine would be to treat acute pain with painkillers without determining, and treating, the cause of the pain. Failure to treat the root cause of the problem in medicine can result in permanent debilitation or death. Likewise, in districts and schools, failure to discover and treat the underlying causes of problems results in treatments that mask rather than cure the dysfunction, resulting in continued and misunderstood underperformance.

It is necessary to get to the fifth level of the diagnostic funnel to finally discriminate between symptoms and actual problems. Clustering the associated VSPI allows us to look at the patterns of behaviors related to the area of underperformance and decide which behaviors, attitudes, and perceptions cause rather than result from the problem. (See Strategy Seventeen.)

A classic example of this distinction was reviewed in earlier chapters. A close examination of patterns of underperformance at Holland Valley High School (HVHS) discovered that minority-student underperformance, frequently blamed on issues of motivation and socioeconomics, was actually the result of opportunities that satisfied basic personal needs—recognition and financial self-sufficiency. HVHS students had the opportunity to develop a sense of pride for accomplishments working in nursing homes that reinforced these benefits with an adult rate of pay.

Similar accomplishments were hard to attain through pursuit of high school academic excellence. The solutions that traditionally targeted the issues of lateness, cutting school, and motivation had failed because these issues were related to but not the root cause of the underperformance. Instead, by working with employers, parents, and students together; making modifications to student schedules; posting of homework assignments and courses online; and increasing communication among all parties, students were employed at times and on days that did not interfere with course schedules.

In another school district that used the diagnostic funnel to identify root causes of underperformance, data revealed a number of concerns about the existing organization, its culture, leadership behaviors, and the influence of student test score results on decision making. Three critical performance categories were identified as having the most need for investigation and potential interventions and are reproduced below.

Careful examination by a district-level team suggested that there were significant adult behaviors that needed to be addressed before the district and schools could effectively meet the academic needs of students. As in most performance-improvement efforts, adult behaviors needed adjustments first. The team identified VSPI that they thought would best reveal improvements that would contribute to future success.

Data Set One—Symptoms of Underperformance in CPC of District-Wide Culture

1. There is a strong sense among teachers and administrators that the cost of taking risks far outweigh any benefits.
2. There is a fear of retribution for failed efforts, especially when the behavior or action is new.
3. Learning is not revered among adults and students.
4. Existing practices are supported and continued beyond usefulness or benefit because a consensus about what to do next never forms.
5. Expectations are not clear.
6. Trust levels are low among stakeholder groups.

Likely VSPI to be measured and tracked as evidence of performance progress:

1. Trust is evident in all interactions among leaders and stakeholders.
2. The culture supports risk taking and creativity needed to solve district and school problems successfully.
3. Adult learning is respected and supported.

Data Set Two—Symptoms of Underperformance in CPC of Leadership (District Leaders)

1. A clear separation exists between leaders and all other employees.

2. A prevalent perception of "we versus them" has developed between and among district and school levels.
3. Little confidence exists in current district committee and team work.
4. A very limited number of stakeholders are engaged in team work.
5. Staff members generally ignore problems outside their control.
6. Traditional boundaries exist among departments and levels.
7. Few employee stakeholders participate in planning and decision making.
8. A shared vision neither exists nor is articulated at any level in the school district.

Likely VSPI to be measured and tracked as evidence of performance progress:

1. Trust is evident in all interactions among leaders and stakeholders.
2. Leaders practice effective listening skills.
3. District and school leaders are fair, compassionate, and act in the best interests of students, parents, and staff.

Data Set Three—Symptoms of Underperformance in CPC of Student Behavior and Performance Data

1. Student performance data are used minimally to justify proposals and recommendations.
2. The board and CSA relationship is contentious, and five consecutive years of failing to meet AYP standards has contributed to that contentiousness.
3. The board's discussion at meetings appears to be motivated by disagreements, politics, or other motives that are not related to education performance.
4. Discussion about "solutions" is based in opinion and reports about pre-packaged or commercial programs that have worked in other places rather than in the needs and outcomes projected for this district and its students.
5. Data are used sometimes to justify decisions, but they do not drive inquiry and lead to the development of solutions.

Likely VSPI to be measured and tracked as evidence of performance progress:

1. The board works effectively with the superintendent to improve performance of district, schools, employees, and students.
2. Board members are able to separate the work of the board from the work of district and school leaders.

3. The superintendent provides a detailed report quarterly about district, school, and student performance to the board so that members are aware of and evaluate the progress made toward agreed-upon goals.

These three examples should not be taken as full descriptions of symptoms or VSPI that can automatically be adapted and transplanted to other schools and districts. Each district and school must develop specific descriptions based on their own data analysis. Nonetheless, it is interesting to see what potential findings and diagnoses were offered by this team.

Findings:

1. Efforts to deal with shrinking revenue and budgetary cuts directed by the central office have contributed to the "them versus us" attitude existing between the central office and schools over lost programs and poor test results.
2. "Top-down" district office direction has left schools few options to address performance concerns.
3. The frequency with which personnel identified trust as a critical issue was a surprise to most members of the team.
4. For a large majority of school and district employees, fear of trying something new was as strong as the fear of failure.
5. Direction to correct these cultural deficiencies was not coming from the superintendent, board, or central office personnel.
6. Current structures, committees, and teams were not the venue through which needed improvements could take place.
7. District employees and stakeholders conceded that they did not know what to do next and started to bicker with one another.

Potential Diagnoses:

1. The expectation of formal leaders that they alone possess the authority and expertise to direct employee actions has led employees to abandon new ideas and experimentation.
2. Formal leaders, probably even the board, are not comfortable with decisions made by anyone but themselves.
3. Planning and problem-solving procedures have not been approved for use by administrators or teaching staff and what is planned is largely ineffective.
4. Administrator behaviors reinforce the lack of collaboration with staff members and the lack of confidence in the work of others.

5. A clear understanding of the district's financial circumstances does not exist among stakeholders to reduce the fighting over diminishing resources.

6. Central office administrators are not listening actively to building level stakeholders to break down perceived barriers to trust and cooperation.

7. A database of district, school, and student performance data, that can focus a dialogue of stakeholder discussion at all levels of the district and schools, including that needed by the superintendent and board, does not exist.

For the purpose of this illustration, all the symptoms, VSPI, findings, and potential diagnoses were not included. Each of the diagnoses could be selected for independent prescriptions, but more than likely the combination of them could be addressed by one prescription with at least some of its parts implemented simultaneously.

Sixth Level: Syndromes and Diagnostic Options

In medicine, syndromes are clusters of symptoms that are not a specific disease, but that tend to occur together or to be related. As such, physicians recognize the cluster and treat the entire syndrome.

Educators, through experience and research, need to identify, record, and share symptom clusters and potential syndromes as well as the actions that have been used to successfully address them. For example, even if the root cause of grade-level underperformance cannot be identified, interventions designed to address a cluster of related symptoms about curriculum standards, lesson planning, and targeted professional development can be implemented and tracked against future performance.

Syndromes usually respond to a single intervention or a few remedies prepared as a package. Prescriptions designed to treat syndromes are very specific for the combination of symptoms and are usually more closely related to the root cause than are treatments aimed at individual and possibly unrelated symptoms. Monitoring the response of each symptom within the syndrome to the same intervention helps identify the most critical symptoms and leads to a better understanding of potential root causes. (See Strategy Eighteen.)

Seventh Level: Root Causes

When symptoms are identified successfully and clustered into syndromes, the root causes of underperformance are more likely identified. This is a difficult discrimination, but when learned, treatments are more effective and efficient than when treating mere symptoms or clusters of them. The great success medical science has had in treating disease has been in the clear identification of its cause and the documentation of the relative success of each treatment developed in response. This is a goal for education. (See Strategy Nineteen.)

Outcomes: Prescription and Prognosis

After sifting and analyzing all collected data, adding new discoveries, and discarding extraneous and distracting information from the performance puzzle, a clearer image of organization strengths, needs, and improvement opportunities emerges. Sometimes, symptoms and syndromes are distinctly recognized early and efforts move quickly during the steps from the top of the funnel to the bottom.

Early diagnostic attempts require a significant investment of time to develop dependable data-collection processes, to build databases that support reliable decisions at each level of the funnel, and to build familiarity and comfort with diagnostic-funnel steps. Practice and experience in these protocols are needed to make an accurate diagnosis and prescription. The knowledge and skill of the diagnostician grow quickly through such practice.

By following the cascading and screening steps through the diagnostic funnel, the relationships among traditional roles and responsibilities (SDF) and the seventeen CPC can be more clearly understood. Board, district, school, student, and other stakeholder performance behaviors can be understood in the context of observed problems. Even so, root causes will not likely be identified in early diagnostic efforts.

In summary, the diagnostic funnel protocol leads to the development, examination, and selection of prescriptions that are far more likely to improve performance than are the solutions developed with less-trusted data at beginning levels of the funnel. In other words, the likelihood of performance success increases when a prescription is prepared with knowledge developed at deeper levels of the funnel.

CHAPTER 6 STRATEGIES

Strategy Twelve: Pre-diagnostic Assessment

Even before conducting a diagnosis of a problem, basic information is required so that the problem can be studied and understood in an appropriate context. Using the data and the VSPI already developed, consider the following questions to ensure that the diagnosis developed will focus on the most appropriate symptoms.

1. How would you describe current performance, and how is it different from one, two, and three years ago?
2. What strategies have been used in the past to address the problems suggested in the VSPI?
3. Why haven't past strategies succeeded?
4. What would improved performance look like and/or how would it be measured?
5. Which stakeholders are most invested in the current practice?
6. Which stakeholders are likely to oppose change?
7. Which stakeholders are likely to support change?
8. What kinds of training are needed to build sufficient capacity for change?
9. Is there sufficient commitment to change among those needed to be involved?
10. What amount of time is needed to demonstrate successful change?

It should be possible to conduct a pre-diagnostic assessment on any number of issues among groups of formal and informal leaders. The pre-diagnostic assessment results should be used to prioritize issues considered for diagnosis and treatment.

Strategy Thirteen: Level One of the Diagnostic Funnel

Using the data available in the data notebooks, consider which kind of information among the following factors help establish the problem definition:

- school?
- grade level?
- subject area?
- socioeconomics?
- ethnicity?
- neighborhood?
- years enrolled in the school or district?
- per pupil expenditure?
- status of curriculum and alignment?
- alignment of testing strategies?
- others?

Strategy Fourteen: Level Two of the Diagnostic Funnel

Level two focuses on questions that dig more deeply into the preliminary definitions of problems developed in the first level.

1. What group is most directly affected by the problem?
2. How is the problem evident?
3. Why is this group impacted?
4. Which other groups may be at risk?
5. What data are needed to clearly define both the problem and the at-risk population?
6. Have any steps been taken to address this problem in the past?
7. What were the results?
8. Is there commitment to a solution?
9. Is there sufficient capacity to implement a solution?
10. Has the problem evolved or is it essentially the same?
11. Are there any stakeholder groups that would oppose a solution?
12. What resources are available?

Strategy Fifteen: Level Three of the Diagnostic Funnel

Second-level results and research-based inventory assessments of specific behaviors are further reviewed at the third level.

1. Are the issues raised in the initial analysis of data also evident in responses of stakeholders to inventories, surveys, and interviews?
2. Which CPC are most closely related to the expressed concerns of stakeholders?
3. What other issues are evident in those specific CPC for identified stakeholder groups?
4. What differences exist among the perceptions of other stakeholder groups?
5. Will those differences support or inhibit possible solutions?
6. Are there common concerns among other stakeholder groups?
7. What behaviors and performance issues exhibited by concerned stakeholder groups most need to be changed as a part of the solution?
8. What other consequences will result from changes in the identified behaviors?

Strategy Sixteen: Level Four of the Diagnostic Funnel

The SDF/CPC matrix, as found in Strategy Six in chapter 3, is a visual representation of the interrelationships that are critical to an exact diagnosis. Based on the data that has been sifted and analyzed through the diagnostic funnel to this point, answer the following questions:

1. Which specific roles and responsibilities are most closely associated with the behaviors and performances that define the problem?
2. Which specific roles and responsibilities are most closely associated with the behaviors and performances that may solve the problem?
3. How can those behaviors and performances be displayed as vital-sign performance indicators?
4. What do the VSPI indicate about

    a. performance that falls outside of the normal range?
    b. what it means when outside the normal range?
    c. practices, expectations, and circumstances that caused behavior to exist outside of the normal range?
    d. need for further examination and assessments that may be necessary to determine the primary causes of abnormal activity and results?
    e. remedies, treatments, interventions, and organizational lifestyle changes that may be required to move the results back into expected and normal ranges?
    f. methods of ongoing monitoring and treatments that may be required even after the organization is brought back into preferred ranges of performance?

5. Are there clusters of VSPI that offer insights into the causes of the problem that have not been considered before?

Strategy Seventeen: Level Five of the Diagnostic Funnel

Questions that will identify the symptoms most closely related the actual problem include the following:

1. What stakeholders exhibit the underperforming behaviors most acutely?
2. How is the experience of the most acutely underperforming stakeholder group different from other underperforming groups?
3. What are the measurable differences of experience and performance within the acutely underperforming group?
4. Do those differences result in the same range of performance as they do among other groups?
5. Are there unique differences between the acutely underperforming group and other groups?
6. Can any of those unique differences account for the underperformance?
7. Are any of the identified unique differences the result of choices made by, or specific needs or characteristics of, members of the group?

Strategy Eighteen: Level Six of the Diagnostic Funnel

Symptoms can be clustered into syndromes of underperformance using the following protocol of questions:

1. Which behaviors/symptoms of underperformance are shared within unique underperforming stakeholder groups?
2. Which behaviors/symptoms share common performance outcomes?
3. Which behaviors/symptoms can be observed simultaneously within underperforming stakeholder groups?
4. Which behaviors/symptoms are found only within underperforming stakeholder groups?
5. Which behaviors/symptoms are found across stakeholder groups when there are indications of underperformance?

Strategy Nineteen: Level Seven of the Diagnostic Funnel

Answers to questions in Strategy Seventeen help to refine the definition of symptoms of underperformance. Answers to questions in Strategy Eighteen lead to the clustering of symptoms into syndromes. Answers to the following four questions, if documented in the data and measurable, begin to move toward discovery of root causes of underperformance.

1. What needs are served by the group's choices that are unique to the group?
2. What is the motivation for the chosen behavior of the underperforming group?
3. Does the group understand the consequences of the chosen behavior?
4. If given opportunity and support, would the group choose to improve its performance?

PRESCRIPTIONS AND PROGNOSES

Prioritizing Solutions to Educational Problems

Performance improvement, like healing from an illness, will not take place without the careful selection and application of the most appropriate prescription and prognosis. The selected intervention is very important, but without a forecast or prognosis of what will happen during the intervention, the diagnosticians and implementers do not learn why the prescription worked or did not. This chapter follows the development and use of prescriptions and prognoses and introduces an electronic format for tracking them.

> *Clinical Cycle Step 6—Prescriptions and Prognoses: In order to develop a plan of treatment with a strong likelihood of success, the physician selects the single best answer to the puzzle of symptoms and syndromes presented by the patient. This answer, the diagnosis, will be the basis for prescriptive treatment that includes a prognosis. The prognosis is essential because it considers what will happen most probably if the condition is not treated and what will happen most probably, both positively and negatively, to the patient as the prescription is administered over time. These probable events and conditions serve as signposts to determine if the prescription is appropriate and is having the desired effect. If not, the original diagnosis and prescription must be revisited and reconsidered.*

PRESCRIPTION AND PROGNOSIS

A prescription is a coordinated set of interventions intended to efficiently and effectively treat root causes, symptoms, and/or syndromes of underperformance. A prescription takes the form of a specific written direction or description of corrective action intended to produce changes in structures, practice, and outcomes that are an improvement over the past. Educational prescriptions must include the anticipated impact of the interventions on interrelationships and activities at every level of the organization.

In efforts to "do no harm" as set forth in the Hippocratic Oath, physicians must consider what the probable progression of an illness will be if left untreated. If the appropriate intervention is more painful or harmful than the condition itself, it may be best to take no action. Large doses of antibiotics, for example, might fight the bacteria that have caused fever and chills, but the gastrointestinal consequences can be so traumatic that the prescription becomes more uncomfortable than suffering the discomfort of a "flu-like" illness.

Decisions to forgo treatment occur under other circumstances as well. In consultation with their physician, many terminally ill patients opt for a higher quality of life in their final months rather than undergoing painful surgeries and treatments that may extend their life briefly but will incapacitate them and prevent them from pursuing activities that give their life meaning.

In districts, schools, as well as other organizations, much harm is done by doing nothing. Organizations over time become less efficient and effective simply because the routines of operation tend to ignore evolving needs. While routines bring stability and confidence to those who work in organizations, routines also cause a resistance to needed change and inhibit growth and flexibility. The use of the clinical cycle for performance improvement is biased toward action.

Well-constructed prescriptions and prognoses create an appropriate balance between necessary action and existing routines. As a protocol of estimation and forecasting, a prognosis requires diagnosticians to anticipate what will happen when prescriptions are implemented with particular stakeholders, using particular techniques, over a particular time frame. Lesson planning, for example, is an exercise of developing a prescription and prognosis for each class, for targeted students, and is delivered over one or more classes. However, a process that leads to accurate predictions of new results expected from the implementation of prescriptions among the SDF and CPC has been missing in education.

Teacher knowledge of student background and skills, content standards, instructional strategies, desired and expected outcomes, and other information determines how the teacher plans the lesson content, structure, and delivery incorporating sufficient student practice and appropriate assessment strategies. The teacher expects certain outcomes and, in the absence of those outcomes, the plan is revised and re-implemented.

When the prognosis fails to predict the responses, reactions, and interactions of the patient (in this case the student) and the prescription correctly, it is important that the prescription be reexamined for its appropriateness. The accuracy of a prescription is most easily observed when specific milestones that were forecast as a part of the prognosis are achieved through stakeholder activities. Achievement of milestones also demonstrates the precision of the prescription in addressing symptoms and possibly the root causes of critical issues.

Every adjustment in a prescription requires an adjustment in the prognosis to improve accuracy in matching the prescription to the issue being remedied. This process takes place with each repetition of the implementation phase in the clinical cycle, the guided implementation phase mini-cycle (GIPMC) first described in chapter 1. The chief benefits to staff members using this approach include the following:

1. gaining a new understanding of the effectiveness of strategies designed to close the gap between present performance levels and actual results;
2. producing "before and after" data that become a part of the database shared with other professionals; and
3. developing commitment and capacity for higher performance that can be taught to others and guided by effective protocols.

WRITING PRESCRIPTIONS

It would appear to be an easy task to write an effective prescription after sifting information through the diagnostic funnel and identifying symptoms, syndromes, and perhaps the root causes of underperformance. For most educators, effective prescription writing improves with practice and, yet, caution needs to be exercised with beginning prescriptions. There are two common assumptions made by new diagnosticians that trap thinking and significantly reduce prescription effectiveness.

Avoiding the first assumption is very difficult. Early diagnostic efforts are often assumed to be accurate simply because they take so much time to develop. New diagnosticians tend not to double-check analyses and test preliminary diagnoses. It is important to receive feedback from stakeholders involved at the critical intersections of the SDF and CPC, measure the vital signs related to symptoms, and be prepared to adjust the diagnosis. Anxiousness to start the prescription must not result in ignoring information relevant to the correctness of the diagnosis.

The second assumption trap is that old prescriptions can be applied to new diagnoses. Physicians are concerned that patients should not "self prescribe" old unused medicines when they encounter symptoms they think they recognize.

Failure to see the doctor for a new diagnosis can produce results that range from poisoning to the delay of effective treatment.

Likewise, educators and stakeholders that are familiar with old remedies often seek to re-implement them. In doing so, they can suffer the consequences of poisoning the organization with inappropriate treatment or delaying implementation of more appropriate strategies. A good example of this second assumption was found in a district exploring strategies to increase student achievement on state-mandated proficiency exams.

The district selected "service learning" as a strategy. Past service-learning projects had made a dramatic impact on the growth of students, increasing motivation and bringing relevance to their course work. The selection of the program in this instance was based in part on the availability of additional money to implement the program. However, there was no research that demonstrated that service learning could be expected to produce higher levels of academic proficiency in language arts and mathematics. (See Strategy Twenty at the end of the chapter.)

CONSIDERING MULTIPLE PRESCRIPTION OPTIONS

It is important to develop a wide range of prescription options. In medicine, options include pharmacology, physical therapy, changes in diet, surgery, and other treatments, depending on the strength of the patient and the severity of the disorder. Districts and schools also have a multitude of options to consider. Options range from training programs, improved communications, changes in personnel practices, new models of supervision and evaluation, realignment of curriculum, improved instructional strategies and materials, formation and training of new teams, hiring or terminating personnel, and others. (See Strategy Twenty-One.)

To avoid the diagnostic and prescriptive traps faced by new diagnosticians, teams need to double-check the diagnosis and to develop multiple prescription options before narrowing the selection. However, with a broad set of options, it is difficult to select with confidence from among several. How can several options be reduced to the most appropriate one?

PRIORITIZING AND REDUCING AVAILABLE PRESCRIPTION OPTIONS

Once a diagnosis has been developed and a variety of prescription options have been identified, it is important to select the prescription that will most effectively and efficiently meet the problem described in the diagnosis. A three-step process has been developed for teams to guide the selection. To establish a reliable connection between the diagnosis and prescription and increase confidence in the results, the team splits into two subgroups to use the "Prescription Priority Worksheets," an abbreviated example of which appears in figure 7.1.

The first subgroup determines which criteria should be weighted more heavily based upon the importance of each to the district or school. That score of 1, 2, or 3 is placed in the "Diagnosis Value" column. The second subgroup selects a prescription value for each criterion based upon its expected impact when used in each prescription option. After all criteria for each prescription option have been considered, the weighted value of each criterion is multiplied by its prescription value. The weighted score of all criteria in an option is added together to produce a total priority score for each prescription option. (See Strategy Twenty-Two.)

Teams using the prioritization worksheets for the first time are often surprised by the outcomes. The application of criteria with specific values often results in unexpected priorities. Many decisions made to improve performance are influenced by opinion leaders, sources of revenue, and past practice. These are not necessarily important factors. Application of criteria and weighted values forces a consideration of factors often ignored; and through this process, prescriptions that may have been largely underused can emerge with a higher priority.

Prescription-development skills are enhanced quickly when the full team discusses results of the prioritizing activity. Consensus can overcome different individual opinions because of the weighted value of specific criteria and their influence on each prescription option. The team is free to select the prescription(s) without being bound exclusively to the priority order developed through the worksheets, but with experience, teams develop greater confidence in their selections and understand better why the selected prescription is likely to succeed. Differentiating among multiple potential prescriptions by weighting criteria for importance and impact, and comparing the relative strengths among prescription options, adds to the team's confidence in the ultimate success of intervention.

DEVELOPING PROGNOSES

It is always easier to predict either the best or the worst possible consequence than it is to accurately predict the actual outcome. Unfortunately, neither optimists nor pessimists have a very successful track record in predicting results ac-

Diagnosis:

Related Critical Performance Categories:

Recommended Prescription:

#	Criteria	Diagnosis Value	Prescription Value			Weighted Score (Diag. Value x Presc. Value)	Rationale
			1	2	3		
1	VSPI Data Supports this Prescription *(See Note 1)*		Very Little	Moderately	Strongly		
7	Board's Readiness to Support this Prescription *(See Note 2)*		Low	Moderate	High		
8	This Prescription will Increase Board Capacity *(See Note 3)*		Very Little	Moderately	Strongly		
9	Leadership's Readiness to Support this Prescription		Low	Moderate	High		
10	This Prescription will Increase Leadership Capacity		Very Little	Moderately	Strongly		
15	Certificated Staffs' Readiness to Support this Prescription		Low	Moderate	High		
19	Parents' Readiness to Support this Prescription		Low	Moderate	High		
25	This Prescription will Improve Cooperative Planning Among All Stakeholders		Very Little	Moderately	Strongly		
30	Overall Costs of Implementation *(See Note 4)*		Low	Moderate	High		
31	Time Required to Implement		Very Little	Some	Significant		

#	Criteria	Diagnosis Value	Prescription Value			Weighted Score (Diag. Value x Presc. Value)	Rationale
			1	2	3		
33	Existing Resources Available to Implement this Prescription		Very Little	Some	Significant		
36	Positive Impact on Student Achievement over the next 1-2 Years *(See Notes 5 and 6)*		Very Little	Some	Significant		
37	Positive Impact on Student Behavior over the next 3-5 Years		Very Little	Some	Significant		
40	The Prognosis for this Prescription is Reasonable and Supported by the Data		No		Yes		

PRIORITY SCORE (Total of individual Value x Score for each criteria)	

LE Team Leader:

LE Team Members:

Data Recorded and Updated by Name/Date:

Additional Considerations: The above criteria are excerpted from a longer set used in setting priorities among prescriptions and the number of each reflects its order in the original. Additional criteria can be added to consider any of the factors in greater detail as noted below in the notes that refer to the set of questions above.

Note 1: Consideration may be given to VSPI Clusters, symptoms, and syndromes

Note 2: It may be important to consider the readiness of any number of stakeholder groups, including parents, students, leaders, faculty, staff, community, etc.

Note 3: It may be important to consider the capacity of any number of stakeholder groups, including parents, students, leaders, faculty, staff, community, etc.

Note 4: It may be important to consider elements of the cost, such as training, materials, staff, etc.

Note 5: In addition to achievement it is important to consider student behavior, attendance, discipline, etc.

Note 6: It can be important to consider change over different time periods, i.e. 1-3 years, 3-5 years, 1-5 years, etc.

Figure 7.1   Prescription Priority Worksheets

curately. Prognoses, to be of real value in monitoring, assessing, and modifying treatment to assure improved outcomes, must consider and predict positive and negative side effects, contraindications, and risks. Very few leaders and planners in education engage carefully in prognosis protocols.

Warnings of drowsiness, headache, nosebleeds, and irritability (less serious side effects) inform the patient that negative effects need to be endured sometimes if the medicine is to have its full, positive, and progressive impact. Humans, patients and diagnosticians alike, have experience in understanding the probable consequences of specific actions. From an early age, children learn that certain actions, words, attitudes, and responses are likely to produce predictable reactions. In a sense, humans practice prognosis all of their lives.

The implementation team must learn how to predict what impact selected prescriptions will have over time and on which individuals and parts of the organization. During implementation, the team measures how much the actual behaviors of individuals and the organization differ from those predicted. Individuals and teams explore reasons for the differences, develop an understanding of why the differences exist, make necessary adjustments to keep the intervention on track, and monitor movements that push the organization ever closer to desired outcomes.

Forecasting skills (making better prognoses) improve with each prescription. Ultimately, the team uses the results of its monitoring of the impact of the prescription and, based on the differences between the prognosis and the actual impact, decides to continue, modify, or even abandon plans, in order to improve performance.

MAKING ACCURATE PROGNOSES

Making accurate prognoses depends upon successful experience in managing side effects and time during prescription implementation. A viable prognosis is based on an accurate forecast of the time needed to develop new capacities (at specific levels of proficiency) among specific stakeholder groups. Prescriptions implemented too quickly may never take root in the daily routines that sustain improvements. Prescriptions implemented too slowly may never develop the critical momentum needed to have real impact on behaviors and practice. (See Strategy Twenty-Three.)

Diagnosticians must carefully and systematically collect, record, and share the results of specific interventions, and organize and reorganize the recorded results by the characteristics specific to each client or patient. This practice improves individual diagnostic abilities; it also results in a significant body of recorded experience that serves as a "text" for diagnostic practice. Some educators become better diagnosticians than do others, but every educator can use the protocols of clinical practice to form diagnoses, test prescriptions and prognoses, and design alternative approaches when expected results are not achieved.

Consider the following positive and negative prognoses for three elements of a sample prescription.

Prescription: Grade-level staff members will be reorganized; grade level leaders selected; and new grade-level teams will be trained in the use of student behavior and performance data to improve planning, decision making, and instructional delivery. This will be accomplished through the following:

Element 1: Creation of new organizational design with grade-level team leaders at each grade level.

Prognoses: There will be expressions of frustration and consternation for approximately four months; there will be strong social pressure to support the prescription in six to eight months, but some private conversations will focus on concerns about appropriateness and effectiveness of the prescription; the seeds of a new organization culture will be sown across the staff in eight months; and the design of training and inservice will change with a greater focus on improvement strategies for the following school year after eight months.

Element 2: Formation and training of new grade-level teams

Prognoses: There will be complaints about insufficient time to accomplish work; concern that team-building activities and processes starting after the first two months are still insufficient; new energy, enthusiasm, and commitment will be evident soon after the determination of the prescription; increases in coordination among grade-level teams will result in more broadly based support for the prescription after four months; new levels of collaboration and support among team members after three months; effectiveness of planning and improved decision making and problem solving will be observed after six months; and grade-level leaders and teachers will operate more closely as a team in eight months.

Element 3: Improved use of student behavior and performance data

Prognoses: Initially, there will be resistance to the use of data in planning and decision making; data will be analyzed superficially for four to five months, not in the depths needed to accurately report symptoms, syndromes, and root causes; over the first six month period, there will be three or four analyses, discussions, and reports of findings from the data; after six months, most staff members would like to skip reviews of data; after eight months, the data will take on new importance and meaning and staff members will feel some discomfort over the realization that prior poor performance should have been recognized and attended to earlier; after ten months, grade-level and other teams begin using the same student performance data to find other performance problems in the organization; and after the same length of time, participants realize that more data is not the same as better use of available data.

Prognoses of negative responses are just as important as positive ones. In most instances, negative responses will be observed first. Ultimately, however, it is the growth in the number of the positive prognoses that indicates an acceptance by stakeholders and success of the changes sought.

New teams are normally optimistic and underestimate how much time will be needed to accomplish positive outcomes. In the examples forecast above for the three elements of the prescription, all of the time frames for positive prognoses would be too short for schools that exhibit poor and inconsistent performance health and whose students have had several years of not achieving proficiency.

However, in schools that have had good success in conducting performance-improvement activities, the time frames for the negative and positive prognoses in the prescription and three prognosis elements are realistic. Prior success and appropriate preparation for additional success reduce the impact of negative prognoses. Additional positive progress will be reported as staff is trained in forecasting reactions to prescription implementation.

TASKS AND TIMELINES

As reactions follow implementation, original expectations can be forgotten or they become difficult to distinguish among projected, unanticipated, and actual outcomes. Tracking outcomes accurately and understanding the differences among forecasted and actual outcomes require the formation of well-constructed prognoses that include tracking of implementation activities.

A "Tasks and Timeline" matrix is a relatively simple presentation of all of the elements of a prescription or intervention plan on which the progression and time frame of the plan can be plotted. Figure 7.2 is a partial Tasks and Timelines Matrix used to plot the activities of a school-level performance-improvement project. The activities are listed down the vertical axis of the matrix. The horizontal axis is comprised of the weeks of the project. Major task checkpoints are plotted in appropriate weeks across the matrix.

The scheduled occurrence of specific activities is identified by filling the intersection of the activity and the week in which it occurs with a code representing the nature of the activity. In this case, a dark square represents the initiation of a specific activity and slashes designate the continuation of that activity over time. Scheduled reports of progress are also marked on the

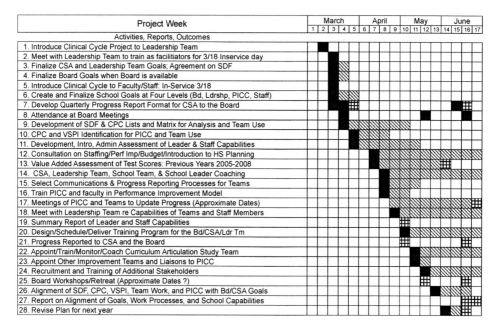

Figure 7.2   **Task and Timeline: Assessing and Establishing School-Wide Capabilities (March-June)**

matrix. Any number of other designations can be made with definitions included in the key.

The Tasks and Timelines Matrix serves as a planning device to organize the selected activities and the time frame needed to complete each. However, it is not unusual for an activity to take either more or less time than originally planned. It is also possible to discover the need to interject new activities or to reorder selected activities. As individuals and teams become more experienced, the accuracy of projected activities and time frames improves. (See Strategy Twenty-Four.)

As changes occur during implementation, the original Tasks and Timeline Matrix should be modified and updated, at least every three to six months. The matrix should represent the current plan and updated expectations for activities and time. A blank row beneath each task can be inserted with a different coding design so that actual results can be recorded as they are measured.

PLOTTING AND MONITORING PROGNOSES

Prognoses must be monitored to ensure that the results of implementation can be clearly understood. The positive and negative effects of the implemented prescription need to be monitored and recorded. When the actual results of the prescription and the positive and negative feedback is different from the original prognosis (expectations), the cause and implications of the difference must be considered. Team discussion of these differences contributes to understanding the differences between forecasted and actual results and helps teams learn to make more appropriate future prescriptions and prognoses. (See Strategy Twenty-Five.)

When outcomes are different from those predicted in the prognosis, it is important to determine if the differences still support continued treatment activities or if differences require modifications to either the prognosis, prescription, or both. When the diagnosed behaviors and activities that contribute to underperformance are aligned well with the prescription and prognosis, improvements in performance occur rapidly and benefit colleagues.

CHAPTER 7 STRATEGIES

Strategy Twenty: Elements of a Prescription and Prognosis

In order to make sure that the prescription is appropriate to the diagnosis and that the prognosis is an accurate prediction of outcomes, begin with the following questions. These broad questions are only the beginning, but each contributes to an initial consideration of the prescription and prognosis. Pick a problem identified in one of the earlier strategies for which a diagnosis has been prepared.

Prescription:

1. What is the target population?
2. What behaviors and perceptions are targets for change?
3. What specific interventions will be applied?
4. How intense a dose of intervention will be applied?

Prognosis:

1. What is the probable outcome if there is no intervention?
2. Over what period of time will the intervention be applied?
3. How often and by what means will progress of the intervention be monitored?

4. What positive and negative side effects might we expect?
5. What are the indications of positive progress?
6. How will we know if we have succeeded?

Strategy Twenty-One: Categories of Prescription Options

The team responsible for developing prescription options needs to think widely and broadly and not be restricted by concerns about cost, convenience, or past successes and failures. (These factors will be considered later.) Potential solutions exist in many forms that have not been utilized before as well as in forms with which educators are more familiar. At least one viable option should be developed in each of the following categories, though there can be more.

- Any of the Seventeen Critical Performance Categories
- Reorganization of Roles and Responsibilities (Specify the SDF)
- Training and Education Programs (consider different stakeholder groups)
- Communications Strategies
- Personnel Practices
- Supervision and Evaluation Strategies
- Realignment of Curriculum
- Improved Instructional Strategies and Materials
- New Performance-Improvement Teams
- Assessment Strategies
- Surveys and Inventories
- Community Engagement
- Others Selected by the Team

Strategy Twenty-Two: Prioritizing Prescription Options

(See figure 7.1—Prescription Priority Worksheets.)

Step One: Determine Priorities among Criteria—For each of the criteria on the Prescription Priority Worksheet, the first subgroup of team members should discuss and assign a value to each listed criterion. Based on its level of importance to address the diagnosis, each criteria should be assigned a "1" (low priority for this diagnosis), "2" (moderate priority for this diagnosis), or a "3" (high priority for this diagnosis). The assigned weights should be recorded in the "Diagnosis Value" column, and not shared with the group assigned to weigh the prescription options.

Step Two: Analyze Prescription Options—The second group assigned to analyze prescription options rates each prescription option by each criterion on the worksheets and determines a score of "1" (low value), "2" (moderate value), or "3" (high value) depending on how well the prescription option addresses the criterion. The score should be circled in the prescription-value column.

Step Three: Compute Results—The leader of the team or a designated member(s) computes the results by multiplying the value recorded for each diagnosis criterion (1, 2, or 3) by the assigned value selected for each prescription criterion (1, 2, or 3), and recording the resulting scores in the weighted-score column. The weighted values are added together to create a composite priority score for each prescription option. The prescription options are then rank ordered by score and reported to the full team for discussion, consideration, and development of a consensus about which prescription will be implemented. The option with the highest composite score is not necessarily the option selected.

Note: The sample criteria in the worksheets presented in figure 7.1 are excerpted from a larger number of criteria. Review the notes at the end of the worksheets to make sure that other criteria needing consideration are included in the comparison of the prescription options.

Strategy Twenty-Three: Developing Prognoses

After the development of a prescription and a preliminary prognosis has been tested by observations, and a review of data and other information has been accumulated as findings, it may be concluded that the prescription is successful or may need to change. To help determine if one or the other conclusion is appropriate, the following questions should be answered by the team:

1. What will be the outcome if current practice continues unchanged?
2. What specific behaviors are expected to change among which stakeholders as a result of this prescription?

   a. In the short term?
   b. In the mid term?
   c. In the long term?

3. What expectations are expected to change, among which stakeholders, related to which performance issues, as a result of this prescription?

   a. In the short term?
   b. In the mid term?
   c. In the long term?

4. Which stakeholders and existing practices will work to support this prescription?

5. Which stakeholders and existing practices will work to inhibit this prescription?
6. What positive "side effects" should be expected?

a. Among which stakeholders?
b. For how long?

7. What negative "side effects" should be expected?

a. Among which stakeholders?
b. For how long?

8. What are the most appropriate time periods for monitoring the accuracy of this prognosis?
9. What outcomes are expected?
10. How will desired outcomes be recognized?
11. What specific behaviors and expectations need to be monitored?
12. How will each critical behavior or expectation be monitored?
13. What differences between the expected and actual will be accepted?
14. What will be done if the differences exceed acceptable ranges?

Strategy Twenty-Four: Constructing Tasks and Timelines

Using the blank matrix provided in figure 7.3, plan the implementation of a project. List each of the specific activities down the vertical axis and indicate the months, weeks, and/or days in which the project will be undertaken across the horizontal axis.

In addition to the key codes for initiation, continuous activity, and reports due, what else might you want to plot? A blank row can be placed after each row of tasks to plot future actual results against those results forecast.

- Team meetings
- Scheduled assessments of progress
- Date of modifications in previous plans
- Data collection or analysis
- New discoveries
- Identification or definition of new VSPI
- Other

Projects that are important to individuals, as well as large and more complex projects that cut across subjects, grade levels, departments, schools, and so forth, can be planned and monitored using the matrix. Practice and experience will increase accuracy and the ability to perceive subtle changes in the progress of activities.

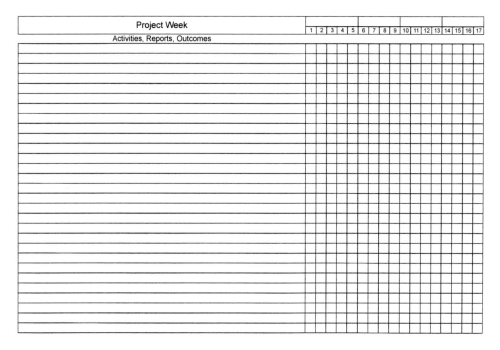

Note: All reporting and meeting dates are approximations and will be finalized as calendars are coordinated.

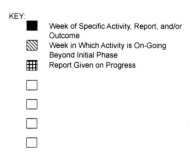

Figure 7.3   Blank Task and Timeline

Strategy Twenty-Five: Plotting Prognoses

If building tasks and timelines with blank rows is too cumbersome, another Tasks and Timeline Matrix can be used to construct a prognosis tracker. On the vertical axis, list the various behaviors and indicators identified in the prognosis. Using the same horizontal time schedule used in the Tasks and Timeline Matrix, indicate when each predicted behavior or outcome was observed. Also include behaviors and other indicators that were observed during implementation that were not part of the prognosis. These can be helpful in refining future prognoses. A sample of this is presented in figure 7.4.

Prescription: Grade level staff will be reorganized, and the resulting teams will be trained in the use of student behavior and performance data to improve planning, decision making, and instructional delivery.

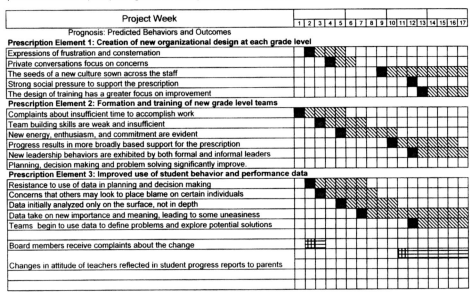

Project Week	1	2	3	4	5	6	7	8	9	10	11	12	13	14	15	16	17

Prognosis: Predicted Behaviors and Outcomes

Prescription Element 1: Creation of new organizational design at each grade level
- Expressions of frustration and consternation
- Private conversations focus on concerns
- The seeds of a new culture sown across the staff
- Strong social pressure to support the prescription
- The design of training has a greater focus on improvement

Prescription Element 2: Formation and training of new grade level teams
- Complaints about insufficient time to accomplish work
- Team building skills are weak and insufficient
- New energy, enthusiasm, and commitment are evident
- Progress results in more broadly based support for the prescription
- New leadership behaviors are exhibited by both formal and informal leaders
- Planning, decision making and problem solving significantly improve.

Prescription Element 3: Improved use of student behavior and performance data
- Resistance to use of data in planning and decision making
- Concerns that others may look to place blame on certain individuals
- Data initially analyzed only on the surface, not in depth
- Data take on new importance and meaning, leading to some uneasiness
- Teams begin to use data to define problems and explore potential solutions

Board members receive complaints about the change

Changes in attitude of teachers reflected in student progress reports to parents

Note: All reporting and meeting dates are approximations and will be finalized as calendars are coordinated.

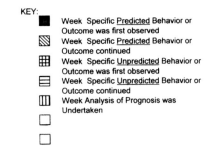

KEY:
- Week Specific <u>Predicted</u> Behavior or Outcome was first observed
- Week Specific <u>Predicted</u> Behavior or Outcome continued
- Week Specific <u>Unpredicted</u> Behavior or Outcome was first observed
- Week Specific <u>Unpredicted</u> Behavior or Outcome continued
- Week Analysis of Prognosis was Undertaken

Figure 7.4   Tracking Prognoses

Consider the following questions when analyzing the matrix:

1. What were the positive or negative behaviors that were anticipated?
2. What were the positive or negative behaviors that were not anticipated?
3. How quickly were predicted behaviors observed?
4. How long did identified behaviors extend if they did not persist?
5. How could the prognoses have been more accurate?
6. What are the implications for predicting behaviors through the rest of this prescription?
6. How different were the expectations from the actual behaviors? Why?
7. If the actual behaviors were significantly different from predicted behav-

iors, what are the implications for the success of the prescription?

8. Do actual behaviors indicate that an inappropriate diagnosis was made?

9. If the actual behaviors were significantly different from the predicted behaviors, what modifications in the prescription or the prognosis can increase probable success?

10. Do the actual behaviors indicate the failure of the prescription to address the problem?

11. Do actual behaviors indicate poor prediction of events and/or forecasting of time used?

12. What actual changes to the ongoing prescription and prognosis will be needed?

8

INCREASING COMMITMENT
AND CAPACITY FOR IMPROVEMENT

A commitment to performance improvement is needed to overcome the inertia of an organization devised for compliance. When only a few employees participate, improvements are few and not widespread. Improvements in performance must be nurtured by the commitment of all employees to increase their performance capacity.

Educators do not receive instruction and practice in the art and science of performance improvement as a component of their undergraduate and graduate degree programs. Therefore, ongoing professional development and training are needed to sustain each cycle of progress. In this chapter, connections are made between the levels of commitment and capacity within the CPC attained by staff members and the readiness of those same staff members to undertake more difficult problem solving.

Clinical Cycle Step 7—Preparation and Training of the Patient: The physician understands that the success of the prescription will depend largely on the patient's ability to follow directions closely, maintain treatment schedules, and correctly report changes in the condition being treated. Side effects, both those that demonstrate that the prescription is working and those that demonstrate it is not, need to be anticipated, observed, and recorded so that the details can be shared with the physician. In the case of chronic conditions, the patient needs to be trained in the continuing monitoring and administration of the prescription. Whether the physician is treating patients with diabetes, heart disease, cancer, or the flu, the knowledge and ongoing commitment and cooperation of the patient are critical to successful treatment.

ISSUES OF RESPONSIBILITY AND ACCOUNTABILITY

When the physician prepares the patient to take responsibility for ongoing treatment, she trusts that the patient will follow the designed regimen to improve health and monitor and report changes in health conditions during the course of the prescription. The physician determines the best course of action based on an assessment of how much responsibility the patient is able to accept for following the prescribed treatments and therapy.

Even though the team comprised of the patient, physician, and other health providers contributes to and is willing to be accountable for the results sought, the team's success is dependent upon the patient's full commitment to recovery. Sometimes, however, patients are not willing to fulfill responsibilities that would enable the health-provider team to perform well and be accountable for the results.

As in the case of the diabetic ex–construction worker whose complex medical problems had to be treated in a sequence of smaller steps that addressed long-term improvement goals, early efforts need to be successful if the patient is to develop hope for success and make a full commitment to the larger range of interventions that follow. Without the patient maintaining hope and demonstrating persistence, the health-provider team cannot hope to manage interventions needed for restoration of health.

District and school teams must create an environment for success similar to that created by the medical team. Successful intervention to remedy poor performance is possible only when employees accept responsibility and are willing to be accountable for results produced. Urgent calls for employees to act more responsibly and accountably for the poor performance of students do not translate into viable action that improves performance. Outside pressure causes introspection and narrows thinking and action to the personal efforts carried out by each employee. Accountability, by contrast, grows in an organization when employees recognize that every individual's performance and effectiveness are dependent on the effectiveness and cooperation of others.

Unfortunately, externally driven accountability systems, that is, high-stakes testing and increasing sanctions for consecutive years of underperformance, are the major thrusts used recently to increase employee accountability for results. Yet, by their nature, these threats do not increase any individual's sense of personal accountability.[1] External demands cause competitiveness, conflict, and a retreat to the safety of individual roles and positions rather than causing increased cooperation.

Despite the widely held belief that accountability can be imposed, there are no effective external accountability systems that can raise levels of personal learning and interpersonal trustworthiness among stakeholders to sustain improvement efforts. Employees should have expectations that their colleagues will perform in ways that will impact their own efforts positively and produce better outcomes.

Concepts of responsibility and accountability are not new to educators or anyone else; they experienced them every day while they were prepared for adulthood. Parents often settle disputes or resolve a breach of the family code of conduct by saying to an older child, "I expected more from you." In other words, the older child is held to a higher standard of responsibility than the younger one. The same is true for older and younger students in schools. There is an assumption that more self-discipline and higher personal responsibility will be demonstrated by the older student.

Once in a job, younger and older employees can have basically the same responsibilities; yet, there may be greater expectations for either the younger or older employee depending on his unique background and experience and the expectations of those working with him. Responsibilities are spelled out in job descriptions; however, the behavioral expectations that push performance quality higher are shared informally through the culture and interactions among employees in positions closely related to one another. A combination of formal responsibilities and informal expectations make up the range of responsibilities and levels of accountability that the employee accepts or rejects.

Supervisors confirm observations of the level of performance quality attained in job roles through evaluation processes. These processes typically dwell on formal roles and responsibilities found within the school and district functions (SDF), which can be identified and monitored easily. This attention to job responsibilities, however, does not prepare employees to pursue collective excellence through self-imposed accountability that is mutually supported among colleagues.

Achieving collective excellence is dependent upon the use of the critical performance categories to guide performance behaviors. In clinical practice, individuals think about their work both within their traditional roles and responsibilities within the SDF as well as those shared across the CPC. As employees utilize the CPC, they prepare themselves strategically to take advantage of the interdependencies and interrelationships that make a difference in personal and organizational performance. (See Strategy Twenty-Six at the end of the chapter.)

Since the concepts of responsibility and accountability have become politically charged, future performance improvements and higher student proficiency rates are much more likely to be attained through the application of commitment and capacity measures. By knowing how much commitment and capacity already exist and what increases in both are needed to improve performance results further, training and professional development programs can be focused on solving problems.

COMMITMENT AND CAPACITY

Plans for performance improvement are too often based on assessments of what needs to be done without sufficient consideration given to the performance and behavioral needs of employees. Leaders frequently have mounted their prover-bial horses to lead the charge only to discover too late that the troops were disor-ganized, did not understand the mission, and were ill prepared to accomplish it.

Both commitment and capacity are essential to determining the readiness of individuals, teams, and organizations to accept the challenges for improved performance health. One without the other is insufficient to achieve improved outcomes. Like the physician that determines the readiness of the patient to manage treatment to improve his or her health, educators must understand the readiness of employees, teams, and schools to manage prescriptions.

DEFINITIONS OF COMMITMENT AND CAPACITY

A working definition of "commitment" is "a promise or obligation to serve, and significantly invest in, an interest greater than oneself; to assume responsibility, individually and organizationally, for change and improvement." Committed people are important to every successful organization. Improvement is impos-sible unless there is sufficient commitment to the effort needed. Commitment is based on the understanding that sacrifice and hard work are investments neces-sary for improved performance. However, commitment itself is insufficient for sustained performance improvement.

"Capacity" is defined as "the competence, knowledge, skill, and resource needed to get things done; the facility or strength to produce desired results." Without the capacity to achieve improved performance no amount of com-mitment will result in success. At the same time, exceptional capacity without appropriate commitment can have only little impact. Successful prescriptions require high levels of both commitment and capacity.

Examples of the importance and power of commitment and capacity are found in every profession, especially sports. Athletic competition often favors individuals and teams that are more than just physically talented. Athletes need to be both committed and capable if they are to learn the skills and practice the strategies that result in winning. One of the great examples of the power of both commitment and capacity is found in the challenge of the decathlon. The decathlete, competing in ten different track-and-field events, must commit to developing a wide range of capacities. (See Strategy Twenty-Seven.)

Growth in commitment and capacity of district and school employees is at the heart of improving performance. School and district personnel need to examine their current skill levels across the spectrum of expectations and further develop performance in every one of them. Shoring up weaknesses and building consistency are important commitments.

THE PERFORMANCE-IMPROVEMENT READINESS INVENTORY

Existing levels of commitment and capacity of stakeholders among the seventeen critical performance categories (CPC) can be used as rough measurements to determine where efforts should be directed to better prepare the organization and its parts for performance-improvement. In addition, those engaged in the effort develop a keen sense of their own commitment to and capacity for the anticipated improvement efforts. (See Strategy Twenty-Eight.)

Levels of commitment and capacity are measured through a diagnostic instrument called the Performance-Improvement Readiness Inventory (PIRI). The PIRI reveals perceptions of commitment and capacity within the seventeen CPC through stakeholder responses. Perceptions of the quality of current commitment to and capacity for performance improvement in the CPC provide indications of strengths, needs, and improvement opportunities among the SDF. (See Strategy Twenty-Nine.)

The PIRI helps educators determine whether there is readiness to advance performance-improvement activities among well-known and underutilized portions of the organization's anatomy and physiology. The PIRI has thirty-four statements, two for each of the CPC. One statement asks for an assessment of the current level of commitment to the expectations included in this CPC. The second statement asks for an assessment of the level of capacity that exists to meet the expectations of this CPC.

In figure 8.1, the relationships among commitment and capacity levels are plotted to reveal readiness for improvement. School employees plot their understanding of performance strengths and needs and, while using information gathered from the intervention matrix, diagnosis, prescription, and prognosis, plan specific training and experiences that raise readiness to accelerate improvement. Readiness does not guarantee improvement, but, without it, higher levels of success are unlikely.

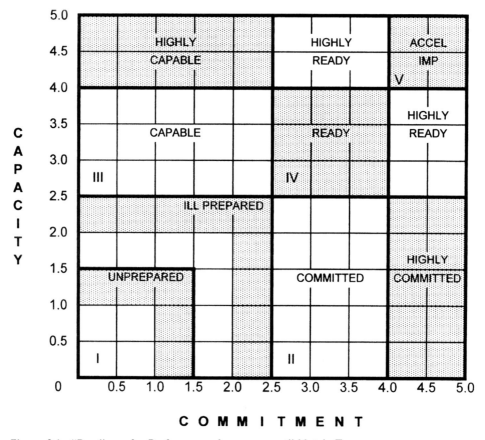

Figure 8.1 "Readiness for Performance Improvement" Matrix Zones

The average score for all the commitment items is calculated and plotted along the horizontal commitment scale. Then the average score for all the capacity items is calculated along the vertical scale. Lines are drawn from each of the two points vertically from the commitment scale and horizontally from the capacity scale. The point at which the two lines intersect provides a score indicating how committed and capable, or how ready, the group is for performance improvement.

By referring to the scores obtained in individual inventory questions, problem solvers receive feedback about the behaviors and areas of mastery that need to be strengthened to increase specific capacities. All districts and schools need to move relentlessly from the bottom left quadrant to the upper right quadrant of the figure. This represents gains in individual and group commitment and capacity.

While considering prescription options, diagnosticians need to ask challenging questions. For example, how much commitment and capacity exist and how much more are needed to make accurate diagnoses, prescriptions, and prognoses? And while these two questions are pondered, should interventions be postponed while readiness is improved? These questions represent the "chicken or the egg" conundrum. Should improvement efforts be delayed in order to increase readiness, or should improvement efforts be implemented and risk success without sufficient readiness?

Actually, districts, schools, and students can't wait. Improvement interventions and increased readiness should be pursued simultaneously. Postponement is not an option; improvement strategies must be initiated in ways that provide the organization and stakeholders the opportunity to develop both commitment and capacity. Bold action through appropriate prescriptions, implemented and monitored, supported by training, and followed by analysis and discussion of results, is one of the best ways to improve capacity and commitment.

READING THE COMMITMENT AND CAPACITY MATRIX

The Commitment and Capacity Matrix scores indicate a general level of readiness for performance improvement. Responses to specific questions in the inventory reveal potential targets among the CPC to improve commitment and capacity further and potential topics for adult learning necessary to balance the two factors throughout the organization.

The goal of every organization should be to achieve both commitment and capacity scores at or above 4.0, meaning that readiness for "accelerated improvement" exists. While this is the preferred state of readiness, and many district and schools are capable of achieving such readiness, few can honestly report scores that high. So, how is it possible to move from a lower section of the matrix to a higher one?

Each of the sections in the matrix can be considered in relation to the performance-readiness status of the organization. Specific responses to PIRI survey items within each CPC provide clues as to where strengths and opportunities for growth may be found. Periodic reporting of commitment and capacity scores to personnel and other involved stakeholders serves as a general progress report and maintains interest in increasing readiness.

"Unprepared"

Districts and schools having both commitment and capacity scores of less than 1.5 on the five-point scale are unprepared to take on the rigors of planned change with any promise of success. These organizations are marked by their inability to react to deteriorating conditions and stop the slide deeper into poor performance. It is likely that commitment and capacity scores are less than 1.5 in most, if not all CPC, although pockets of health may be found.

Improving performance will not be possible without first increasing commitment and capacity to meet the everyday challenges of program delivery and basic compliance with laws and regulations. This includes training in the roles and responsibilities fundamental to meeting the basic expectations among school and district functions (SDF). Only when personnel and organizational performance levels are above 1.5 for both commitment and capacity does a sufficient foundation exist to introduce CPC into job responsibilities.

Districts and schools that have both commitment and capacity scores between 1.5 and 2.5 on the five-point scale are still ill prepared to take on the rigors of comprehensive organizational performance improvement. But, they have staff members with enough commitment and/or capacity to learn what can be done to perform better. These organizations are marked by uncoordinated behaviors that can produce pockets of success, but success is not widespread nor can it be sustained. An inability to predict outcomes reliably from plans to improve performance is the norm for these districts and schools.

"Committed" or "Capable"

Districts and schools can be either "committed" or "capable" without being both. When a score in one factor is between 2.5 and 4.0 and the score of the other is less than 2.5, there is insufficient balance to sustain significant performance improvement. Capable organizations have the required expertise but lack the dedication and unity of purpose needed to perform better. Committed organizations enjoy sufficient dedication to make necessary improvements but lack the expertise needed to improve performance.

Too often, failure in these organizations occurs because strategies that will produce a better balance of both commitment and capacity have not been directed at the weaker factor. Districts and schools with scores that fall below 2.5 in either of these categories must examine individual CPC scores and determine where the largest disparities exist. Finding out specific reasons for low commitment or capacity should lead to the design of focused interventions that create strengths among more employees for more-balanced improvement efforts in the future.

This strategy is very important to the long-term performance health of the school and district. Less-committed or less-capable staff members tend to receive fewer expectations for performance quality and receive a "lighter" workload than those with higher commitment or capacity levels. If strategies are not implemented to alter the imbalance, the more committed or capable become overwhelmed and move on.

Significant differences between commitment and capacity within a single CPC suggest the need for a prescription that increases commitment in that CPC by building awareness of the importance for action or by developing capacity through adult learning and practice.

"Highly Committed" or "Highly Capable"

Usually, highly capable teams are at least committed; and highly committed teams are capable. But, when a team is recognized as highly committed or highly capable and ill prepared in the other factor, the imbalance is too great for successful performance-improvement efforts. The organizations and stakeholders exhibiting either of these two combinations of factors produce only small improvements with mixed levels of success. Either group can have a reputation and be respected as hard working or intelligent, even though general success is missing.

This imbalance of "highly committed" and "highly capable," places employees at greater risk for failure than those that are "capable" and "committed." The imbalance afflicts a significant number of districts and schools. It is most frequently found in the physical exodus of talented staff members from poorer and urban schools to suburban schools. For others in these same districts and schools, a retreat from collaborative efforts to the strict adherence of job responsibilities takes place. Unless district and school organizations and individual stakeholders understand growth needs and begin to develop equivalent strengths in both factors, little excitement and accomplishment are possible.

"Ready"

Scores ranging from 2.5 to 4.0 in both commitment and capacity identify districts and schools that are ready for significant performance-improvement efforts. These districts and schools are either ready to assume or have already assumed the challenge of improving performance continually. They examine their performance quality regularly and determine in which CPC and SDF they need to develop increased commitment and/or capacity.

The challenge for districts and schools in pushing performance into the high ready range is to build consistent levels of commitment and capacity among a substantial majority of personnel. Like the decathlon champion that realized that he did not have to be the world's best in any one event to be a champion, schools do not need several superstars to raise student achievement. If available, superstars would help; however, students will perform well where all employees perform consistently high across all categories.

The outside call for accountability to overcome student and staff underperformance can cause a negative side effect on the path to ready performance levels. When ongoing performance-improvement efforts have been initiated and a large number of employees are still unable to reach high readiness levels, commitment diminishes and performance quality trends toward the average of the group.

On the other hand, once a series of improved performance outcomes have been achieved and become a more normal expectation, efforts made to close the commitment and capacity gaps are viewed by employees as legitimate and supportable. Ready organizations that continue improvement have individuals and groups that lead by example and teach others how to perform better. This is an important cultural phenomenon within "ready" organizations. Staff members are recognized by their peers as resources that support the development of commitment and capacity in others to the "highly ready" level.

"Highly Ready"

"Highly ready" districts and schools are further along in their development of commitment or capacity than "ready" districts and schools. When diagnosticians know that their districts and schools are highly ready, they can focus on customizing and individualizing improvement plans, reaching for optimized performance in either one or more parts of the CPC that produce higher commitment and capacity for better performance.

Once new commitment and capacity levels have been established through specific interventions, employee and stakeholder levels of confidence in their new knowledge and skills are transferable to new, more complex problems. A commitment and capacity for greater success has been demonstrated, and a stronger foundation has been built for meeting future challenges. Learning in such circumstances is not abstract but is specific to the behaviors needed for further performance improvement. Consequently, organization and personnel performance behaviors are altered or replaced with new and more effective ones.

"Accelerated Improvement"

Districts and schools demonstrating "accelerated improvement" emphasize optimizing strengths among all SDF and CPC. These schools and districts are approaching world-class status and prepare themselves to take advantage of these strengths like Olympic athletes. Districts and schools that enjoy scores in both factors above 4.0 on the five-point scale possess a balance of highly developed commitment and capacity for improved performance. Achieving this status should be the goal of every organization. However, once this status has been achieved, continuous learning and performance-improvement efforts are still needed to maintain the state of accelerated readiness.

In the review of the responses to the individual items in the PIRI, there should also be an analysis of the CPC with the highest balanced scores and the CPC with the lowest balanced scores. High, balanced CPC scores are an indication of great strength and can be used to plan improvements in other performance areas. Low, balanced scores are an indication of serious weakness that necessitates significant training and wholesale change in practice to meet fundamental requirements of operation. (See Strategy Thirty.)

Professional development that supports growth in commitment and capacity of school personnel and other stakeholders involved in performance-improvement processes is essential to moving continually toward accelerated improvement. Periodic assessments of current levels of commitment and capacity determine if prior performance-improvement efforts have produced knowledge and skills needed for solving more difficult problems that have prevented higher student achievement. Increasing commitment and capacity levels provides an encouraging view of the staff's willing acceptance of responsibility and accountability for better performance and higher student achievement.

CHAPTER 8 STRATEGIES

Strategy Twenty-Six: Moving from Responsibility to Accountability

While a simple strategy or workshop is not enough to move individuals in job role responsibilities to accepting real accountability, it is helpful to engage team members in discussion about the interdependencies in team work.

1. What is the most important responsibility of this team?
2. What is my most important individual responsibility in supporting the work of this team?
3. What is the most important collective responsibility of all team members in supporting the work of this team?
4. Are there members of this team whose work will make my work for the team more or less difficult? More or less effective?
5. Are there members of this team whose work will be made more or less difficult by my work? More or less effective by my work?

6. Is it possible for us to work together in ways that make each of us more effective?

7. How can we keep each other better informed to support each other's work?

8. What do we need to share to better understand the implications of our own decisions on the work of the other?

9. Are there any routines that the team should adopt that will promote support among team members for each other's work?

Strategy Twenty-Seven: A Sports Legend

One of the authors began his career in a school with a proud legend of individual optimization. The school enjoyed great success in academics and in sports, including football, lacrosse, field hockey, and other sports, winning state championships and sending players to college who ultimately became All-American and professional athletes. One young man was a very good athlete but would never be the best at any one sport, including track, his favorite.

He told his coach about his desire to compete in college and, his dream, the Olympics. His coach was worried that the student would struggle to find a single event in which he could excel sufficiently to compete at the university level. The coach advised the student to consider the decathlon, an event that combined ten different individual events, including sprints of one-hundred and four-hundred meters, javelin, discuss, shot put, hurdles, long and high jumps, pole vault, and distance running. The coach told the student that if he focused his performance in any one event he might not win, but, if he could optimize his overall performance, he might be good enough across all events to do well when all scores were combined.

The winner of the decathlon is often considered the best of all track-and-field athletes. Past champions have included the great Jim Thorpe. The young man worked hard and achieved his dream. At the 1968 Olympic Games, Bill Toomey set the world's record for the score in the decathlon, meaning that he finished with scores and times closest to the world record in each of the ten events. He achieved the status as the greatest track athlete without setting a record in any individual event. He was simply closest among his competitors to the world record in ten different events. His legend in the school was that it was far more important to be as good as one could be across a broad range of abilities than to simply be best at one thing.

What legends exist in your district and school that promote excellence? How can they be more widely shared?

Strategy Twenty-Eight: Informal Assessment of Commitment and Capacity

As a first step to understanding the specific levels of commitment and capacity of employees and other stakeholders, consider the following questions.

1. What are the three greatest strengths of this district/school? What commitments and/or capacities are represented within each of the strengths?
2. What are the three greatest needs of this district/school? What commitments and/or capacities are needed to address each identified need?
3. What two changes in adult behavior would do the most to improve student achievement? What commitments and capacities will be required to achieve each change?
4. What additional commitments and/or capacities should the superintendent/principal and board develop to better meet the needs of:
   a. the students?
   b. adult learners?
   c. informal and formal leaders?
   d. the district?
   e. the school?
5. What two recommendations would you make to reduce expenditures? What commitments and capacities are required to achieve each recommendation? What additional commitments and/or capacities would be freed for use elsewhere?

Strategy Twenty-Nine: Preliminary Assessment of Commitment and Capacity

Performance-Improvement Readiness Inventory (PIRI)

The PIRI is designed to be used by an individual or a group of any size. When used by a group, average scores are reported for each subgroup and/or the entire respondent group.

Directions: Read the definition of each CPC in the PIRI found in figure 8.2. Following the definition, indicate first your perception of the *commitment* of the district/school to the behaviors and attitudes based in that CPC using the following scale.

1 = no existing commitment
2 = limited commitment
3 = broad commitment

Critical Performance Category	Commitment Score	Capacity Score
1. Alignment of Work Processes: *Precise adjustments made to district and/or school structures, work processes, and efforts that improve performance to increase student achievement and counteract ineffective processes and efforts that hinder attainment of desired results.*		
2. Business/Financial Acumen: The knowledge and skill needed to guide the financial support of district and school operations, provide support for performance improvement activities, meet performance goals, and shape the management and control of funds for protecting the public's investment in the educational enterprise.		
3. Customer Focus: *The philosophical and operational expectation that employees will focus their attention and efforts on the needs of students and other customers of the district and schools.*		
4. District and School Wide Culture: *The collective attitude, values, and actions that nurture the organization and its stakeholders as they learn, interact, and perform the challenging tasks necessary to meet and exceed expectations and to attain optimum performance.*		
5. Effective and Integrated Governance: *The distribution, delegation, and use of the authority legally invested in the Board of Education, Directors, or Trustees and integrated through district and school level structures and positions to accomplish desired district and school performance results.*		
6. Human Resource Excellence: *Every employee will perform in a superior fashion and surpass performance expectations. District and school policies and procedures that govern the selection, training, supervision, and evaluation of employees, along with recognizing, rewarding, and compensating exemplary performance, should all focus on preparing and sustaining every employee for success at the highest performance levels.*		
7. Information, Measurement, and Reporting System: *An operating system designed to maintain, update, and distribute the organization's life-blood of information and data about district, schools, and students to continually focus the attention of employees, students, and other stakeholders on the level, meaning, and characteristics of current performance in order to design and sustain efforts to establish new levels of success.*		
8. Leadership: *The purposeful day-to-day activities planned and accomplished by employees who have responsibility for the organization, or any part of it, to produce desired outcomes; these employees have authority to drive the organization to higher performance levels; and they are willing to be held accountable for the results achieved.*		
9. Planning and Planned Change: *Authorized processes used by individuals and groups to think about, organize, and implement strategies to create better ways to achieve optimum results for the district, schools, and students.*		
10. Professional Learning and Instruction: *The life-long process of acquiring and using the knowledge, skills, and attitudes needed to be an outstanding district and school employee with the intent of becoming a better resource and communicator, and teacher and leader of students and adults. Employees have responsibility to define performance expectations and offer programs and services that support the development of knowledge and skills for on-the-job success.*		
11. Programs and Services that Accelerate Learning: *The system of programs and services that is planned, designed, implemented, evaluated, and upgraded to increase student knowledge, understanding, and skills. The implementation of programs and services represent the district and school's promise that all students will succeed. At least annually, the system is assessed to determine if all students are prepared to meet current and future academic goals. Discrepancies between the results obtained and the performance goals sought should establish the basis for ongoing diagnosis and the performance goals sought should generate treatments to the system that produce an accelerating rate of learning.*		
12. Staff, Student, and Family Interactions: *All the personal and interpersonal behaviors and communications that support the fulfillment of the legal and professional obligations of a district and school; provide direction, resource, and energy to improve performance; facilitate and guide students through learning activities; and make working together enjoyable and beneficial.*		
13. Structures that Nurture Improvement: *Offices, departments, and committees that are authorized to resolve legal, regulatory, and policy obligations, and councils and teams that have responsibility to improve organizational performance and increase student achievement.*		
14. Student Behavior and Performance Data: *All the quantifiable data and qualifiable information about individual students and student groups, collected and organized to enhance understanding of present behavior and performance, and used to improve organization and personal practice. The data are compared with the results obtained in similar and best performing districts and schools and used to establish the baseline upon which improvements and progress will be measured.*		
15. Team Work and Problem Solving: *A team is a learning and problem-solving group with specific responsibilities to resolve issues of purpose and understanding; conflicts of philosophy, values, and opinion; relationships and alignment of processes to complete tasks; to improve operational performance; and to increase student achievement.*		
16. Technology that Supports Programs, Personnel, and Students: *Computer hardware, software, communications systems, and related technologies that support school and district efforts to accomplish work tasks; communicate with and among stakeholders; help board members, staff members, students, and parents assess current performance levels; and support the establishment, implementation, and monitoring of prescriptions to close the gap between current and expected performance levels.*		
17. Universal Acceptance of Expectations: *Clear and comprehensive expectations are developed, deployed among stakeholder groups, accepted as appropriate and legitimate, used to improve organizational performance, and guide the improvement of student behavior and achievement.*		
TOTAL SCORE		
TOTAL SCORE DIVIDED BY ~~5~~ 10		

Figure 8.2 Performance Improvement Readiness Inventory (PIRI)

Next, indicate your perception of the *capacity* of the district/school to exhibit the behaviors and attitudes based in that CPC.

1 = no existing capacity
2 = limited capacity
3 = broad capacity

Add the total commitment scores and the total capacity scores. Divide each total score by ~~five~~ ten. Plot the commitment and capacity scores on the matrix provided in figure 8.1 on page 106.

Strategy Thirty: Analyzing Placement on the PIRI Matrix

From the results of Strategy Twenty-Nine, record the commitment and capacity scores below.

Commitment Score: _____   Capacity Score: _____

Sector Score (i.e., "Committed," "Capable," "Ready," etc.) _____

Consider the following questions in analyzing the PIRI score and the readiness to accept the challenges of improving performance:

What CPC has the greatest disparity between commitment score and capacity score?

What CPC has the least disparity between commitment score and capacity score?

Which CPCs can be viewed as strengths because of high scores in

- commitment?
- capacity?
- both commitment and capacity?

Which CPC can be viewed as weaknesses because of low scores in

- commitment?
- capacity?
- both commitment and capacity?

Which roles (SDF) need the most professional development in which CPC to increase "readiness"?

If you used the performance-improvement opportunity matrix in chapter 3 (figure 3.5) on page 104, what professional learning opportunities will you now emphasize in which SDF and CPC to move the organization further in its quest for performance success?

USING PROTOCOLS AND MILESTONES TO PROMOTE CONSISTENCY AND THOROUGHNESS

Building problem-solving skills and solving complex problems is a goal of clinical practice. In addition to having a performance-improvement game plan that utilizes the right data, develops an accurate diagnosis, guides the implementation of the right prescription and prognosis, and prepares employees with appropriate training, it is very important that everyone use protocols and milestones to produce consistency and thoroughness in practice. This chapter guides the reader and teams through use of protocols and milestones to accelerate performance-improvement steps.

> *Clinical Cycle Step 8—Protocols and Milestones (patient self-monitoring): The patient becomes the eyes and ears of the physician in monitoring treatment and recovery. Having been trained to know what to look for and what to expect, the patient is prepared to monitor personal progress toward recovery. Training can be as simple as adopting the schedule of medication; testing, recording, and reporting specific levels of sugar in the blood; or as complex as schedules of multiple medications, strenuous therapy, and keeping a daily log of food and caloric intake. The patient and physician communicate periodically to ensure that there is continual monitoring and mutual understanding.*

PROTOCOLS GENERATE COMMON UNDERSTANDING
BETWEEN PATIENT AND PHYSICIAN

During performance-improvement efforts, employees fill the roles of both the diagnostician and patient at the same time. Individual staff members must assess their own skills and expertise in light of current conditions and proposed initiatives and assess the performance of colleagues and the school as well. It can be confusing and seem like a mixture of administrative and teaching roles and responsibilities. Yet, it is through such a paradox that commitment and capacity of all staff members are developed further.

Simple remedies require very little attention to detail. Small aches and pains usually respond to a single dose of aspirin, acetaminophen, or ibuprofen. As remedies become more complex, however, the details of a medication schedule, dosage, and monitoring need to be coupled with diet, physical therapy, and rest. The very best treatments for illness are only as effective as the care and precision with which they are delivered and monitored.

The physician establishes protocols to prepare the patient for the responsibilities of his own treatment and identifies milestones that alert the patient to changes that can be expected. Protocols and milestones assure the doctor that there is an organization to the patient's efforts to guide personal care. Also, when changes occur during treatment, protocols and milestones give the patient confidence that he is following the correct steps needed to achieve improved health.

Protocols are the detailed steps through which treatment is started and delivered. Milestones are the points of change in the condition of the patient during treatment that the physician expects and identifies for the patient. The uncertainty that always accompanies health interventions and performance change is less threatening when the entire predicted sequence of outcomes is known from the beginning.

Patients battling cancer are better able to face the pain and the threat of the disease because they can track their own treatment and its progress. Knowing ahead of time that chemotherapy results in hair loss prepares patients mentally and emotionally for dramatic physical changes during and after treatment. The patient can better face the challenge of treatment knowing that features affected by chemotherapy will return to normal.

If educators do not understand what will happen on the performance-improvement journey and how much time will be needed to see improvements, they are unlikely to stay dedicated to efforts long enough to make a difference in outcomes. Like the patient that faces extended treatment, teachers and administrators are much less discouraged by slow progress when they understand that time is needed for the prescription to have the desired impact. Prescriptions prepared to improve team work, lesson planning, and instructional strategies, for example, need time in practice and experience to show benefits before new prescriptions are offered to increase student achievement.

Staff members and teams develop patience for the time needed for progress by linking performance-improvement designs with outcomes through protocols and likely milestones. In too many districts and schools, however, protocols are not defined, milestones are not identified, and staff members do not know if they are making appropriate progress toward new outcomes. Educators need to forecast likely changes accurately and share information about milestones reached among stakeholders to build confidence in the protocol's use.

The adoption and use of protocols and milestones generate a shared understanding among team members of what to expect during prescription implementation, including the likely impact the solution will have on others. By establishing and using protocols and milestones, prescriptions and prognoses are more tightly linked, improving practice and leading to the achievement of desired outcomes.

SIMPLE, COMPLICATED, AND COMPLEX PROBLEMS

A reliance on past practice, unchanged training, and a lack of preparation and documented research all contribute to making problems more difficult to resolve. In medicine, recurring infections after surgery present a special problem for patient recovery.

Atul Gawande, M.D., chief researcher of an international study of surgical-infection prevention, wrote about the growing complexity of problems in medicine and across many other professions as well. In *The Checklist Manifesto: How to Get Things Right*, he cites the work of Zimmerman (York University) and Glouberman (University of Toronto), who have classified problems into three separate categories: simple, complicated, and complex.[1]

Gawande found that each level of problem classification needed to be approached differently to develop successful solutions. The professors reported that simple problems are similar to following a recipe for baking a cake. Complicated problems are similar to sending a rocket into space and bringing it back. Complex problems are similar to raising a child.

Simple and complicated problems are related in some ways and become easier to handle over time. With practice, the accumulated expertise and problem-solving techniques can be used repeatedly with success. Complex problems, such as child rearing, offer different challenges, however.

Although success may be experienced in raising one child, more often than not, practiced strategies are unsuccessful with the second child.[2] Complex problems do not respond to the same routines due to changing variables and underlying influences that defy the simple repetition of old strategies. Educators need to understand which kinds of strategies and protocols can be used successfully in specific situations.

Simple problems in education include preparing a meeting agenda, an annual calendar, or a schedule of events; establishing bus routes; ordering supplies; preparing monthly reports; publishing a newsletter; and so on. Simple problems yield themselves to relatively simple solutions applied by individuals and teams and shared with others to follow. Over time, only minor changes will be required for continued application of simple solutions to simple problems.

Following a routine consistently for solving simple problems requires little judgment and decision making. Even if there are modifications, future cycles through the sequenced activities should produce consistency and ongoing success. Solutions to simple problems do not result in improvements in student achievement, but contribute indirectly through time and resources saved and available to address more complicated and complex problems. (See Strategy Thirty-One at the end of the chapter.)

Complicated problems, like sending a rocket into space and bringing it back safely, require substantial planning and coordinated activity. The first time processes are used to achieve the goal, every thought and step is new. Trial-and-error efforts accumulate information and data about what works and doesn't. Each successive try produces new insights into the problem and new solutions are learned and practiced.

Opening new schools and closing older buildings are complicated problems that often beguile educators. Nonetheless, the processes followed to accomplish these tasks can be improved with each new try. Complicated problems require more time and attention than do simple problems; and the risks for not solving complicated problems are much greater than are those for unsolved simple problems.

When district or school practices are in disarray or unreliable, such as after frequent turnover of leaders and staff members or in the case of newly opened charter schools, there is usually a variety of related complicated problems. They include, but are not limited to, hiring staff, developing a budget, setting goals and implementing strategies to achieve them, evaluating performance, establishing priorities among limited resources, resolving disagreements and establishing unity of purpose, and succession planning.

Solving complicated issues makes it possible for the school or district to improve, but it does not guarantee better performance or increases in student achievement. At the same time, only districts and schools at a consistent level of performance health as a result of solving complicated problems will ever be able to resolve complex problems that lead to improved performance.

Routines used in solving complicated problems can be repeated successfully as long as the problem remains largely the same over time, for example, developing a budget, changing attendance boundaries, opening a new school, closing a school and redistricting students, and adding or reducing employees based on opening or closing school buildings. Even though complicated problems involve a lot of variables, the protocols are very similar to the protocols for simple problems, and the routines are more detailed. (See Strategy Thirty-Two.)

Solutions to complex problems, like raising a child, defy the kinds of routines used in solving simple and complicated problems. In education, complex problems include, but are not limited to, improving staff performance; making team work productive; improving governance practices after each school board election; linking board performance with staff and student performance; discovering the root causes of underperformance; and aligning people, SDF, and CPC to improve student achievement.

Solving complex problems requires significant time, energy, and resource. Like complicated problems, lots of data and stakeholder interactions are studied and used to guide decision making. But, unlike simple and complicated problems, complex problems interfere with the most important outcomes that a district and school are supposed to address. If complex problems are solved successfully, there will be improvements in the performance of personnel and organization and student achievement. If complex problems are not solved, staff-performance and student-achievement increases are going to be stalled indefinitely.

Protocols designed to solve complex problems require a flexible approach based upon the analysis of data about changing conditions and influences on the performance of adults, students, and the organization. Accumulating and sharing the evidence of what has worked, and why, contributes to the successful revision of solutions. Sound judgment and decision making are critical to achieving optimized performance and learning. Complex-problem protocols should be reviewed frequently with the expectation that solution processes will change and never be fully established as routines. The clinical cycle is an effective protocol for solving complex problems. (See Strategy Thirty-Three.)

PROTOCOLS AND PROFESSIONAL JUDGMENT

Dr. Gawande's research demonstrates that simple protocols used before, during, and after surgery reduce infection among recovering patients because every member of the surgical team could be sure that everyone else's job had been accomplished. Doctors, nurses, and technicians tested each other to be certain that every step had been taken and was checked by the team. There was no room for even minor errors or shortcuts.

There were, however, complaints within the group of professionals. The checklist approach seemed unprofessional to the higher-ranking professionals, and routines were thought to replace the use of professional judgment. However, the reduced rates of infection, the shorter patient stays in hospitals, and the higher surgical success rates proved that these protocols were important assets that should be in place in all hospitals.

Dr. Gawande explained, "I want to be a good doctor for my patients. And the question of when to follow one's judgment and when to follow protocol is central to doing my job well—or to doing anything else that is hard. You want people to make sure to get the stupid stuff right. Yet you also want to leave room for craft and judgment and the ability to respond to unexpected difficulties that arise along the way."[3]

Every element of the protocol needs to be monitored. At any point, if the next element of the protocol doesn't fully address the remaining problem, an adjustment needs to be made. Just as the prognosis is monitored to make sure the prescription is on track, protocols need to be monitored to determine if the solution is on track to treat the entire problem. Practice and experience with protocols instruct users that even when the problem seems to be a repeat of previous problems, protocols need to be examined carefully to make sure they align with each new problem.

Gawande's research of complex protocols took him outside his own field of medicine and into the construction of buildings. "A building is like a body," the construction manager said. "It has a skin. It has a skeleton. It has a vascular system—the plumbing. It has a breathing system—the ventilation. It has a nervous system—the wiring."[4] All together, he explained, projects today involve sixteen different trades. Protocols are used to make certain that all those engaged in a project are doing their work correctly and that the building comes together appropriately, even though the manager could not possibly understand the details of every individual task.

Protocols in construction management are based on the assumption that every person is fallible, but proper coordination of the work of many people is less so. The process of identifying separate work tasks and forcing communication about them among several specialists represents a different philosophy for the medical and education professions.

Improvements in performance come from pushing the power of decision making away from the center through accepted protocols. Efforts to dictate every step from the center fail when chaotic conditions reign, problems are complex, and the knowledge required exceeds that of any individual. In organizations, people do not succeed in isolation. Instead, a combination of freedom and expectation to coordinate and measure progress toward common and individual goals is required.[5]

In many fields—medicine, business, military, building construction, hospital emergency rooms, Formula One racing, and education, among others—team work represents a collection of assigned tasks, knowledge and experience, coordinated communication checks, and appropriate decision making to obtain the best possible results for all. There is less chance now than ever before for isolated individuals to succeed in education. People and the organization must succeed together.

URGENCY AND PROTOCOLS

Protocols serve another increasingly important role in assuring that effective solutions are developed and implemented for problems of varying degrees of complexity. Nearly universal use of computers and voice, text, and video communications creates a growing expectation that answers should come as quickly as the questions. Such expectations discourage careful consideration required to produce a sound response.

As urgent as a problem may be, a quick response that is incomplete or inaccurate will waste more time than will carefully considering the problem in the first place. Protocols provide the framework for careful consideration of each type of problem. Time taken to develop solutions based on protocols requires careful analysis of the problem and its relationship to the larger group and organization.

Further, as each step is engaged or completed, the effectiveness of the solution is examined and adjustments are made that would be impossible in solutions implemented too quickly. Protocols require investing the time and the separation needed to ensure that responses to problems are meaningful and appropriate. As has been so aptly pointed out: "Why do we never have time to do it right, but we always find the time to do it again?"

COMPLEX PROBLEMS AND PROTOCOLS

The ultimate power of protocols lies in the effective support they provide in tracking and monitoring individual prescriptions. They frame the analysis of data and support the physician, patient, and team members in assessing the quality and accuracy of their decisions. Also, the use of commonly applied protocols across any number of teams enables comparisons of work processes and progress. Teams working on multiple prescriptions produce documented experience and outcomes that provide invaluable information to help modify steps in the protocol.

While the steps within protocols are expected to be used consistently by individuals and teams, how can school and district leaders be assured that they are appropriately implemented? The answer is simple and, at the same time, complex—through extensive and ongoing training, practice, and review. There is truth in the old joke about the cab driver in New York. When asked how to get to Carnegie Hall, he replied, "Just buy a violin, and practice, practice, practice."

Every employee must be expected to develop expertise related to performance improvement, including the use of various protocols. This commitment can only be successful if school and district leaders encourage their use and support practice with them.

MILESTONES OF EXPERTISE

Milestones are the changes in behavior that indicate that the expected impact is occurring as protocols are followed. In one school intent on increasing student achievement, an assessment of staff expertise identified several areas where additional skills needed to be developed through the school's professional-development program and through individual study and practice. A "decathlon" of ten areas of expertise was established.

In figure 9.1, the ten areas are presented with a rubric of expertise in ten levels from "Preclinical Practice" skills through the "Clinical Professional" level. School administrators provided the first ranking of teaching personnel. After eight months of preparation and training, a self-assessment by all personnel provided insights into the perceived progress made in less than a year.

In figure 9.1, administrators ranked all teaching personnel as having expertise at least at level two in all ten areas of expertise, nine areas of expertise at level three, and a rapidly decreasing number of areas of expertise until only two categories were identified at level seven. No other expertise mastery was identified above level seven. When teaching-staff members had an opportunity to assess their own levels of expertise on the same scale, different perceptions were noted.

Teaching-staff members assessed their levels of expertise to be no lower than level three in all ten categories. And they thought that staff members had substantial expertise at levels six, seven, eight, nine, and even level ten. Approximately half the faculty thought that staff members were at levels six, seven,

	Areas of Mastery									
	Data Analysis	State Curriculum Standards	School Curriculum	Instructional Strategies	Lesson Planning	Resources	Technology	Team Work	Decision Making/ Routine Building	Use of Clinical Practice Protocols
Pre-Clinical Practice: (Training and Preparation)										
1. Familiar/conversant with topic	X	X	X	X	X	X	X	X	X	X
2. New learning introduced for practice	X	X	X	X	X	X	X	X	X	X
3. Participate in simulation(s)/guided practice	X	X	X	X	X	X	X	X	X	
Clinical Practice: (On-going Practice and Development)										
4. Plan for new skill use—team and PIC informed		X	X	X	X	X	X	X		
5. Initial effort to practice new skills individually and with grade level team		X	X		X		X			
6. Informal—Peer observation &/feedback about new skill use			X		X		X			
7. Implement new skills for improved practice			X				X			
8. Formal (supervisor) observations/feedback confirm skill level—Team and PICC approval										
Clinical Professional:										
9. Makes continuous improvement and experimentation—Recognized as a resource										
10. Expert—Demonstrated ability to teach skills to and lead others										

Figure 9.1   Assessing Clinical Expertise

and eight in seven of the ten areas of expertise; and even a substantial number thought that one-fifth of staff members were clinician coaches or experts in three of the ten areas.

Prior to the initiation of training, neither a school-wide or team aggregate score was at the top level of clinical practice, level eight, or at the clinical professional levels, levels nine and ten. Fortunately, a few individuals were rated at levels nine and ten in one or more areas, qualified to serve as instructors in the professional-development program and as resources to help colleagues improve their expertise year-round. A strategy to improve staff performance consistently across all grades and subjects was formulated utilizing these strengths.

Ratings of individual and team expertise on the rubric established an understanding among the faculty of the range of perceived expertise that existed and their own placement within the range. The clinical basis for the rubric tied expertise to the application of the clinical practice model and provided incentive and interest in development of specific skills. Subsequent administrations of the rubric were completed and those results reported increasing school-wide levels of expertise and growing availability of resources for performance improvement.

In an effort to more clearly understand how to achieve higher levels of expertise, administrators and staff members began to develop a variety of criteria or milestones that described professional behaviors in more detail at each of the preclinical, clinical practice, and clinical professional levels. Each of the ten areas of expertise was subdivided into more specific skill-based topics that became the focus of workshops varying in length from two to twelve hours. These more-frequently observed milestones were used in formal and informal observations of classes, in staff member and administrator discussions, and in peer discussions in teams.

Workshop presenters planned learning activities based on the level of existing expertise of workshop participants. Teachers and administrators set a goal to improve at least one level of expertise for each workshop attended. As milestones were accomplished, new levels of expertise were recorded and celebrated. (See Strategy Thirty-Four.)

Everyone engaged in performance-improvement efforts should constantly assess his or her learning and experiences in the application of that learning to improving performance. This is a professional's responsibility—building continually higher levels of commitment and capacity and sharing this growing expertise in problem-solving and performance-improvement efforts. Colleagues that learn from others and teach one another contribute to the development and awareness of increasing levels of expertise that are demonstrated in solving simple, complicated, and complex problems.

Adding new, higher floors to the foundation of professional expertise improves teacher and administrator decision making, which impacts student achievement positively. Creating and using protocols and milestones contribute to greater interest in and commitment to the acquisition of expertise and the use of processes that support professional growth and problem solving.

CHAPTER 9 STRATEGIES

Strategy Thirty-One: Protocols for Simple Problems

A simple problem can be resolved using a simple protocol. Make sure that the protocol fits the problem and that the protocol results in resolution of the problem and the development of a routine that can be used for solving the same or similar problems in the future.

Select a routine or simple problem (e.g., develop a budget, calendar, or newsletter; schedule bus routes, etc.) and use the following protocol to develop a solution.

Simple Problem Protocol:

1. Define the problem.
2. Define the preferred outcome.
3. Identify the actions needed to achieve the preferred outcome.
4. Identify stakeholder groups impacted by the problem and the solution.
5. Identify the resources needed and available for the solution.
6. Set a reasonable time frame for implementing the solution.
7. Identify key stakeholders to be involved in implementing the solution.
8. Provide training to involved stakeholders, if needed.
9. Make available the resources required at each step.
10. Establish reporting processes and timelines.
11. Implement the solution.
12. Determine any dissatisfaction with the results and modify one or more of the previous steps.
13. Compare the preferred outcome with the actual outcomes.

Strategy Thirty-Two: Protocols for Complicated Problems

A complicated problem requires a more-detailed protocol than do simple problems. Be certain that the protocol fits the problem and that the protocol results in resolution of the problem; look to develop a routine that can be used for solving the same or similar problems in the future.

Select a complicated problem (e.g., opening or closing a school, realigning attendance districts, reorganization following significant expenditure reductions, etc.), and use the following protocol to develop a solution.

Complicated Problem Protocol:

1. Form an expert team to define the problem and develop written procedures to direct its work.
2. Gather information and research related to the problem.
3. Develop goals and objectives for an implementation plan.
4. Define the roles and responsibilities of participants.
5. Forecast best, expected, and worst-case scenarios.
6. Design and perform tests and pilot trials to evaluate potential solutions.
7. Select the modified solution based on trial results.
8. Establish the sequence of activities, including deadlines and intermediate dates.
9. Initiate the action plan to accomplish goals.
10. Share interim results with various stakeholder groups for reaction and feedback.

11. Monitor results and modify implementation strategies to improve results.
12. Report goal accomplishment and make recommendations to improve the next effort.

Strategy Thirty-Three: Protocols for Complex Problems

A complex problem requires a more comprehensive protocol, as found in the clinical cycle. Select a complex problem (e.g., improving staff performance; making team work productive; discovering the root causes of underperformance; aligning people, SDF, and CPC to improve student achievement, etc.), and use the following protocol to develop a solution.

Complex Problem Protocol:

1. Leadership and staff develop *awareness* of a problem.
2. An expert team is formed to *gather data.*
3. The team *reviews and consults* about the data.
4. The team forms a *hypothesis* regarding the root cause of the problem.
5. The team develops and refines *diagnostic options* using the diagnostic funnel.
6. A *prescription and prognosis* are developed.
7. *Preparation and training* are provided to stakeholders who will participate in the implementation of the prescription.
8. *Protocols and milestones* are identified to determine the effectiveness of the prescription.
9. The team *monitors and measures* the impact of the prescription.
10. The team *reports* findings to and *consults* with stakeholders.
11. The *new state* of performance health is identified and defined.
12. The new state is *confirmed* in measures of improved performance.
13. New awareness of performance health is shared among appropriate stakeholders.

Strategy Thirty-Four: Assessing, Benchmarking, and Monitoring Adult Expertise Development Using a Clinical Practice Rubric

Success of performance-improvement efforts through the application of the clinical practice model requires the ongoing development of adult expertise. A blank copy of the spreadsheet used in figure 9.1 is provided as figure 9.2 and includes the clinical rubric used to benchmark and monitor the development of expertise.

	Areas of Mastery									
Pre-Clinical Practice: (Training and Preparation)										
1. Familiar/conversant with topic										
2. New learning introduced for practice										
3. Participate in simulation(s)/guided practice										
Clinical Practice: (On-going Practice and Development)										
4. Plan for new skill use—team and PIC informed										
5. Initial effort to practice new skills individually and with grade level team										
6. Informal—Peer observation &/feedback about new skill use										
7. Implement new skills for improved practice										
8. Formal (supervisor) observations/feedback confirm skill level—Team and PICC approval										
Clinical Professional:										
9. Makes continuous improvement and experimentation—Recognized as a resource										
10. Expert—Demonstrated ability to teach skills to and lead others										

Figure 9.2   Rubric for Adult Mastery of Clinical Expertise

Identify areas of expertise that specific teams and individuals need to develop to achieve higher levels of performance and use the rubric to assess the present status of expertise in those areas. Individuals can self-assess and can aggregate scores for their teams. Teams can also discuss and develop consensus levels of expertise. Aggregate scores provide averages of self-assessments, and consensus scores are impacted by discussion.

Have individuals complete their own assessments, and then have team discussion. The differences between team scores that are averages of member scores and scores developed through team discussion provide interesting feedback to teams and individuals about their ability to assess personal strengths and in determining priorities for professional development.

Are self-assessment rankings sufficient for the next performance-improvement cycle? Do consensus rankings reflect a higher or lower level than the self-assessment rankings? Why? What are the implications for professional development?

10

MONITORING AND MEASURING
IMPROVEMENT PROGRESS THROUGH
INDICATORS, CONTRAINDICATORS,
AND SIDE EFFECTS

Teams that practice performance improvement require skills at forecasting and plotting milestones. The progress made during prescription implementation and the use of prognoses through forecasts of positive indicators, contraindicators, and positive and negative side effects of progress must be documented to increase the likelihood of success. Prescriptions and the changes they produce will cause pain within the organization. This chapter explores how to react to performance-improvement pain.

> *Clinical Cycle Step 9—Monitor and Measure: Progress toward recovery is marked by positive indicators and contraindications experienced by the patient during prescription administration. Indicators and contraindications track the impact of the prescription on both the malady and the patient. Adverse reactions are carefully monitored to insure that the cure is in fact not more deadly than the disease. The patient and the physician are partners, and the patient reports regularly the specific measures and observations that allow the physician to reassess progress and prescription appropriateness.*

Physicians and patients need to know that the diagnosis, prescription, and prognosis continue to be appropriate for the condition experienced by the patient. The prognosis contains a forecast of expected outcomes and the events that the patient is likely to experience during treatment. If the patient returns to the physician's office, new readings of vital signs can reveal if there has been a positive measurable impact on the patient's health and if it is returning to normal or improved levels.

If the patient takes medicine but experiences no changes in physical condition, both patient and physician have to wonder if the diagnosis was accurate and if the medicine is effective. The doctor explained to the patient the kinds of changes that should be expected as a result of treatment, and she forewarned the patient that not all of the expected consequences would be positive. These expected changes are milestones that both doctor and patient use to monitor progress. The changes, updates from the hospital bed, office visit, and/or calls and e-mail are noted in the patient's file.

A similar approach is taken by educators using the clinical cycle for performance improvement. A prescription is accompanied by a prognosis that identifies milestones to be met during the course of the intervention. Keeping track of changes and recording related measurements are vital to maximize learning from the experience of implementing the prescription.

Vital-sign performance indicators (VSPI) provide one method to display prescription progress over time. Recording progress information on VSPI documents what improvements have occurred over time and may include specific milestones. VSPI do not, however, document all milestones that are reached as an outgrowth of prescription implementation and prognosis monitoring. This chapter introduces additional clinical documentation processes that are similar to those utilized by physicians and hospitals.

FORECASTING AND PLOTTING MILESTONES

It is important to make sure that team members engaged in problem solving have the same shared expectations and commonly defined set of targeted outcomes. These expectations are translated into specific milestones plotted on timelines and recorded as they occur or are missed on the way to targets. Like the forewarned and forearmed cancer patient, this step in the clinical cycle prepares employees and organization for what will be experienced along the way and establishes a climate that supports decisions based upon current information.

A recent school project reinforced the importance of this component of the clinical cycle. After an extensive discovery process, critical issues were identified using the diagnostic funnel, potential diagnoses were developed, options were narrowed through use of the priority worksheets, and a prescription was developed. The prescription had five major parts, each assigned to a separate team.

The five parts of the prescription were designed to be connected to student achievement, but none of them dealt with it directly. One team had the task of increasing levels of performance expectations among several stakeholder groups that were pulling in different directions. A second team was responsible for refining student rules for improved student behavior. A third team reviewed current programs and services to prepare recommendations to strengthen opportunities for student success.

The fourth and fifth teams had tasks that appeared even less directly tied to achievement. One team had the task of designing and leading an administrative reorganization of positions and a reassignment of personnel in these positions. The last team was responsible for addressing negative stakeholder perceptions that the board and leadership teams were moving in directions that did not support one another and were detrimental to the school's performance.

A common set of milestones was identified for all teams for what was expected to be a two-year project. In figure 10.1, general tasks for each team were identified at the bottom of each of the team columns, and milestones on the left margin were identified for each three months of the project. All teams launched their improvement efforts at the same time. After six months, teams reported significant differences in progress.

After six months, Teams Two and Three had reached the third milestone originally targeted for all teams by the end of the first three months. Teams Two and Three had similar responsibilities and experiences; they conferred frequently to generate plans, to integrate their work, and to align expected outcomes. However after six months, both teams became frustrated and concluded that they lacked direction and cooperation necessary to get goals accomplished.

Team Five had exceeded performance expectations by completing the fifth milestone at the end of six months, three months ahead of schedule. Team Four had the greatest difficulty moving beyond a diagnosis and prescription and

Time	Step	Level of Milestone Accomplishment	Charted Progress of Team				
24 months	10	Student achievement improvement is sustained					
21 months	9	Continuous improvement practices are evident					
18 months	8	New data confirm or question the effectiveness of practices					
15 months	7	Trust levels among stakeholders are increasing					
12 months	6	Employee confidence in new structures, practices, and roles & responsibilities is growing (supportive professional development and training provided)					
9 months	5	Performance data show positive trends					▨
6 months	4	Understanding of governance, leadership, organization, personnel, student, and programs/services needs and changes is growing	▨				▨
3 months	3	Implementation efforts started	▨	▨	▨		▨
	2	Diagnosis, prescription, prognosis, and remedies have been described	▨	▨	▨	▨	▨
	1	Critical Issues have been identified	▨	▨	▨	▨	▨
		Critical Issue Team	1.0 Student Behavior and Discipline	2.0 Organization	3.0 Integrated Ldshp & Gov.	4.0 Programs & Services	5.0 Increasing Shared Expectations

Figure 10.1　**Tracking and Monitoring Milestones: Discovering that Milestones are Imprecise**

accomplished only the second-month milestone through six months. Recommendations for changes in programs and services were not completed in time for budget development, and the team reported that the school was not likely to better prepare students academically next year than it was doing this year.

Teams One and Five worked with internal and external stakeholders to build and unify expectations for improved student behavior and performance. These teams collected data through surveys that were discussed at meetings to identify strengths and needs, to decide action steps, and to develop measures of progress. Commonly held expectations were established for the three staff, student, and parent stakeholder groups and used design strategies that began to improve student behaviors. Only Team One reached milestone four within the projected time period.

Administrators and teachers from all five teams met two times during the first six months to discuss their experiences. They determined that the original expectations in the prognosis for the performance of the five teams were not appropriate for the selected prescription. Even with the early success of Teams One and Five, the common milestones and time projected for all five teams proved to be inadequate. The experience demonstrated that a prescription with five parts is appropriate only if the prognosis contains a forecast of accomplishments and milestones that is customized for each team and its part of the prescription.

Milestones are like road signs; following accurate signs takes travelers toward the desired destination. Following the wrong signs, or using signs that are not specific, carries little assurance that the destination will be reached. It became evident to members of the teams that the milestones originally selected to monitor progress were not tied closely enough to the mission of each team to accurately track progress. Milestones were rewritten to be precise and ultimately more effective. In this case, the original milestones were too general to be effective.

Experience in forecasting and using milestones to measure progress can be easily gained through practice. For any selected project, define each team's mission, break down the mission into manageable pieces, and describe the behaviors of the teams and expected key accomplishments along the way. Discuss the progress of each team with all team members to build a level of comfort with tracking progress through the development of milestones. (See Strategy Thirty-Five at the end of the chapter.)

INDICATIONS, CONTRAINDICATIONS, AND SIDE EFFECTS

Reaching the next milestone is an "indication" that the prescription is appropriate for getting closer to the performance goal. As teams document their progress, anticipated changes can also be accompanied by undesirable changes. Physicians often warn patients that the prescription may cause drowsiness or upset stomach even as it does its intended work. Pharmaceutical company television commercials extol the benefits of their drugs but warn that some patients may experience very serious complications, such as blurring vision, nausea, and even coma as a result of use of the drug.

While "indications" are changes that demonstrate that the prescription is working, contraindications are unintended negative results that suggest that the prescription is not having the impact that is desired and may fail or result in harm. In medicine, contraindications are identified, carefully defined, and tracked to make sure that the unintended consequences of the prescription do not cause irreparable damage to the patient. Recognizing contraindications as early as possible is important. In prescriptions designed to improve performance, contraindications are often ignored despite very serious negative consequences.

For example, in a school committed to getting off the state's underperforming "watch list," the prescription included stronger grade-level team efforts to align standards, curriculum content, instructional strategies, and classroom assessments. In one part of the prescription was a design to increase and improve teacher cooperative planning within grade levels. At the beginning of the training in grade-level team work, a teacher resigned rather than be compelled to use new techniques and implement them with colleagues that she thought did not want to work with her.

At the time, the teacher was confronting a series of personal and family issues and was overwhelmed by the new performance expectations. Out of empathy for their colleague, some other faculty members began to withdraw and disengage from training activities. This contraindication prompted leaders to meet with faculty and reassess the requirements of the training schedule and the time frame for expected outcomes—milestones were adjusted.

In another instance, a program designed to increase rigor and enrollment in high school science courses produced two strong contraindications before the program was started. School leaders, parents, students, central office administrators, the board, and public were engaged in a debate about increasing the number of science courses required for graduation. This proposal was met with protest from other subject departments fearing that increased enrollment in science would decrease enrollment in other elective programs.

Even after the board approved the additional science course requirement, the debate was reignited during the course-selection process, in which fewer students selected courses beyond minimum requirements. Student fears about increasing the difficulty of the science curriculum were accompanied by concerns that student rank in class would be affected negatively if the more rigorous science classes were taken. In consequence, while the quality of the program was supposed to improve, fewer students enrolled in upper-level science courses.

The prescription for improved science-course rigor and higher science-course enrollments was temporarily halted while administrators and faculty discussed the preferred programmatic outcomes for all subjects and grades. The decision by many students not to enroll in higher-level science courses and the reaction of nonscience-department faculty members were clear contraindications to the prescription.

"Side effects" are not as severe as contraindications and may be positive or negative. Side effects are unintended consequences of a prescription that need to be understood and can be documented for improved prescription management. A negative side effect of some medications may be a headache, while a contraindication could be memory loss or loss of consciousness. Positive side effects sometimes lead to new applications of prescriptions. Viagra, for example, has made millions of dollars for its manufacturer and the company's stockholders for its side effects not related to its intended treatment of heart disease.

A side effect may be tolerated if the overall effect of the prescription is long-term improved health. Some negative side effects can cause the patient to break the regimen of treatment, however. Too severe a stomach ache and dizziness or the breakout of an unsightly or unbearable rash may cause the patient to be less conscientious about taking a pill every four hours. So, side effects can be harmful, even if they do not indicate a failure of the prescription.

Positive side effects, however, are welcome additions to the treatment. Some medications intended to treat depression, for example, may also increase attention and energy, two very positive attributes that will assist the patient in his efforts to overcome the original depression. In districts and schools, efforts to improve parent communications have shown positive side effects of decreased student tardiness and absenteeism, increased attendance by parents at teacher conferences, and improved homework completion.

UNDERSTANDING AND TRACKING INDICATIONS, CONTRAINDICATIONS, AND SIDE EFFECTS

The Food and Drug Administration in the United States has the most stringent drug-approval protocols in the world. A critical element of the approval process for new pharmaceutical drugs is the identification and measurement of side effects and contraindications. Literature for an approved drug must include detailed descriptions of the negative side effects and contraindications of which the patient needs to be aware—not good or easy reading, but necessary information.

In districts and schools, there is no requirement to document the unintended consequences of planned improvements, but think how useful such information would be to planners and to those that would be affected by the plans implemented. Tracking milestones and, more specifically, the indicators, side effects, and contraindications that occur during the administration of each prescription and prognosis should be practiced. (See Strategy Thirty-Six.)

Over time, teams tracking milestones develop improved forecasting skills that can be shared with colleagues to enhance performance-improvement skills school- and district-wide. New prescriptions and prognoses are improved from the findings of teams that developed and tracked indications, contraindications, and side effects in other projects. These crucial skills are needed by educators to advance performance improvement and student success.

THE PAIN OF HEALING

After experiencing a serious accident, it is impossible to heal without pain. Even when painkillers are administered, there is necessary discomfort. Pain is an important indicator of healing and a certain amount is tolerated as a sign of progress. Too much pain is never a good thing, and the physician is always careful to treat and reduce it without masking or diminishing the body's response to treatment. It is often difficult for patients who are fearful of developing drug dependency to "stay ahead of the pain." Knowing when and how much medicine to take is important in effective pain management during healing.

It is important to understand differences between the pain and discomfort of healing and the pain and discomfort of injury, illness, and disease. The differences can be subtle, but the physician must recognize the source of the pain the patient is experiencing and share those observations so that the patient can participate in the monitoring of recovery.

There is also discomfort and pain experienced when efforts are made to improve performance. While the pain should not be physical, it is unrealistic to believe that significant changes in thinking and behavior can occur without the discomfort of uncertainty, new expectations, and possible failure. The organizational pains experienced as a result of making changes for improvement may sometimes be manifest as negative side effects of a prescription, but rarely are "growing pains" contraindications of a prescription for improvement.

In fact, there can be very little improvement without discomfort, so it is important that these kinds of pain and discomfort are anticipated, discussed, explained, and do not result in overreactions that can be counterproductive. Just as an athlete knows that efforts to build strength will cause muscle soreness, educators need to understand that efforts to improve performance will cause some professional discomfort. The secret of success is to understand how much discomfort is appropriate and how much is a sign of counterproductive overexertion.

Athletes work with trainers who design improvement programs geared to the specifics of the individual's present and desired state of fitness. Programs target specific muscle and organ systems to bring the athlete to peak condition and then maintain that condition for a specific length of time. It is not sufficient to strengthen one system without building corresponding strengths in the supporting network of systems to balance and maintain the new level of fitness in pursuit of higher performance levels.

Leaders of districts and schools should also consider which commitments and capacities need to be strengthened in efforts to improve performance. An assessment of existing commitments and capacities is important in the assessment of discomfort resulting from change. Are stakeholders experiencing discomfort because they are required to build new commitments and capacities, or are they experiencing discomfort because they are overworking tired practices that cannot grow stronger under present circumstances?

When the discomfort in districts and schools is the result of "overworked muscles," it is important to slow the pace of improvement efforts and make sure that the commitments and capacities needed to support and sustain improved performance have been developed. An overreliance on strengths used to solve past problems wears down personnel and fails to develop new capacities, especially among unfamiliar CPC organ systems.

Most contraindications and negative side effects of performance-improvement efforts develop out of new prescriptions that require changes in behavior or practice. Other times, potential pain and discomfort exist under the surface and only become evident when the practices that mask the pain are removed by the treatment process.

Administrator and teacher behaviors and decision making are accepted as appropriate as long as too many new stressors are not introduced into the workplace. Unfortunately, as the collective weight of stressors of change and performance expectations become heavier, negative side effects arise and interfere with the normal interactions of individuals. For example, with less time for the principal to informally interact with staff members, students, and/or parents, the principal may be perceived as less friendly and more critical of the performance of others.

In a very similar way, teachers expected to participate in new initiatives while meeting the everyday expectations of instruction and higher student learning can, in their haste to accomplish everything, be perceived as uncaring by students. These negatively perceived teacher behaviors are likely to result in a lack of cooperation and trust, and reduced student motivation. These contraindications and negative side effects are more difficult to resolve because they are not the result of an outside or new influence that can be modified but are the personality and background of an individual that may or may not be willingly modified.

Facilitating changes in the personal behaviors and responses of employees is difficult and requires an investment of time. Most likely, personal, one-on-one coaching and feedback about experiences, observations, and data will help to promote a different response over time. It is important to differentiate between those behaviors of discomfort and pain that arise in response to the prescription and those that are personal expressions caused by the stress of increased expectations. (See Strategy Thirty-Seven.)

Employees expected to assume leadership responsibilities deserve opportunities to learn about personal and organization responses to change. Developing skills to understand "growing pains" and to build capacity to identify and deal effectively with them dramatically improves personal, team, and organizational capabilities to diagnose, prescribe, and forecast potentially negative reactions and interactions in efforts to improve performance. While there is a bias for action in the clinical cycle to improve performance, there should be a sensitivity to contraindications and negative side effects that could derail progress.

CHAPTER TEN STRATEGIES

Strategy Thirty-Five: Tracking Team Progress through Milestones

Using a matrix like the one presented in figure 10.1, identify the milestones that will guide, track, and monitor the progress of teams. Use a prescription that requires two or more teams. The number of milestones for each team will vary.

Milestones can be developed for simple, complicated, and complex problems. Using the same complicated problem identified for Strategy Thirty-Two in chapter 9, develop projected milestones that will indicate progress for the team. If you feel adventuresome, pick a complex problem and prepare appropriate milestones. In either case, prepare a list of all the milestones that are potential indicators of progress, both positive and negative, to be experienced by participants. Then discuss why any parts of the description of actual results were different from the milestones expected.

1. Identify the specific steps or milestones for each team.
2. Establish appropriate expectations for the time frame within which each team should accomplish each step.

3. Identify specific behaviors, accomplishments, and other indicators that indicate that the milestone has been reached and then maintained.
4. Bring full teams or their representatives together bimonthly to discuss and compare their experiences with project progress and milestones reached or not reached.
5. Determine the reasons why different teams move through the milestones at the same or different rates.
6. Determine if there are intermediate steps in the milestones that have not previously been identified that would be helpful in tracking progress.
7. Share with other teams, any new data used by each team and their findings to help all teams discover the best ways to measure team progress.
8. Can the milestones be refined?
9. Are there other data that need to be gathered and reported?
10. Does the amount of time needed to accomplish any single milestone suggest the need to modify the prescription and/or prognosis developed by any team?
11. What new protocols emerge from the shared experiences of the teams?

Strategy Thirty-Six: Tracking Side Effects and Contraindicators

The quality of prescription implementation can be maintained only if those responsible for its administration and monitoring understand and track the unintended consequences it produces. A chart, like the one provided in figure 10.2, can be used to track these consequences, to better understand them, and to share the findings with other teams that can benefit from such observations. From one of the teams in Strategy Thirty-Five, examine and pick the milestones that produce side effects and contraindications for this exercise.

Not every milestone will produce side effects or contraindicators and some may be left blank or filled in at a later date. Over time, however, the use of prognoses and milestones will produce a record of side effects and contraindicators common to certain expectations, regimen, and populations.

Milestones: Fill in each milestone from first to last chronologically. For each milestone, record the side effects and contraindicators experienced and noted by the team.

Indicator: What behaviors and conditions have emerged in response to the prescription that suggest the prescription is working? What needs to be done to support those behaviors or conditions?

Positive Side Effect: What unanticipated behaviors and conditions have emerged in response to the prescription that have added benefits? How can they be maintained?

Prescription:				
Milestone Step 1	Indicator	Positive Side Effect	Contraindicator	Negative Side Effect
	Recommended Action	Recommended Action	Recommended Action	Recommended Action
Milestone Step 2	Indicator	Positive Side Effect	Contraindicator	Negative Side Effect
	Recommended Action	Recommended Action	Recommended Action	Recommended Action
Milestone Step 3	Indicator	Positive Side Effect	Contraindicator	Negative Side Effect
	Recommended Action	Recommended Action	Recommended Action	Recommended Action
Milestone Step 4	Indicator	Positive Side Effect	Contraindicator	Negative Side Effect
	Recommended Action	Recommended Action	Recommended Action	Recommended Action

Figure 10.2 Tracking Indicators, Contraindicators, and Side Effects and Recommended Actions Perscriptions

Contraindicator: What behaviors and conditions have emerged in response to the prescription that suggest the prescription is failing or have negative impact on other important parts of the organization? What needs to be done to counteract those behaviors or conditions?

Negative Side Effect: What unanticipated behaviors and conditions have emerged in response to the prescription that have negative impact on the prescription or general organizational health? How can they be eliminated?

Strategy Thirty-Seven: Monitoring the Discomfort of Improvement (Growing Pains)

An important aspect of monitoring performance progress is to accept and understand that "growing pains" are inevitable and that they will arise from the uncertainty caused by the gaps that exist between current levels of commitment and capacity and those levels needed for higher performance in the future. Answers to some simple questions are needed to make certain that the discomfort doesn't become an obstacle to continued growth. (Consider the results obtained in Strategy Thirty-Six in answering the following questions.)

1. Are stakeholders involved in the improvement process experiencing "growing pains"?
2. Is the discomfort of the "growing pains" a nuisance or is it sometimes debilitating? To whom?
3. What are those "growing pains" and how can they be measured and monitored?
4. What aspects of the improvement process are being delayed or diminished by the discomfort?
5. What existing commitments need to be strengthened to deal effectively with the identified "growing pains"?
6. What new commitments need to be developed to deal effectively with the identified "growing pains"?
7. What existing capacities need to be strengthened to deal effectively with the identified "growing pains"?
8. What new capacities need to be developed to deal effectively with the identified "growing pains"?
9. What positive attributes are being developed as a result of the "growing pain" experience?
10. What negative attributes are being developed as a result of the "growing pain" experience?
11. What new organizational strengths can be identified as a result of the exercise that resulted in the discomfort?
12. Should the exercise be formalized in other parts of the organization to develop similar strengths elsewhere?

11

MANAGING PERFORMANCE-IMPROVEMENT PROCESSES

In its simplest form, performance improvement is the work of an individual who is dissatisfied with his own performance and wants to achieve better results. Very few people know about the plans, and even some of these people may not ever find out about the results. In organizations like schools and districts, successful performance improvement requires everyone's participation and requires structures and communication processes to meaningfully coordinate individual and collective efforts.

Through use of protocols in the clinical practice model, educators learn what prescriptions to propose, the results they are supposed to obtain, the implications of interventions, and resulting outcomes for the organization. A network of district and school performance-improvement coordinating councils and a number of teams at both levels should be established to advance performance-improvement goals. The network coordinates efforts of all teams so that surprises are minimized and effectiveness maximized.

Clinical Cycle Step 10—Report and Consult: In the simplest of situations, such as treating poison ivy or the common cold, the patient and physician are able to successfully treat the illness without additional shared input. More-significant issues require that both the physician and the patient consult with specialists in fields related to the condition as well as with people in the patient's family and workplace that will be living and working with the patient. Those whose own lives will be affected by the patient, his condition, and treatment need to know what to expect and how they can and should contribute to successful treatment and recovery of the patient. The physician describes the treatment and anticipated reactions and behaviors of the patient for others to guide their contributions to the patient's recovery. The greater the complexity of the patient's condition, the more carefully others will need to manage their contributions. Having expert advice and coordinated consults are important for stakeholders as well as the patient.

The physician understands that the full recovery and health of the patient is dependent, in large part, on the understanding, support, and acceptance of the patient's support network. Family, friends, and colleagues influence the patient, and they provide the support needed to maintain positive outlook and dedication to the prescribed treatment on the long road to recovery.

Teams in districts and schools responsible for implementing and monitoring improvement prescriptions can also benefit from an organized support network among stakeholders. The work of teams is central to the implementation process, but ultimately, without support for the team within the broader district and school community, performance-improvement initiatives will have only limited success.

How does team work get started? How is the work of teams coordinated? How should teams be supported? And how do teams share the results of their ongoing efforts in order to generate greater understanding and support for ongoing improvement efforts? At district and school levels, a group of staff members should serve as authorizers and coordinators of performance-improvement strategies.

These coordinating groups are made up of "specialists" organized to provide the intellectual, professional, emotional, and other resources needed by teams and their members. These groups are comprised of formal and informal leaders that have an understanding of the relationships between coordinated improvement efforts and the outcomes sought. They maintain a balance among the efforts of multiple teams; ensure that the available resources are expended efficiently and effectively; and provide guidance and support so that the efforts of each team mutually support the work of all other teams.

THE PERFORMANCE-IMPROVEMENT COORDINATING COMMITTEE

The Performance-Improvement Coordinating Committee (PICC), or by whatever name it is known, has the responsibility to manage and coordinate all district and school performance-improvement efforts. The PICC organizes and reviews team improvement efforts and the communication among teams regarding their progress and findings. The work of the PICC can be compared to the board of physicians that directs and oversees the clinical operations in a hospital. The basic design for performance improvement is displayed in figure 11.1.

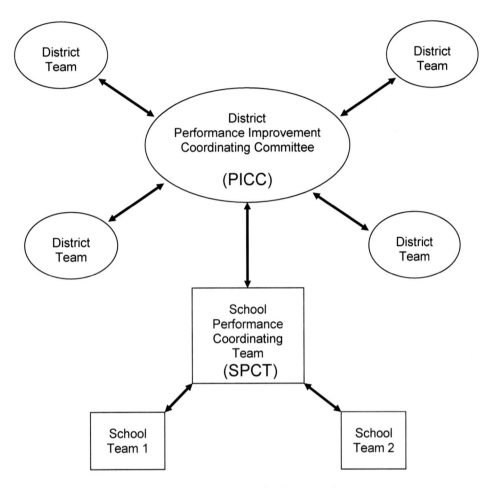

Figure 11.1 Organizing for District and School Performance Improvement

The PICC establishes the "ground rules" by which teams will carry out performance-improvement efforts and report the results of their work. A "team reporting handbook" exists to help guide the process. The PICC provides general direction for all team operations, but each team is expected to customize prescriptions, prognoses, milestones, and reports to their specific mission and to secure the approval of the PICC before implementing prescriptions.

The PICC is formed early in the diagnostic process. It is being introduced in this chapter because its comprehensive role can be better understood following the description of the clinical practice cycle in previous chapters and its prominent role in the reporting and consulting processes. The PICC, operating like the board of medical specialists, consults within its membership and with teams to solve shared problems. The leader of each team serves on the PICC and is the liaison and coordinator of activities and ideas among team members, other teams, and the PICC.

The PICC holds every team accountable for meeting expectations of outcomes and time use, and ensures that scarce resources are shared equitably. At the school level, a School Performance-Coordinating Team (SPCT) has most of the same responsibilities that the PICC has at the district level. The SPCT is likened to a satellite medical practice that coordinates the work of teams and committees charged with improving performance at the school level.

Together, these pieces constitute the district's performance-improvement network. The PICC is comprised of the leaders of each of the district implementation teams, as well as district and/or school leaders and individuals whose expertise is helpful (e.g., technology, curriculum, professional development, personnel, etc.). The network is not complete, however, without the connections to a coordinating body in each school, often cochaired by the school principal. The network, comprised of the PICC, district teams, SPCT, and any related teams, is also illustrated in figure 11.1.

PICC coordination of team activities begins with the distribution and discussion of the team reporting handbook. The handbook introduces common questions that help team leaders and members think about and better understand the team's mission and processes that will govern the team's work in its first clinical cycle. The PICC encourages a discussion of roles and responsibilities within each team and approves the team's description of its anticipated work. (See Strategy Thirty-Eight at the end of the chapter.)

The PICC and the SPCT endeavor to develop increased "sensitivity" to the subtle changes in momentum (the force for change generated by the combined energy of the teams) and balance (the equitable sharing of responsibility among teams for the overall performance-improvement effort). Too often, teams charged with responsibilities to improve program and performance operate in isolation from other teams with similar objectives. Medical specialists try to prevent such isolation by regularly consulting with each other to make sure that treatment by one physician for a heart ailment does not interfere with another's treatment of poorly performing lungs, or the normal function of other organs.

The efforts of the PICC to coordinate the work of teams is intended to make sure that performance-improvement efforts in one system, CPC and SDF, will not have a negative impact on performance levels in other systems. In more traditional performance improvement, there is little or no coordinated team effort to preserve accomplishments and produce synergy for professional learning and further performance improvements. The PICC, by contrast, provides support to all improvement efforts, reduces confusion regarding roles and responsibilities, manages momentum, and balances the work of teams to produce best results.

The PICC approves team plans, monitors and receives reports of progress, and disseminates findings, results, and experiences of each team so that all teams benefit from the accomplishments and experience of others. The efforts of the PICC assure that the burden of responsibility for understanding and use of the clinical cycle, as well as accountability for performance results, are broadly shared among teams. Ultimately, this network of coordinating groups and teams facilitates and manages improvement processes district-wide through the application of standard processes and protocols. (See Strategy Thirty-Nine.)

The PICC focuses early efforts on solving small, simple, and complicated problems, training participants, establishing consistent practices, and building routines. Initial challenges draw upon existing levels of commitment and capacity among involved staff members and are not so complicated that failure is likely. Success in dealing with smaller initial challenges builds confidence in team-work processes and increases stakeholder trust in protocols. (See Strategy Forty.)

The eventual success of performance-improvement efforts is dependent upon clearly establishing the principles and processes for each team's work early on and reinforcing efforts in conducting the clinical practice cycle with training and professional development. The PICC authorizes all intervention plans based on the appropriateness of diagnoses, prescriptions, and prognoses, and approves revisions based on new data and team recommendations. (See Strategy Forty-One.)

Teams provide opportunities for performance improvement through the broad participation of many different stakeholders. District leaders establish one overall coordinated performance-improvement process, managed by the PICC, SPCT, and team network, that performs consistently through protocols, but they also encourage creative and innovative problem solving. Internal course work and professional development workshops are offered every year to better prepare participants for tackling more-difficult and complex problems to further improve performance.

TRACKING PROGRESS THROUGH VSPI

Vital-sign performance indicators are important in the diagnostic and prescriptive process. They also are critical in the process of reporting progress, consulting with specialists, and consulting with stakeholder groups across the district and school. Just as a physician rechecks vital signs related to organic systems to see if the treatment is having desired positive effects, educator behaviors, attitudes, and work quality also need to be rechecked and considered, as progress results are measured and reported on VSPI.

Examples of some VSPI, established as benchmarks and tracked over time in one district's efforts to improve performance, are presented in figure 11.2. These VSPI are related to the diagnosis and prescription presented in chapter 5. The key symbols here are the same as used there, except that an additional two notations have been added to the VSPI as indications of progress over time. Not all VSPI demonstrate positive change from the initial measurement over the two additional reporting periods. In fact, some VSPI show regression in reported behaviors.

A striking example of that regression was in the measure of student, family, and teacher interactions in a district study, displayed in the last VSPI in figure 11.2. Teachers reported receiving fewer contacts by parents over the six-month period in question. Teachers attributed the decline to parent perceptions that teachers were busier with performance-improvement team work, and parents were therefore hesitant to communicate as frequently as in the past.

Parent dissatisfaction with the frequency of interactions and communications was a negative side effect of progress made in other areas. While trust levels between leaders and stakeholders improved, it did not improve initially between teachers and parents. With parent-teacher conferences scheduled within a month, teachers developed plans to address this issue and to make clear that they were available to parents by phone, e-mail, and in person. Teachers made a concerted effort to call and e-mail parents more frequently.

In medicine, the physician wants to make sure that the regimen of drugs and exercise given the patient is having the desired impact. Vital signs should indicate a return to ranges that are normal for the patient when in a general good state of health. In districts and schools, leaders and teams need to know if performance is improving and has changed compared to similar and best-performing districts and schools. Teams monitor performance change and outcomes on the VSPI that were identified as critical during the formation of the diagnosis and prescription and determine whether performance is within an acceptable range or not. (See Strategy Forty-Two.)

At the same time, the physician may notice new indications of illness or reactions to treatment that were not anticipated. These side effects and contraindications, as discussed in the last chapter, need to be monitored by VSPI to make sure that the patient's health does not deteriorate. In most cases, negative side effects disappear or have less impact through the course of treatment, but when they worsen, the doctor must reconsider continuing or revising the prescription.

Similarly, teams determine how to quantify and measure negative side effects and contraindications. Too many basically sound solutions fail because the negative side effects and contraindications are not addressed as they become known. Under most circumstances, only minor alterations or small additions to the

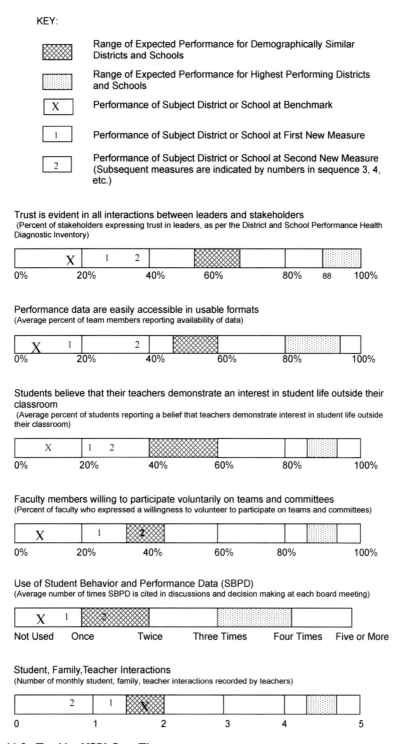

Figure 11.2 Tracking VSPI Over Time

prescription are needed to address negative conditions and accelerate efforts to make real progress.

Stakeholders negatively affected by the intervention cannot be expected to support the continuation of prescription implementation without attention to their concerns. Coordinating bodies and teams need to discuss anticipated negative side effects and how they should be monitored, and when they occur, confer with affected stakeholders quickly, discuss anticipated side effects, and how they should be addressed.

FINAL REPORTS OF CONSULTING SPECIALISTS

Team members become significant experts and resources to assist the growing capacities of other staff members. Consultation is a part of the professional clinical obligation of those with experience and knowledge. Assistance to others should be provided willingly and without judgment. The shared expertise contributes to growth among staff members and goes beyond the work of teams. It is the responsibility of the SPCT and PICC to consciously establish and maintain a culture that nurtures learning and sharing among professionals.

Formally, both the SPCT and the PICC require teams to document the results of performance-improvement efforts and to report them in VSPI and other formats that make sense to stakeholder communities. Implementing prescriptions and prognoses are the early protocols used to solve problems and improve performance. Additional protocols during treatment measure progress through milestones, through indicators of success, and through measures of side effects and contraindications.

All of these protocols build success among medical practitioners. Patient health and social welfare depend on the common understanding among medical professionals of the root causes of diseases, their symptoms and manifestations, the populations they affect, and the best ways to respond to them. The medical profession has produced an advanced body of knowledge through the practice and accumulated experiences of physicians, including formal medical training, reading, experimentation, and ongoing professional development.

These contributions to knowledge and practice have been firmly supported by interested government agencies, collaboration with medical and pharmaceutical businesses and research institutions, and the application of individual, corporate, and university patents used to start new scientific companies in medical and related fields. Most important, the common understanding shared among medical professionals is continually challenged, modified, and changed through new discoveries shared within the profession.

Medicine has a history of introspection and consideration of work done in the field that is discussed, tested, and shared widely. Physicians consult "desk references" such as the *Merck Manual, Harrison's Principles of Internal Medicine, French's Index of Differential Diagnosis,* and *Oxford American Handbook of Clinical Medicine,* each reflecting the history of experience of a large number of the best medical practitioners in a wide variety of specialties.

Making sense from the combinations of symptoms and recognizing the syndromes or root causes of poor performance lead to precise diagnoses and reliable prescriptions with predictable outcomes. This becomes possible only through ongoing collection, study, sharing, and reconsideration of data about treatments and outcomes. Educators need to build similar expertise through compilation, publication, discussion, and studied reapplication of improvement successes and failures as has been accomplished in medicine.

Written descriptions and presentations of performance-improvement experiences of teams through the clinical cycle produce a body of knowledge about the causes of problems and the different ways they can be addressed. Ultimately, the results of district and school efforts to improve performance become incorporated into the traditions, legends, and literature of district and school problem solving. (See Strategy Forty-Three.)

The incorporation of discoveries made in team experiences is long overdue in the professional learning of educators. This process should begin with the compilation and publication of the results of team work. A systematic compilation of reports forms the core of the district and school "performance improvement manual." Descriptions of effective performance-improvement strategies combined with documentation of the outcomes they produce can be gathered in desk and online resources for consultation as well.

Medical references contain the compiled successful experiences and empirical research carried out by physicians, who report them to assist present and future colleagues. The *Merck Manual* was first compiled in 1899 and is presently in its eighteenth edition. In 1899, this book marked the first description of clinical practice in medicine, and, hopefully, the distillation of successful practice in education into a similar manual will help drive improvements in school performance.

CHAPTER 11 STRATEGIES

Strategy Thirty-Eight: Getting Teams Started through the PICC

The PICC can initiate the coordination of teams by having each team explore its mission in the context of the following statements and questions. The responses and answers provided by each team are then shared among all teams and the PICC.

The Role of the Team

1. Define the most important role of this team in implementing its charge.
2. Define the least important role of this team in implementing its charge.
3. What charge or characteristics of this team promises to make it successful?
4. What charge or characteristics of this team could inhibit its success?

The Responsibilities of the Team

1. What responsibilities does this team need to accept in order to be successful? How do we measure and report those responsibilities?
2. What responsibilities does this team need to share, and with whom, in order to be successful? How does the team measure and report those responsibilities?
3. What responsibilities does this team need to delegate, and to whom, in order to be successful? How does the team measure and report those responsibilities?
4. What responsibilities does this team need to abandon or disown in order to be successful? How does the team measure and report those responsibilities?

The Team's Relationship with Stakeholders

1. Which stakeholder groups will consider the success of this team as a positive?
2. Which stakeholder groups will consider the success of this team as a negative?
3. Which stakeholder groups will have no interest regarding the success of this team?
4. Which stakeholder groups will stand to benefit the most from the success of this team?

Strategy Thirty-Nine: Checking Team Progress through the PICC

Once teams have begun their work, the PICC receives regular reports (i.e., monthly or bimonthly, and annually) on the progress of the development of the team's prescription, prognosis, and milestones. In their early efforts, teams provide a periodic self-assessment progress report using the following rubric:

1. Team members have discussed and are in agreement with team purposes.
2. The team is in agreement with the PICC and/or the SPCT regarding the team's purposes.
3. Team members are clear about the team's overall responsibilities and those for performance improvement.
4. Team members understand the roles and responsibilities of other teams and the relationships among the teams.
5. The team has reported its agreements on how to assess progress of the prescription to the SPCT and/or PICC.
6. The PICC has approved the assessment criteria and components to be used by the team.
7. The team has reviewed data to understand performance levels.
8. The team has discussed meaning found within the data.
9. The team has made suggestions to strengthen the presentation of the data to improve their meaning.
10. The team has discussed the implications of the data with other teams or team leaders.
11. The team has discussed strategies to address concerns found in the data.
12. The team has produced a written description of what the data mean to the team.
13. The team has outlined a plan to improve performance.
14. The team has assessed knowledge and background of members and knows strengths and needs in order to implement a successful prescription. (performance-improvement plan).
15. The team has outlined a plan to improve adult performance.
16. The team has presented plans to affected stakeholders for discussion, encouragement, and direction.
17. The team has held discussions about plans with other teams and is ready to submit the plans to the PICC.
18. The team has received PICC approval to implement the plan.

Strategy Forty: Checking on Progress through the SPCT and PICC

The PICC reviews and checks the initial results of the teams' implementations of their prescriptions by requiring a simple team report that includes responses to the following questions. After the PICC review of reports, it coordinates steps to improve alignment of the prescriptions of all teams to accelerate progress.

1. Has the initial prescription proven effective? Why?
2. Are initial findings appropriate and meet expectations?
3. Are initial findings consistent with milestones and is there evidence that performance has moved closer to desired outcomes?
4. Within findings, what indications of success were found? What contraindications and side effects were found?
5. What is recommended to enhance the indications? What is recommended to address the contraindications and side effects?
6. Should the prescription continue without change?
7. Should the prescription be altered or replaced? What new commitments or capacities need to be developed and aligned with the new prescription?

Strategy Forty-One: Reporting the Interim Results of Team Work

At least annually, preferably semiannually, and sometimes quarterly, each team should report its progress to the SPCT and/or PICC. The PICC should, in turn, publish an annual summary of team reports to the larger school and district community. Each report should include the following:

1. statement of the diagnosis;
2. statement of the prescription;
3. statement of the prognosis;
4. milestones anticipated as a part of the prognosis;
5. milestones reached;
6. key VSPI, and how the measures of data related to each have changed over time;
7. observations about implementation processes and efforts;
8. assessment and revision strategies discussed and recommended;
9. revisions made to prescription, prognosis, milestones, and processes;
10. results obtained, including supporting data;
11. recommendations for improving results;
12. recommendations for improving protocols, and processes; and
13. recommendations for continuing professional development to increase commitment and capacity.

Strategy Forty-Two: Monitoring, Measuring, and Reporting VSPI

Monitoring the VSPI that were used in the diagnostic process provides important evidence of the progress and success of the prescription. The VSPI provide an important way to document and report performance changes to other stakeholders, especially those who have responsibilities for other prescriptions or different parts of the same one. The PICC authorizes the use of particular VSPI and needs to develop answers to the following questions to make the VSPI data and information as meaningful as possible.

1. How often should activities in each VSPI be remeasured?
2. Which VSPI should be remeasured together to provide cluster benchmarks?
3. Are there implications in the remeasured VSPI for the work of other teams?
4. Were there negative side effects or contraindications of the prescription that influenced the outcomes reported on the VSPI?
5. What VSPI were identified and tracked to monitor negative side effects or contraindications?
6. After reporting and considering the remeasured VSPI, do other VSPI need to be developed?
7. With which teams and stakeholder groups should the results of the remeasured VSPI be shared?
8. What do the remeasurements mean to the ongoing prescription?
9. What are the implications in the VSPI results for preparation and training of teams and staff members?

Strategy Forty-Three: Team Final Reports

The annual report of the PICC summarizes prescriptions and outcomes as reported by teams in reports that include the following:

1. a summary of the success of the team in meeting its original charge;
2. the SDF and CPC that were the focus of the team's work;
3. the revisions in the prescription that were recommended and implemented during the work of the team;
4. the VSPI that were tracked during and at the conclusion of the implementation of the prescription;
5. the changes in the original prognosis that resulted from the team's work;
6. side effects and contraindications that were experienced and the changes in the prescription that resulted;
7. observations and recommendations regarding the distribution of resources in the district/school;

8. the team's prognosis for the continued success of the implementation for which it has had responsibility;
9. the new knowledge and data generated by the work of the team that can be generalized to the entire district/school;
10. observations of the team that enlighten the next discovery phase and the work of future teams; and
11. other observations or recommendations of the team.

12

LEADERSHIP FOR MORE
EFFECTIVE ORGANIZATIONS

This chapter is the first of three devoted to leadership roles and responsibilities for performance-improvement processes. The organization striving to reach new performance highs and higher student achievement requires leader abilities and behaviors that take the organization far beyond compliance. This chapter looks through a wide-angle lens at factors that lead to success.

While leaders need to report to stakeholders annually about progress and what is planned to move past current accomplishments, they must recognize that performance-improvement processes can leave less-prepared and less-talented personnel behind. These personnel have a sense of being at risk that should not be ignored.

Clinical Cycle Step 11—New State: There is a point in the treatment process when the patient and the physician understand that a new, and hopefully improved, state of health has been achieved. At this time, the physician determines what, if anything, needs to be done to preserve the improvements, and whether additional improvements are possible. It is essential that the patient understand that the changes in lifestyle made to achieve the new state must be maintained to preserve the new state.

The label on the container reminds patients to take all of the medication that their physician has prescribed. As the patient begins to feel well again, perhaps even better than he did before he was ill, it is easy to stop keeping the regimen designed to treat the illness. Despite any difficulties, maintaining

strict adherence to the prescription until it is certain that all indications of illness or infection have been healed, and this has been confirmed by the physician, is very important.

Doctors are often frustrated in attempts to convince patients that preserving
improved health requires a commitment to an improved lifestyle, avoiding those
circumstances that led to illness in the first place. Too many recovered patients
slip back into old habits of diet and lack of exercise and become vulnerable
again to illness and disease that could have been avoided. Past routines did not
prevent the illness and a return to them will not prevent a resumption of the
same malady.

Organizations have the same bad habit of falling back into old patterns of
planning, decision making, and leadership behaviors once the problem that
inspired new efforts appears to be resolved. In a larger societal context, people
with very little in common will rally to a common effort in times of crisis, only to
return to old patterns of bias and selfishness once the crisis has past. This chapter explores the major roles and responsibilities of leaders seeking to prevent
organization backsliding and promote performance improvement.

The "New State" in Clinical Cycle Step 11 calls for the careful assessment of
the improved state of the organization and a commitment to the practices and
routines necessary to maintain it. The commitment to those routines requires
that the definition of the new state and the routines be clear and widely shared
with those expected to participate.

Once a preferred new state of performance has been reached by administrators, teachers, and students, the commitment, routines, and new capacity levels
that produced the new state should keep performance health strong. Yet, without alertness to potential new problems and an increasing willingness to find
and apply new solutions, the new state will slip back into a former, less healthy
one. Avoiding this very common problem requires personal and organizational
flexibility not normally found in districts and schools. It has to be built into the
culture.

ROLES OF LEADERSHIP

Management and leadership behaviors have been a central focus of clinical
practice in schools in several of the preceding chapters, but the focus was on
teams, the PICC, and group processes and not on any individual formal and informal leader. Chapters 12 and 13 explore two iconic American leadership styles
found in folklore and literature that reflect a cultural bias for individual strength
and courage, and mask the importance of collaborative leadership styles.

Both styles also reflect a dependence on team effort, commitment to the success of everyone involved in an enterprise, and enormous potential rewards for meeting goals. Each is often cast as an American hero, but the hero has been misrepresented as standing alone and isolated from the work of others. In fact, the heroics of these two characters demonstrate how the complexities of their respective challenges were more effectively dealt with through their leadership of responsible and accountable team work.

A WESTERN TRADITION—THE CATTLE DRIVE

There is a uniquely American tradition that can offer great insight into the processes of leadership in an organization whose challenges are ever changing even as the ultimate goal remains the same. From the period immediately following the Civil War until the early 1880s, Texas cattle ranchers were faced with the challenge of maximizing the profit on their beef cattle. Cattle in Texas were so plentiful that they were sometimes not worth the cost of raising them; their value on the local market was depressed by the huge available supply.

The most profitable eastern U.S. markets for beef could only be reached by rail, but railroads did not yet extend to Texas. Since the railroad was not prepared to come to the cattle, the ranchers endeavored to take their cattle to the railroad. For about twenty years, one of the great adventures of the American West was found in the cattle drives that moved tens of thousands of beef cattle each year from ranches in Texas to railroad depots in Kansas and Missouri. An entire mythology grew up around the experience of cowboys on these drives through Native American lands, open ranges, and all of the dangers inherent in river crossings, thunderstorms, stampedes, and rustlers.

Few educators will ever plan to drive cattle, but the organization of the drive offers insight into how the trail bosses balanced the "big picture" responsibly, with circumstances that frequently changed the nature of the original problem. The only things that the trail boss and crew knew for sure were that their goal was to get the cattle to a railhead and that they could never anticipate all of the challenges that would arise. In addition to moving the herd, the boss and crew also had to allow sufficient grazing to fatten the cattle for market and get them to the train on time.

Based on his experience, knowledge of the trail, and the general attitudes of his men and cattle, the trail boss set out to succeed over every obstacle. Involved stakeholders in education are not to be compared with the cattle that were driven to railhead. Quite to the contrary, stakeholders are represented by the cowboys who accepted the challenge to guide, protect, and move the herd in a way that will bring the greatest possible value. The moving herd represents the district or school with many actual and potential problems with which it must contend while pushing to the goal of universal student proficiency.

The beauty of the drive is found in its organization. The trail boss was the leader. He was the most experienced and knowledgeable of the cowboys and had made the journey many times before. It was his duty to organize the work of all the others on the crew and, each day, to ride ahead and find the best path for the day and the next place to safely bed the herd. He was assisted by a team of individuals with specific responsibilities whose coordinated efforts resulted in the most efficient and economical movement of the herd.

The ratio of cowboys to cattle varied from one-to-twenty in rare situations and up to one-to-four hundred in the most difficult times.[1] The ratio was determined in part by the experience and skill of the cowboys and in part by economic circumstances. Point riders led the herd within a reasonable proximity of the recognized trail, according to the instruction of the trail boss. Swing riders, alongside the herd toward the front, and flank riders, alongside the herd toward the back, worked to control the herd by keeping it moving, calming them in times of storm or river crossing, and making sure there were none that wandered away and were lost.

The least experienced or least respected cowboys rode "drag." Following the back of the herd to both keep it a single unit and to round up strays, they literally ate the dust of the herd, resulting in their daily coating with thick dust. In addition to the herd riders, there was a wrangler who protected, guided, and moved the group of horses that the cowboys needed. Every rider might have as many as six different mounts in order not to exhaust one or two horses on the journey.

While each cowboy was responsible for feeding and caring for his own mounts, the wrangler was responsible for protecting the assets and resources of the drive. Finally, there was the cook and driver of the "chuck wagon," who prepared the meals, procured supplies, and even acted as the ad hoc judge in arguments and contests.

The trail boss had an ever-changing problem to solve. The herd had to be "given its head" within limits if the drive was to be successful. He knew that while some of the challenges would be similar to those faced before, other challenges would be new. He understood that he could not anticipate every problem. He would need to solve new problems as they arose, relying on his experience, training, and skills as a rider and leader.

He surrounded himself with capable individuals of varying experience and skill, and with specific assignments. The trail boss had to balance his experienced judgment with the habits and behaviors of the cattle and riders in order for the drive to be both effective and efficient. In spite of all of the measures taken to control and move the herd, all of the riders knew that the herd determined the route taken. The cattle could sense where the best grass and water were and where the most efficient path of progress lay.

The riders would try to keep the cattle moving in a general direction with little wasted time, resource, and effort, while exerting as little direct control as possible. Meanwhile, any number of surprises could ignite a stampede that pushed the herd off its preferred path and caused a loss of important body weight, numbers of cattle, and, possibly, missing the train. In short, the trail boss demonstrated effective leadership by balancing achievement of the ultimate goal with constant resolution of smaller problems influenced by ever-changing circumstances.

The thinking of the trail boss was influenced by experience with prior herds and riders. The trail boss made assessments of present rider skills to facilitate the drive, the organization and deployment of riders and skills needed for the new terrain and number of cattle, and estimates of the reactions to known and likely hazards and events. The trail boss used three different time frames in his assessments of the variables of riders, herd, and conditions.

Past experiences, present circumstances, and potential future outcomes were simultaneously considered by the trail boss and more experienced riders. While reacting to current conditions, information, and emerging problems, the boss and riders made adjustments based on their capacities and instinctual reactions to herd behaviors. There was hope that the problems confronted would not overwhelm team capacities.

The best trail bosses visualized and understood the undulating, but purposeful, flow of people and herd among terrain and events to the railhead goal. Most of the work was routine and monotonous; yet, the real test of preparation and implementation came when trail boss and riders alike were tested by sudden or unexpected changes in circumstance. The thinking process, organization design, and skills utilized by the trail boss suggested order and competence, even amid the chaos of constant change.

Trail boss leadership was effective. Many people enjoyed beef in their diets because changing challenges between Texas and Kansas or Missouri were overcome by the combined knowledge and skill of the trail boss and riders. In summary, the important leadership practices demonstrated included the following:

- a clearly stated, shared, and unequivocal goal that guided planning and execution;
- personnel practices that built teams with a mixture of necessary tasks and talents;
- roles and responsibilities that were specific and included the expectation of appropriate and independent action based on conditions;

- factors, such as terrain, locations of grass and water (resources), threats from people and weather conditions, and potential team cohesion and resilience, were calculated into plans to achieve the goal; and
- the management of time, which was critical for the maintenance of momentum and a balanced team effort to accomplish the goal.

Successful cattle drives were led by men who had a vision of the "big picture." They visualized the goal and how it would be accomplished, and they understood the challenges involved. Trail bosses pulled together important ingredients that connected herd, riders, terrain, and conditions essential for success on the trail.

Modern-day education leaders are very much like the "trail bosses" of the nineteenth century as they facilitate and drive personal and organizational efforts to higher levels of performance and student achievement. They have expertise in leadership craft and understand the goals and performance expectations that others hold of them. But, like the riders when faced with a sudden flash of lightning and crash of thunder that transformed the quiet drive into a stampede, today's district and school leaders need to expect, prepare for, and resolve crises to restore the more-stable learning climate so essential to student success.

Processes of gathering; organizing and analyzing information; developing, selecting, and implementing a solution; and monitoring and revising that solution during implementation must become standardized through protocols that bring assurance and confidence to people affected by new circumstances. (See Strategy Forty-Four at the end of the chapter.) Establishing trust among all stakeholders is extremely important to leader success in performance improvement and clinical practice. Yet, trust is an elusive commodity under difficult circumstances.

Risks on the trail were at a much higher level when decisions were made to push the herd against its selected path. During a stampede, skilled individual and collective decision making was required even when there were no opportunities to communicate. When the trail boss and riders worked together on more drives, they forged a clear vision and understanding of what was expected during the drive and how to respond when problems arose. Expectations and values that guided the successful trail boss and influenced the behavior of cowboys can also be applied by educators to keep the drive together for higher student achievement.

Risks for educational leaders have increased significantly in the last decade. Leaders are vulnerable when staff members and students perform poorly, and they are equally vulnerable when changes are introduced to improve performance. Diminishing this double set of risks requires that leaders and staff members understand and discuss how to intervene in problems and track performance improvements. Leaders and staff members need to know when to maintain current practice to preserve gains and when to commit to new interventions needed to move forward.

Teams, the SPCT, and the PICC have integral roles in achieving a new and improved state, but the people on them collectively may be reluctant to assume the risks necessary to push for higher performance. The principal and the chief school administrator cannot delegate the key responsibility to decide to consolidate improvements or to press forward for even higher goals. Team structures and processes do not relieve leaders of the most basic duty—the decision to accept the risk or to avoid it. Clinical practice provides the experience that leads to valuable insights on how leaders make this choice.

BETTER OR JUST DIFFERENT?

In order for a state of existence to be better, it must be different, but the mere fact that it is different does not guarantee that it will be better. To assess the changes that result from planned intervention, it is essential to measure the differences between former performance levels and the new state. The VSPI used to diagnose and define the problem and track performance change through multiple cycles of prescriptions and prognoses provide a historical record of the changes in behavior, perception, and performance that result from the efforts to improve outcomes.

Changes measured by and recorded on VSPI are the evidence that the new, improved state exists and is not merely different. Improvements measured on VSPI establish a new highest level and the new higher floor of performance. If this is the normal range for this performance category, the team determines how to maintain performance at that level. (See Strategy Forty-Five.)

Over time, routines that are the practices and protocols that maintain current performance are adopted and form the foundation for reaching even higher performance and achievement levels. Just as heart rate, blood pressure, and arterial flow need to be continually checked in patients that have recovered from open-heart surgery, continued monitoring of VSPI serves to alert school stakeholders to recurring concerns and new successes.

Maintaining gains while working to achieve ever-higher levels of performance is the ongoing goal of leaders. Leaders remain attentive to ongoing efforts and indicators of progress as each new performance level is pursued. Yet, these same leaders, in order to achieve the next performance level, begin to focus on how people, structures, and resources in the organization will flow together to achieve the next goal. Leaders must plan mentally and emotionally how resources can be directed to obtain higher levels of commitment and capacity needed for the next challenge.

Even as situations and obstacles change, the ultimate goal remains the same for both the trail bosses of the Old West and today's district and school leaders. In addition to bringing each student to academic success, the enduring challenge to educational leaders is to maintain high levels of energy and commitment among stakeholders, particularly teaching personnel, to overcome each new obstacle as it blocks progress to the goal.

RECOGNIZING AND ADDRESSING AT-RISK ADULT POPULATIONS—ANTICIPATING WHAT HAPPENS ON THE TRAIL

An important positive side effect of successful performance-improvement efforts is the growth of commitment and capacity among stakeholders that participate in the performance-improvement project. Unity of purpose and pride in accomplishments develop within the community of successful stakeholders and produce an expanding confidence to accept new challenges. This confidence spreads among most performers, however, it also separates them from other stakeholders and represents an important negative side effect that can be addressed by teams and structures but cannot be ignored by leaders.

It is important to understand that successful improvement efforts create divisions among stakeholders. Those who did not actively participate, those who participated in simple and superficial ways, those who felt that they were disadvantaged by the changes, and those who demonstrate that they remain outside of the range of new performance expectations become a population that is "at-risk" in the new state of the organization. Some of these individuals are like the inexperienced "drag and flank riders" toward the back and rear of the herd that lack the experience to contribute to the herd's direction; some do not contribute to the work of the team; others get in the way.

Maintaining new performance levels requires the development of new skills and higher confidence among all stakeholders, especially those that are at risk. Leaders and teams must commit to reducing the number of at-risk stakeholders. It is not enough to observe that different levels of readiness for performance improvement exist among stakeholders. Conscious efforts are needed to close the gap.

Ironically, the separation of stakeholders into successful and at-risk groups is both an indication of productive results from successful prescriptions and a contraindication of the unity and readiness required for the next clinical cycle. Once at-risk stakeholders have been identified, it should not be difficult to prepare and implement efforts that reduce differences in commitment, capacity, and experience between newly empowered team members and the at-risk persons or groups. Many steps can be incorporated into ongoing professional development and training, human resource practices, and supervision and evaluation processes. (See Strategy Forty-Six.)

Specific strategies for closing the gap should be based on the reasons that the person and group are at risk. Stakeholders that consciously choose to separate themselves from the improvement process are likely to respond to professional development designed to identify their own strengths, needs, and performance-improvement opportunities. Based upon an inventory of strengths and needs, new training opportunities can be identified. Opportunities can also include new team assignments more closely aligned with their interests and background to counter reasons for their lack of commitment.

Stakeholders that participate superficially want to appear involved but do not dedicate the time and energy required. Consequently, they remain uninformed and far less experienced in new protocols. It is important to bring this group into fuller participation and not drive it away by ignoring its behavior. Guided practice with experienced colleagues and supportive training will usually bring these at-risk stakeholders into successful team work.

At-risk stakeholders performing below the new performance expectations will usually agree to join with those committed to problem solving if asked and provided the opportunity. Their other alternatives are few—either fight the system or leave it. Those that choose to remain outside of the high-performing group engage in a tug of wills over lost comfort, a concern over lost power, or some other battle. This is usually a temporary disagreement as they grow to understand that a better future rests with joining the new community of improved performers or that a better future resides somewhere else.

After identifying at-risk stakeholders, leaders need to be personally engaged to actively recruit them into the mainstream. The first important step to bringing at-risk performers into the organization's new state is to open a dialogue. Careful consideration must be given to the reasons that any individual or group feels disadvantaged, and efforts should be made to remove any perceptions of bias or inequity in efforts to have the at-risk persons meet the new expectations. (See Strategy Forty-Seven.)

Finally, human resource practices need to be assessed, and where necessary redesigned, to make sure that the recruitment and hiring processes include consideration of the behaviors, perceptions, and attributes that will ensure that new employees are prepared to fully participate in new and future states of the organization. Processes that place people at risk during performance-improvement projects need to be carefully analyzed and reconsidered. Otherwise, they could be a future root cause of organizational underperformance.

The accomplishments of successful, or highly committed and capable staff members, will be limited as long as ill prepared, uncommitted, or incapable personnel are working along with them. Gaps in performance quality of staff members will continue to widen unless conscious efforts are made to close them. Feedback about performance quality to staff members based in observations and evaluation data produces understanding. Opportunities for practice of new skills under the guidance of skilled clinicians help move understanding to growth.

Leaders need to establish processes to recruit and hire candidates who have a commitment to lifelong professional growth, have demonstrated evidence of work using the ethical guidelines in chapter 4, have a predilection for team work, and demonstrate problem-solving skills. These new employees, as well as existing employees at every existing skill level, should have opportunity to acquire additional capacity. Programmatic support should provide mentoring, coaching, and professional-development workshops and courses that give every employee a chance to contribute to accelerating improvements.

ANNUAL REPORTING

Every district and school has responsibility to report information to federal, state, and local governments every year concerning the collection and expenditure of monies; student attendance, behavior, and achievement of proficiency benchmarks; and compliance with law and regulation. Districts and schools engaged in improvement efforts based in clinical practice also have a responsibility to share their vision of improved outcomes, the challenges they face, and interventions that have produced the latest results.

The district's or school's annual report is a proactive communication with the investors and stakeholders in local education. The annual report provides the opportunity to credit teachers, leaders, staff members, and volunteer stakeholders for efforts that made improved outcomes possible. Additionally, leaders use the report to build shared expectations among powerful allies of performance improvement by communicating a desired future state and levels of commitment and capacity needed to attain it.

The annual report is a leadership view of the new state and serves as the documented record and notice of what exists and what is needed to move forward. In medicine, it is essential that patients understand that the changes in lifestyle made to achieve a new state of health must be maintained to preserve the gains realized. Likewise, internal and external district and school stakeholders must understand that changes in behavior, attitude, commitment, capacity, and perception are needed to preserve the new state of performance and serve as a launching pad for greater gains.

The annual report reflects how leaders view the important work they lead and focuses on the current view of performance in the new state of the organization, changes in performance over time, and how various stakeholders have contributed. Where performance has faltered, honest presentation of the reasons and consequences provides the basis for support for new plans and revisions. The information used to develop the annual report, in large part, comes from the annual PICC and SPCT reports that have specifics about teams and their accomplishments and more detailed plans about future efforts.

Information about the identification of problems, the interventions designed to address them, and the improvements that result summarizes recent ongoing efforts to improve performance and supports the establishment of a performance-improvement culture. Understanding that leaders and staff members are dedicated to identifying and solving problems and that they are willing to document yearly progress generates confidence among stakeholders and encourages others, even those at risk, to participate in performance-improvement efforts. (See Strategy Forty-Eight.)

Part of the responsibility of every medical professional is the necessity to record, monitor, and share the results of treatment efforts. Scientific discovery is predicated on trial and error, controlled experimentation, hypothesis testing, measurement of progress, interpretation of results, and reporting implications for further research. Annual reports serve as a record of the success history of teams and of districts and schools using the CPM. This history encourages ongoing experiential learning, supports higher levels of success, and provides a record of improvement efforts that can be a resource for future diagnoses and prescriptions.

The cattle drive and trail boss are metaphors for districts and schools headed by intrepid leaders moving assuredly toward the goal of improved performance and higher student achievement. The leader's job is to prepare personnel to guide the organization in the right direction keeping as close as possible to the path selected to achieve the goal. If problems arise that divert staff and student attention and direction, prior training and experience of leaders and staff members help pull the organization back on path.

CHAPTER 12 STRATEGIES

Strategy Forty-Four: The District/School as a Cattle Drive

Consider the leadership responsibilities of the educational leader to be like those of the trail boss on the cattle drive, while leaders and team members answer the following questions:

1. Have team members been assigned according to their skills and experience and the needs of the team? How should future team assignments be made?
2. How much deviation from the prescribed path to the primary goal will be tolerated by leaders?
3. What influences are most likely to be tolerated in causing the deviation? Why? How much?
4. How are resources protected or conserved along the path to the goal?
5. Who is the "referee" that makes judgments about opinions and behaviors of staff members that could divert efforts from the goal?
6. Are protocols in place and are roles assigned in case there is a "stampede"?
7. Is a new "trail boss" being trained?
8. Are members of the team sharing responsibilities in order to learn how to function in other roles?

Strategy Forty-Five: Defining the New State of Performance

The definition of the new state of performance should be understood as the new foundation for ongoing practice. The PICC should issue a report defining the new state of performance based on the information provided in final reports of all of the implementation teams. The report will:

1. identify the highest levels of performance measured on the VSPI cited by each team;
2. define the "new state" of performance as these highest performances;
3. define what the new "floor" (i.e., low level) of acceptable performance is in this new state;
4. specify the routines, practices, and protocols needed to maintain performance levels above the new floor;
5. establish a schedule to monitor, remeasure, and report performance on each VSPI identified;
6. specify the stakeholders responsible to monitor, remeasure, and report on each VSPI identified;

7. specify the steps to be taken when performance falls below the new foundation level; and

8. specify the stakeholders responsible to take the steps to address the drop in measured performance.

Strategy Forty-Six: Identifying At-Risk Groups

It is important to identify groups of stakeholders that developed a sense that they were placed "at risk" as a result of the changes instituted in the improvement process.

1. Which stakeholder groups chose to not actively participate in the improvement process? Why?
2. Which stakeholder groups participated superficially?
3. Which stakeholder groups established and maintained behaviors outside of the new expectations? Why?
4. Which stakeholder groups felt that they were disadvantaged by the changes? Why?

Strategy Forty-Seven: Programs to Reunite At-Risk Groups and Individuals with the Organization

For each of the at-risk groups or persons, identify specific programs to reunite them into the mainstream of the district and school performance-improvement community, engage them in the ongoing improvement effort, and maintain their focus on improved performance. For each at-risk group or person, identify the:

1. Reason for at-risk status;
2. VSPI related to at-risk behavior;
3. Recommended intervention to address at-risk characteristic (e.g., training, professional development, etc.);
4. Desired outcome;
5. Desired VSPI measures that demonstrate diminished sense of risk;

Strategy Forty-Eight: The Annual Report of Improvement Efforts

The SPCT and PICC annual reports of improvement summarize many team efforts to diagnose problems, prescribe interventions, predict outcomes, monitor and assess progress, and report findings of improvement. Report the work of teams with a summary of:

1. team leader and members;
2. initial problem;
3. diagnosis;
4. essential VSPI;
5. prescription;
6. prognosis;
7. summary of team efforts;
8. measured outcomes;
9. description of the new state;
10. implications for further improvement efforts; and
11. contact information for follow-up questions and suggestions.

LEADERSHIP IN THE FLOW
OF ORGANIZATIONAL CHANGE

Formal leaders have the responsibility to observe, think about, discuss, and decide how organizational change will take place. Initially, only formal leaders are conscious of the flow of organizational change and have authority to change the flow to accommodate conditions and to seek different results. During periods of upheaval and crisis, leaders have an obligation to use their authority and knowledge to interrupt the negative flow to establish stability through which positive results can be obtained.

Once stability and new performance results have been achieved, leaders and others utilize teams and protocols to spread understanding of the flow of change and to influence it innovatively and creatively. This is a realistic outgrowth of widespread participation of staff members in clinical practice. New synergies support continued performance improvements when stakeholders at different levels of the organization implement prescriptions to obtain higher performance levels in the critical performance categories (CPC), the organization's organ systems.

Clinical Cycle Step 12—Confirmation: The improvements achieved through the treatment process have resulted in a new and improved state. The physician establishes new benchmarks to serve as a new baseline if further improvement is a goal. The new benchmarks are measured and confirmed to insure that they can be maintained. If the new benchmarks cannot be confirmed, reasons must be sought and the treatment regimen reexamined to determine if any part of the previous treatment needs to be re-implemented or if a totally new treatment is needed. If the benchmarks can be maintained, new goals can be established and the new state is determined to be reality.

In the previous step ("New State"), the physician and the patient concluded that a new and hopefully improved state of health was achieved as a result of treatment. In the course of disease management, not all patients make it to confirmation of improved health. Some succumb to their illness or must learn to manage their life in a weakened state of health. Understanding the improved state of health is based on knowing what has changed and why, what must be done to maintain the improved state, and what new needs and opportunities exist to improve further.

The district and school, their stakeholders, structures, activities, and conditions undergo many changes while academic goals remain largely the same. Even armed with early clinical practice experiences, educators may not have confidence in their understanding of the new state and what must be done to maintain and improve it. Educational diagnosticians need to focus on the internal organizational anatomy and physiology to learn about the impact of treatment, the responses of those affected, and the change or lack of it in the recesses of the organization.

PILOTING THE RIVER OF PERFORMANCE CHANGE

A second particularly American leadership style offers insights into recognizing, understanding, and anticipating the impact of ongoing changes in the organizational landscape. The river pilot is a hero of American folklore with much of the same leadership experience and mystique as the cattle drive trail boss. In addition to the visualization and organization skills utilized by the trail boss to move the herd to targeted destinations, the river pilot needed to observe and react to the smallest of details on the river surface that indicate danger below that could bring the boat to an abrupt stop.

Piloting is a daunting task, explained well by Mark Twain in *Life on the Mississippi*. In great detail, Twain discusses the importance of the pilot's knowledge of the river to the safe passage of the boat, its crew, passengers, and cargo. That intimate knowledge results from careful observation and a great deal of practice. "One cannot easily realize what a tremendous thing it is to know every trivial detail of twelve hundred miles of river and know it with absolute exactness."[1]

The exactness itself, however, is fluid. The desire to know the river exactly must include a sense of the changes that occur but often go unnoticed. "Here were leagues of shore changing shape. My spirits were down in the mud again. Two things seemed pretty apparent to me. One was, that in order to be a pilot a man had got to learn more than any one man ought to be allowed to know; and the other was, that he must learn it all over again in a different way every twenty-four hours."[2]

Twain likened knowing the river to memorizing every aspect of a long street in New York City so that if a person were dropped anywhere along its route, she would immediately know where she was. "Next, if you will take half of the signs in that long street, and *change their places* once a month, and still manage to know their new positions accurately on dark nights, and keep up with these repeated changes without making any mistakes, you will understand what is required of a pilot's peerless memory by the fickle Mississippi."[3]

Nothing less is needed to master the river of progress planned for districts and schools and among students over time. School and district leaders learn about, anticipate, and track new influences on performance and reorganize resources (structures, people, teams, processes, time, money, etc.) to better deal with the challenges that their experience and knowledge help them anticipate.

The riverboat captain has to be aware of how conditions are influenced by the weather, currents, shifting debris, and other actions of nature and man in order to navigate around them safely to pilot the boat to its destination. Educational leaders must similarly anticipate how intended and unintended circumstances influence the path to improved performance and make adaptations based on personal and organizational knowledge so that every student's academic journey is successful.

School leaders, like the trail boss and riverboat captain, must acquire more information "than any one man ought to be allowed to know." In schools, it is the interplay of the currents of student and staff behavior, curriculum content, class and grade experience, and staff skills amid the broader flows of parent and community expectations, state and federal standards and expectations, and other variables that influence student learning directly and indirectly. Educators must learn about, weigh, and manage all of these in order to achieve performance goals. (See Strategy Forty-Nine at the end of the chapter.)

The thinking processes and considered actions of the physician, trail boss, and riverboat pilot provide interesting examples of leaders that demonstrate the knowledge, team empowerment, and fluid creativity that drive performance outcomes higher in the most difficult and challenging of circumstances. Still, districts and schools are unique institutions, and the educational diagnostician must develop the level of understanding that will make plans and actions appropriate even as the challenges change and evolve.

MAKING THE ORGANIZATIONAL "BLACK BOX" TRANSPARENT

The concepts that bring focus, connectedness, and success to the improvement process include the interrelationships of stakeholder functions and responsibilities, stakeholder behaviors and activities, and performance health as measured in VSPI. These make up the three dimensions of organization space that impact performance.

The first dimension is comprised of the roles and responsibilities designed into school and district functions (SDF). The second dimension is made up of the critical performance categories (CPC) that cut through and across the organization and form the basis of interactions among individuals and groups. These two dimensions provide a height and width for a matrix or map of the surface of our educational "black box." This matrix-map provides the framework that allows a critical appraisal of existing commitments and capacities needed for performance improvement.

While the matrix-map is useful, it is incomplete without depth, and fails to provide a glimpse of the activities within the organization. Diagnosticians are still limited to treating only the symptoms of the larger problem until they can get inside the black box of district or school.

MEDICAL ADVANCES OPEN THE HUMAN BLACK BOX

Knowledge of structural anatomy alone does not provide the physician with sufficient insights into the physiology, the interactions of internal organs, of the living body. Likewise, an understanding of district and school structures and the people who work within them is only a precondition to learning about the interactive processes in which those structures and people are engaged. Choosing a successful path to desired outcomes requires an understanding of the interconnections among behaviors, structures, expectations, and processes that should be expected in the school.

With the advent of effective anesthesia and better management of infection, physicians and medical students moved from dissection of cadavers to the surgical examination of living patients. But the potential for significant complications led many physicians to use exploratory surgery only as a technique of last resort to solve a patient's physical problems. Instead, the training of physicians emphasized a studied, less intrusive approach of rigorous data gathering, clinical observation, increased reliance on test results, and deliberative discussion with colleagues to understand what was happening inside the patient.

Early medical instrument technologies served as extensions of the physician's own senses during examination processes and provided more-detailed information for the diagnostic process. Increasingly, physicians came to rely on the evolving accuracy of laboratory and other testing that allowed physicians to understand the significance of deviations from normal expectation and further refine diagnoses. An experienced physician understands the limits and merits of each of the tests, and synthesizes them with the physical information and history, and interprets all of the data in light of known facts of anatomy, physiology, and chemistry to test hypotheses, and finally to reach a working diagnosis.[4]

More recently, remarkable new technologies have made possible nonsurgical diagnosis for treatments even down to the level of the cell. "Optical coherence tomography," for example, uses an "ultra thin fiber-optic cable to deliver infrared light inside organs like the stomach, the heart, and lung to produce high-resolution images. Laser scanning can produce cross-section images of living tissue, offering immense promise for detecting oral and cervical cancers. The hope is that personalized medicine will ultimately improve the effectiveness and lower the cost of medical care for us and future generations."[5]

Pennsylvania Hospital in Philadelphia, among several across the nation, has a space-age device using rays from three different points, each of which individually does no harm to healthy tissue. When the three are focused to converge on a single point, however, there is sufficient energy to eradicate the cancerous cells in the strength and precision that a particular cancer requires. The success of these technologies is dependent on mapping and the programming of treatment processes in three dimensions, rather than just in two-dimensional planes or slices through tissue.

The next generation of noninvasive treatments with the flexibility to serve the individual needs of patients is already in the prototype stage. Combinations of computer technology and miniature devices can deliver medicine to specific internal locations without damage or discomfort, for example. The "Philips iPill: The Ingestible Electronic Drug-Delivery system,"[6] can replace large equipment and still assess internal conditions, and modulate responses that fit unique circumstances within the patient's gastrointestinal tract.

Treatment and benefits are accomplished without adverse reaction and require only that the patient swallow the pill.[7] Monitoring pill progress electronically provides indications of dosage effectiveness and of need to make adjustments. The three-dimensional problem identification and solution strategies developed in medicine provide insights into new strategies that can be used for improved problem solving in education.

UTILIZING THREE DIMENSIONS TO SOLVE PROBLEMS IN DISTRICTS AND SCHOOLS

Public education has the potential to develop the technology to diagnose, treat, and respond to conditions quickly and accurately. For public education to be as successful in improving school and student performance as medicine has improved patient care, education needs a stronger foundation of research and development based upon internal views of processes and activities available through three lenses focused on the interactions of the SDF, CPC, and stakeholder activities.

The use of only two dimensions (SDF and CPC) offers an organized view of the interactions of roles and performance categories. It is a dramatic improvement over the traditional examination of only job functions, but it fails to provide entrée into the mass of the organization where the previously unseen critical internal relationships and actions can be observed and considered. An examination of the third dimension in which the behaviors, perceptions, attitudes, and other manifestations of stakeholder interaction occur is needed to precisely pinpoint where and how interventions can be most effective.

Research into what works will require investigations of minimally three sets of variables simultaneously: 1) expectations for stakeholder roles and responsibilities among the SDF; 2) stakeholder activities and performance that support improvements among the CPC; and 3) stakeholder interactions and behaviors at the intersection of the SDF and CPC at one or more levels of the organization.

The river pilot balanced previous experience, accumulated knowledge, and observations of present conditions to decide how to bring boat, cargo, and crew safely to their destination. He had limited clues about what changes may have occurred under the surface. Educational diagnostician decision making now can improve from the use of more modern technology that supplies information about stakeholder interactions and behaviors at critical intersections, even beneath the surface, for the benefit of administrators, teaching staff members and students.

THE ENGAGEMENT AND ACTION DIMENSION

Educators are able through clinical practice to move from broad treatments of the organization, often treating the illness with gross measures that harm some healthy practices, to a more precise treatment of underlying causes of underperformance. The third dimension of depth reveals exactly where and among which group of stakeholders and in what context the critical issue is most significant. This dimension is best identified as a specific stakeholder group at a particular level in the organization, concerned with a specific issue.

This third dimension is the dimension of "Engagement," the action that occurs within the intersections of the SDF and the CPC. We understand the third dimension as engaged stakeholders identified, for example, as the "band parents," "the first grade students," or the "high school science teachers," engaged in specific, measureable activities. The work of these stakeholder groups is identified further by their location, responsibilities, plans, and actions.

In theory, there is an infinite number of combinations of stakeholders when we group them by interest and activity in combination with their more general identity. The level (i.e., community, district, board, school, grade, etc.) also serves to specify the group in a manner that will ultimately allow greater precision in the development and implementation of a remedy. The identified group is not necessarily the cause of the critical issue, although that is possible.

The third dimension reveals and illuminates the group whose behavior, attitudes, production, effort, and so on, most directly affects or is most affected by the critical performance issue that needs treatment. In figure 13.1, the seventeen CPC found on the horizontal axis and the SDF found along the vertical axis are the same as those found in the matrices used in chapter 3. The depth can be visualized as a set of drawers; one at the intersection of each SDF and CPC. Within each drawer are found the stakeholder activities, behaviors, and perceptions that can be measured and monitored as VSPI related to these SDF and CPC.

Once the critical SDF and the CPC have been identified, the drawer behind that intersection can be researched to find the right group of stakeholders and

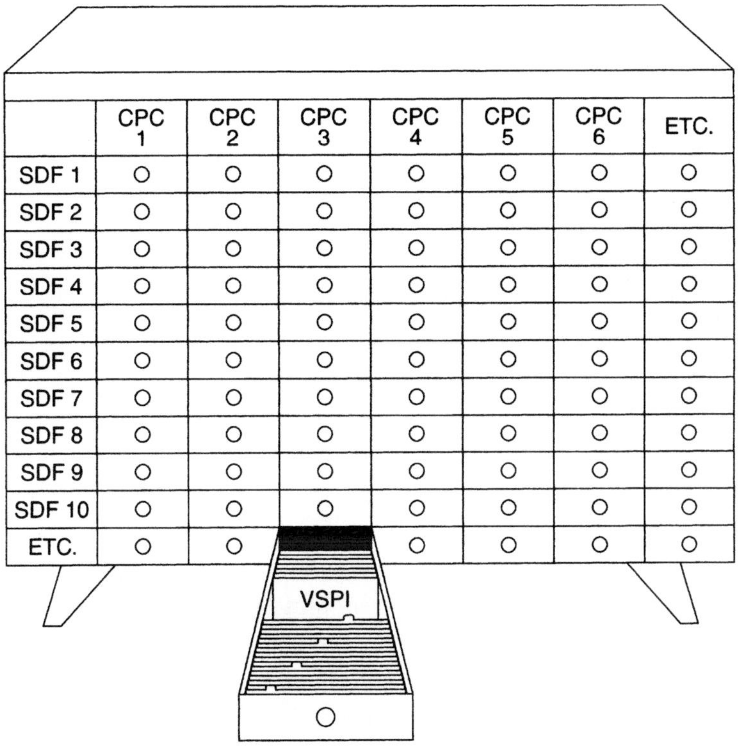

Figure 13.1 The Three Dimensions of Clinical Practice: each drawer in the apothecary contains the VSPI related to stakeholder behaviors and interactions at the intersection of the specific SDF and CPC

their specific behaviors that need to be influenced in order to change and hopefully improve performance. Identification of three dimensions in combination,
like the energy rays converging on cancer cells, pinpoint precisely the work
function, the critical performance issue, and the stakeholder group engaged to
improve the organization's effectiveness.

For example, a problem of an over-expended athletic budget could lead to the
unnecessary purchase and adoption of new budget software when the real issue
rests in the specific identification of leaders and coaches (stakeholders) of the high
school athletic department (SDF) who ordered more equipment than they had
budgeted, failing to adhere to their business and finance responsibilities (CPC).

A critical issue about poor elementary school reading scores, and the plan
to raise them, too often leads to decisions to adopt a new curriculum when the
source of the underperformance could be more precisely identified as a professional training function (SDF) related to the use of student performance data
(CPC) by first grade teachers (stakeholders).

Likewise, a critical lack of community support for new facilities may be
blamed on the general opposition of senior citizens when in fact it should be
more precisely dealt with as a board function (SDF) related to customer focus
(CPC) on the needs of retired community members (stakeholders) who have
never received the analysis of the higher costs of maintaining deteriorating existing facilities. In short, the new plan would have less of an impact on their future
taxes and should be supported.

In all three cases, an emphasis on incorrect or less-precise descriptions of the
problem will usually lead to more costly, less-effective solutions and will not resolve the underlying behaviors that are ultimately responsible for the problem.
Interventions need to be guided by the thorough diagnosis of the underlying
causes of underperformance, including the identification of the stakeholder
group central to the problem and the solution. Failure to identify the root causes
of problems leaves the real problem unsolved and recurring.

The third dimension, the "Engagement and Action Dimension" of districts
and schools, is usually unseen or ignored within the educational black box. Most
of the meaningful work gets accomplished there, in the depths of the interactions, but it is the area that is least known and understood. Within this dimension are found the organization's cultural inhibitors to progress, the informal and
undocumented behaviors that maintain the status quo, as well as the positive
and enthusiastic energy and resources that make improvements possible.

Descriptions of work within the depth of the organization can be examined
and discussed as VSPI. Many of the strategies used earlier in this book addressed
the interactions among the SDF, one or more CPC, and stakeholders that were
thought to contribute to outcomes. Educators need to develop the observation

skills that identify the unique combinations that have an impact on performance and to connect the appropriate intervention for each unique combination. (See Strategy Fifty.)

LEADERSHIP IN EDUCATION

Like the riverboat captain that needed both a peerless memory of the river and an awareness of many small changes that required quick adjustments to plans to achieve safe passage, educational leaders need to observe and assess three dimensions continuously in order to facilitate a positive influence on performance quality. Today, the individual's memory is insufficient to the task. Clinical practice provides the techniques and protocols for the collection, analysis, and use of adult, student, and organization data to examine, understand, and treat problems within the black box of the district and school.

All school employees need to understand the internal anatomy and physiology of the school and its parts, and the interactions among the parts, in order to confirm the current state of performance reality. With confirmation of the new three-dimensional realities, educators can analyze current performance, diagnose obstacles to improvements, and prescribe interventions that meet unique circumstances and create the next new state.

Confirmation of the "new state" of the river is dependent on the pilot's ability to understand the benchmarks and signposts, even as they change relative to the greater course of the river. Clinical practice leadership requires a multidimensional understanding of the organization and all of its parts, not only as they are but also as they are influenced by other performance changes and are disguised or become more complex.

Effective leaders (diagnosticians) usually are, and should be, the first to realize that the new state is real, how it is manifest in the behaviors and activities of stakeholders, and if the behaviors and activities need further change. These leaders have "antennae" that are extremely sensitive to the school environment. What makes these leaders different from others is that they collect information in a variety of ways and they decode it rapidly and correctly to enhance decision making.

With their superior antennae, river pilots thrived in a risky environment. However, in today's district and school "pressure cooker" environments, even leaders with similar antennae cannot sustain institutional performance improvement alone. Staff members, individually and on teams, need to acquire information that produces understanding of the interactions and behaviors in all three dimensions in order to make decisions that will sustain and improve performance anywhere in the district and school.

CHAPTER THIRTEEN STRATEGIES

Strategy Forty-Nine: Learning to Pilot Change

Learning to "pilot" improvement processes through the ever-changing environment is a real challenge. This strategy repeats some of the questions that guided discussion in previous strategies, and those questions are offered again in this context, but now the team is not required to quantify responses. Instead, the team is expected to discuss the on-and-under-the-surface currents that need to be addressed if performance improvement is to take place beyond the current new state.

The following questions initiate the consideration of time on the impact of team efforts:

1. At what points in the process did we experience the emergence of unseen obstructions (sandbars—contraindications and negative side effects, for example)?
2. What kinds of interference and obstructions are we facing now?
3. What kinds of interference and obstructions should we anticipate?
4. What early signs indicate a need to address interference to improvement plans?
5. If different kinds of interference exist, what strategies should we consider?
6. How has the movement of time influenced the path to improvement?
7. How have interventions changed the path we have taken for improvement?
8. What other influences could alter the course of the path to improvement?
9. What implications exist for training team members as a result of obstructions and influences?
10. What can be done to eliminate some of the interfering influences in future efforts?
11. What personal behaviors, information collection, work locations, and interactions would help reduce concerns about obstructions, interference, and negative influences on the flow to higher performance?

Strategy Fifty: Pinpointing Locations for Intervention

In this chapter, three different examples of the interactions among the three dimensions of space were provided. The examples of stakeholder groups included high school athletic director and coaches, first grade teachers, and senior citizens. From Strategies Ten, Fourteen, Fifteen, Twenty, Thirty, or Thirty-Seven select a problem that has examples of all three dimensions (SDF, CPC, and stakeholder interactions.) Create a statement that summarizes these critical points where interventions that include internal relationships and actions can be made to improve performance.

The purpose of this strategy is to produce a more-precise description of the problem and create a smaller, more-precise prescription that will boost performance and reduce energy and resource consumption of larger interventions.

1. Statement of the problem (from Strategy ___):
2. Identify the school and district functions (SDF) that will be addressed.
3. Identify the critical performance categories (CPC) that will be addressed.
4. Identify the stakeholder group(s) and behaviors that will be addressed.
5. Identify the organizational levels at which the three dimensions interact.
6. Rewrite the information collected for steps 2, 3, 4, and 5 more precisely.
7. Write a prescription to address the stated problem.
8. Repeat these steps for each problem identified.
9. What observations can be made about the new prescriptions?
10. What findings about the interactions of the organization and stakeholders can be made?
11. What are the implications of these observations and findings for future performance-improvement efforts?

14

LEADERS AS PERFORMANCE-IMPROVEMENT HEALTH SPECIALISTS

Leaders determine the organization's capacity for performance improvement by examining repeatedly performance-health issues, considering the influence of time on performance-improvement efforts, and conducting cycles of planning effectiveness. Effective leaders are the first to know the performance-health levels throughout the organization. And, leaders use clinical practice protocols to help others learn about the organization's performance health and to manage performance-improvement processes.

The completion of the full clinical practice cycle should bring the patient and the physician to a shared commitment to maintain an improved state of health. Completion of the cycle does not mean that there are no additional concerns or that the patient will not experience other problems that will bring him back to the physician for consultation at a later date. It is expected, however, that the chronic or critical issue that first brought the patient to the physician has been dealt with and has either been corrected or its consequences can be managed.

Following full recovery, new regimens of exercise, medication, health monitoring, and wellness maintenance should become routines in the patient's life. Like the human patient, districts and schools that have experienced improved performance need to adopt new routines as well. Stakeholders that have completed the clinical cycle have become knowledgeable and practiced in the processes of diagnosis, prescription, prognosis, and assessment and revision. For recovered patients, a maintenance plan is appropriate; for districts and schools, it is not enough.

The objective must be not merely to maintain improvements, but to boldly move to higher levels of performance health. Too many well-intentioned reforms fail to produce higher achievement because the new staff and student behaviors promoted in the reform cannot be maintained in the existing system. It is the existing system, even as it slowly changes, that inhibits efforts to improve further.

It is unreasonable to expect to sustain and improve higher achievement unless adult behaviors and organizational structures can support it. In a new state of health, the focus has to be on students, but adult learning and decision making, particularly related to basic functions and critical categories, require continual improvement. Leaders must identify and understand the constraints of the system and overcome them through clinical processes.

This is the third of three chapters that look at leadership thinking and practice needed for performance improvement in schools and districts. The first look, at the long cattle drive, encouraged a large view of the organization and its personnel along an undulating path to its railhead goal. Movement of the herd changed with the terrain, winds, streams, rivers, and other obstacles. The riders maintained a loose control over the herd. They managed and balanced time, distance, and available resources along the trail to bring the herd in at the appointed time.

Leaders were experienced in the drive, understood and trained their crew, and encouraged riders to learn their roles well to be both flexible and decisive in maintaining the general heading of the herd and the delivery schedule. Leaders developed plans and stuck to them in spite of unexpected circumstances because arriving late was not an option. The flow of improvement processes is never a straight line of events and accomplishments either. Fits and starts describe most school and district attempts to move toward academic goals.

The second chapter on leadership thinking and practice reviewed how riverboat pilots observed and responded to the smallest details for safe arrival at a distant dock. The Mississippi River pilot had an uncanny visual memory whose mental snapshots of river segments could only be rivaled today by the GPS positioning satellites and very large computer data storage. Like river pilots, today's educational leaders are inundated by a growing data stream. More often than not, the data available outstrip the leader's and organization's capacity for comprehensive reviews and appropriate responses.

Unlike the river pilot, today's educational leaders can establish teams and groups to collect and analyze data and take action to offset negative findings and improve performance. In clinical practice, leaders utilize data to generate diagnoses, identify underlying causes of problems, develop pinpoint interventions— and save time and resource during the process. The amount of data is immense, challenging the leader's ability to mine the right data and still have time to lead staff and organizational change to improve performance.

Like river pilots, education leaders are sensitive to the subtle, and not so subtle, changes within the organization and its environment. However, it is not necessary for leaders to know everything within the data and the organization. Leaders need to know where to look to find value in some of the data that provide evidence to support decisions that will move the organization forward. This very important role of line administrators—superintendents, assistant superintendents, and principals—cannot be performed by teams or delegated to others without sacrificing confidence and trust among stakeholders.

Formal leaders must assume responsibility to weigh together the larger picture of goals, direction, and organization design with the smaller views of personnel, technology, data, student behavior, achievement, and so on. The clinical practice model (CPM) expands the leader's view of the details while the model's protocols and strategies support learning how to weigh them more carefully and quickly. Leaders of efforts to improve performance need to visualize the direction of the entire organization while at the same time integrating that vision with what is happening internally among its parts.

Whether it was bringing a thousand head of cattle to market through swollen rivers, tying ropes to shoreline trees to help navigate the boat around raging currents, or organizing a community's manpower to rebuild a burned-out family, heroic leaders of the past did not and could not do the work alone. The work was truly a team effort that could only be accomplished by committed and competent workers who cooperated with experienced and knowledgeable leaders.

Formal leaders in districts and schools are responsible for establishing the same level of commitment, capacity, and cooperation, while implementing structures, councils, teams, and so forth, to help personnel achieve high levels of success. Ultimately, principals, assistant superintendents, and superintendents determine if teams are functioning better than they did before, if changes have made the entire organization better, and if the organization is in a position to perform at a higher level.

Formal leaders anticipate and plan for future growth by synthesizing the important data, that is, understanding and applying the concepts of performance health and the impact of time on performance and cycles of planning effectiveness, to form a view of the organization's future and how to get there. These efforts to tie the present and future together provide leaders with the perspective on when and where to push the organization in order to move it toward a healthier state of performance. Benchmarks and milestones help leaders understand the dynamics of organizational change and establish a readiness for decisions that will push the organization forward.

DEGREES OF PERFORMANCE HEALTH

Performance health is a concept that measures how well adults and/or students work together within designed structures and activities to achieve goals. Leaders can forecast outcomes consistently from frequent assessments of work quality in a variety of performance areas. Just as the performance-health level of a small part of the organization can be measured and reported in VSPI formats, the performance health of the entire organization can be categorized as one of four degrees, like the degrees of severity of skin burns, as shown below.

The Degrees of Performance Health

Fourth Degree: Chaotic and Unpredictable
Third Degree: Inconsistent
Second Degree: Consistent
First Degree: Optimized Excellence

The fourth degree, the most critical degree of performance health, is *Chaotic and Unpredictable*. This state is marked by constant ill health and underperformance. In this state, a well defined and commonly shared plan for improvement rarely exists. Time is spent responding to crises, and existing action plans produce results that are wildly different from those expected. There is little confidence in problem-solving capacity and no tradition of success. Both time and energy are used up in fighting the same problems over and over.

These schools are like young athletes learning to play a new sport. Natural ability and physical coordination may bring some success for some athletes, but without learning and practicing specific skills needed for the sport, overall performance remains poor. Young athletes without the skills needed for the sport or with limited natural ability appear awkward and are painfully unaware of what should be done to perform at a higher level.

The third degree of performance health is *Inconsistent*. Districts and schools demonstrating inconsistent performance experience frequent setbacks in improvement efforts. Beginning steps to improve performance need to be repeated often as plans are disrupted by newer problems. Turnover among formal and informal leaders occurs almost as frequently as it does in schools performing at the chaotic level, requiring retraining and more preparation time before implementing plans for performance improvement.

When improvement plans are implemented, efforts and results are inconsistent grade to grade, staff member to staff member, subject to subject, and student subgroup to subgroup. Like athletes that experience only occasional success, these schools and personnel have yet to understand the skills they have learned and when to apply them to attain better performance.

The second degree of performance health is characterized by stable leadership and faculty and existing formal and informal improvement practices that contribute to *Consistency*, the state of most healthy districts and schools. Many routines and protocols have been established that maintain focus on the well-being and performance of students. Frequent assessments are used to update knowledge about the current state, maintain consistent performance, and provide data to support decision making and improvement planning.

The organization is like the experienced athlete and team performing at consistently high levels, which translates into more wins than losses. Both the athlete and the school employee know what behaviors will produce success, and there is ongoing practice, conditioning, and skill development. Data about organizational performance health are gathered for analysis and used to plan improvements. These data can be compared to films of practice and games that are used to view performance, examine and break down skill strengths and weaknesses, and devise strategies that improve individual and team performance.

The first, most sought after and most elusive, degree of performance health is *Optimized Excellence*. Teams and individuals in these districts and schools perform at a very high level and demonstrate the ability to consistently apply knowledge in innovative ways. Many people within these organizations have performed in positions other than their own and are able to substitute for others when needed. Changes in veteran leadership and staff do not diminish high performance nor slow the pace of improvements. Administrators and faculty in districts and schools characterized by optimized excellence behave as the best athletic teams do.

The best teams commit time and energy to continually improve individual and organizational skills. Those who optimize performance skills and results know their organization, its strengths, and needs well, and recognize emerging improvement opportunities. The culture is marked by high expectations and a belief that improvement is always possible. The attitude, beliefs, and levels of resilience under pressure support success at critical times. A high level of synergy exists and what looks impossible to those in organizations at lower performance levels is seen merely as another challenge.

Almost all districts and schools exhibit various aspects of performance health that fall into the fourth, third, and second degree levels simultaneously. Sometimes there are examples of optimized performance, but not enough to characterize the organization, or even large parts of it, as performing at that level. Long-term success requires that districts and schools achieve and maintain consistency and begin to pursue optimization. Outstanding superintendents and principals work to visualize the desired performance-health level of the organization several years into the future and work in the present to move both parts and the entire organization there.

Great teams are dependent on the contributions of all players, regardless of roles. While the attainment of the next higher level of performance is the specific responsibility of board, superintendent, and principals, districts and schools cannot reach the optimized level or even stay at the consistent level without everyone participating in cooperative, positive, supportive, and effective ways. Using common planning and decision-making criteria and processes provides every team member with background and skill to perform consistently. (See Strategy Fifty-One at the end of the chapter.)

Leaders must recognize and understand movement from one performance-health level to another and the efforts that made that movement possible. Building the skills of educators individually, on teams, and throughout the school and district is a process very similar to the preparation of successful sports teams—a combination of building the individual skills of each athlete and building the skills of a functioning team. The PICC and SPCT contribute to team development but only succeed when principals and superintendents lead and coach others to improve the performance-health characteristics of the entire organization and its parts.

IMPACT OF TIME ON ORGANIZATION PLANS AND BEHAVIOR

A second concept, equally as powerful as the degrees of performance-health is the influence of time, the fourth dimension. The passage of time impacts all organizations including districts and schools. Gertrude Stein said, "The trouble with Oakland is that when you get there, there isn't there anymore."[1] No matter how hard educators work to get "there," over time, the original plans for changes in outcomes may not relate any longer to success in a new reality. Conditions change and time itself causes new variables that make the plan obsolete.

Time influences processes, outcomes, and the thinking and actions of stakeholders, and introduces many variables into planning for improvement. The mere passage of time can require changes in expectations and practice. Consequently, leaders are forced to think about and utilize time as a catalyst to attain desired outcomes and prevent outcomes that should be avoided. Like the classical example of the river, the flow of time creates a continuum among past, present, and future, changing behaviors in ways that cannot always be seen or anticipated.

Successful diagnosticians learn to recognize and understand the course of the river of time, the patterns and precedents of its flow, and early indications of unexpected influences that require recognition of the new, unprecedented, and unexpected. It is important for leaders to visualize the movement of many organizational parts and determine how they will come together at a future point in time. Plotting a direct line to the goal may look good on paper, but the pace of movement among structures and people varies and needs to be a part of the calculations that are included in effective prognoses.

In space travel, it is necessary to calculate the time, direction, and gravitational influences to arrive at a specific point in space at a specific time when you anticipate that your target will have moved there. Are similar considerations any less important in K–12 education? By confirming the influence of time on prescriptions and making time a planning factor, educators acquire valuable experience by which they can predict with reasonable assurance the time period needed for prescriptions to succeed.

IMPROVING PLANNING EFFECTIVENESS

Identifying goals, implementing strategies to achieve them, and reaping the rewards for reaching them is fundamental in the training and minds of those that seek paths to a better future. In most districts and schools, improvement plans are usually adopted from a combination of selected programs designed to address perceived needs of students and staff members somewhere else. They are often imperfect fits for badly defined problems. Research has shown that individuals selected to pilot new programs invariably report positive results as a reflection of the importance of their time and energy and their belief that they have succeeded.[2] These perceptions are not supported by real gains.

Planning ineffectiveness is not limited to education. In a search of clinical methodologies, we, the authors, interviewed people from many fields, including engineering, law, medicine, higher education, retail, nonprofit, social service, and government, to name a few. In all of these fields, there was strong agreement reported by representatives that standard planning processes were rigid and largely unsuccessful. A high degree of frustration and resentment existed about how planning was conducted and substantial dissatisfaction existed with both the process and outcomes. Invariably, plans were relegated to shelves even as work to effect change continued. (See Strategy Fifty-Two.)

The pie chart in the upper left corner of figure 14.1 represents the consensus among interviewed professionals regarding how time is spent in problem identification and development of a solution, implementation of strategies, and the assessment and revision of results. As illustrated, most project time is spent in problem identification and in finding a solution, the two processes often conducted simultaneously and inseparably. The problem is often redefined to fit available solutions.

Some individuals described their workplace as having a cultural need to spread responsibility for defining the problem, resulting in a political definition of the problem but no real attempt to solve it. Such groups are not planning teams; they are cultural centers of affirmation. In some organizations, these groups determined where to place blame for past failures rather than finding appropriate solutions to current problems.

The clinical practice model changes these traditional and common processes. In each repetition of the clinical cycle, the skills of diagnosis, prescription, and prognosis are refined and more time becomes available for implementing solutions, practicing improved skills, and measuring progress.

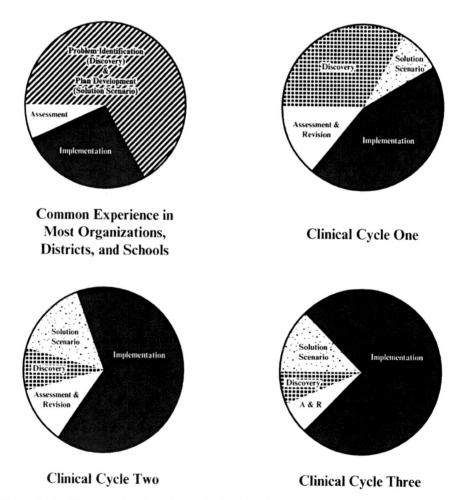

Figure 14.1   Changing the Use of Time in Planning for Improvement

THE "PAC MAN" CYCLE OF PLANNING

One of the earliest popular video games was Pac Man. In the game, the Pac Man character pursued target characters through a maze and scored points by capturing them before he was overtaken by the characters from the side or behind. Pac Man was a circle with a mouth that opened and closed as a wedge in the circle. The clinical practice model for improved planning is named for this video character because as time spent in implementation increases, the "Implementation" section of the pie chart grows and the pie chart comes to resemble Pac Man.

The standard and reliable diagnostic protocols of the clinical cycle have been designed for teams to focus time on the implementation of the prescription, the practice of new behaviors, and the accurate measurement of the real impacts, both positive and negative that result. The other three pie charts in figure 14.1 illustrate the change in the use of time through successive cycles.

The first major shift in thinking in the development of the last three time-allocation pie charts is the separation of the "Discovery" process from "Solution Scenario." The simultaneous problem identification and solution development of the traditional model result in a redefinition of the problem to fit available solutions and the selection of existing solutions to fit inexactly described problems. Effective clinical practice requires that a clear, sound, and complete definition of the problem be developed in isolation of other considerations in the diagnostic funnel.

Solution-scenario development, to be effective, requires that the solution specifically address the definition of the problem through adequate analysis of all information (diagnosis) and the formation of the most appropriate prescription. This is a challenging process that requires learning and practice, and as a result, takes more time in early cycle attempts. As expertise is developed among stakeholders in defining problems and developing specific solutions, the proportionate amount of time needed for discovery and solution scenario is decreased significantly and allows more time for implementation, the second major shift in thinking.

Over subsequent cycles, time spent in planning processes becomes a more reasonable investment for educators, and the clinical skills and tools of stakeholders improve. Time spent in planning becomes efficient and economically sound. Less time is spent defining problems, diagnosis becomes more precise, and prescriptions become more accurate and are identified, shared, and implemented appropriately. Completing one clinical cycle builds a familiarity with CPM practices and protocols and establishes a new knowledge of how to practice.

Participants recognize that thinking and performing have changed dramatically through the completion of subsequent cycles. The second cycle brings more stakeholders together that understand the cycle. Less time is spent deciding what to do and how, and more time is spent thinking and discussing the meaning of new performance data in developing the next diagnosis and prescription. By the end of the third cycle, many participants can analyze, discuss, and present their findings; make diagnoses, prescriptions, and prognoses; and identify the milestones, potential contraindications, and expected side effects.

By the end of the fourth cycle, strong improvements in prescription and prognosis accuracy and reliability are seen. Forecasting the impact and effects of interventions becomes a new strength among experienced participants. These stakeholders become coaches of others and are recognized as experts in team work and problem solving. Before long, empowerment and professionalism permeate staff and other engaged stakeholders. As the number of clinical cycles completed increases, the concepts and protocols of CPM become internalized and performance improvement can become a much more routine activity.

DECIDING TO IMPROVE—LEADING THE WHOLE AND ITS PARTS

Leaders need to see both the whole organization and its parts. In reality, some see the big picture; others see the detail. Many leaders are unable to see a combined image because daily decisions require inordinate time and energy and become a bigger influence on thinking than the nature of the evolving organization and its challenges is. As Dr. Groopman cited, decisions made by physicians were most influenced by the last bad decision that led to patient death, disability, or prolonged sickness and slow recovery.[3] Recent bad decisions take up enormous mental and emotional space and time, which prevents a focus on new tasks and challenges.

We can be assured that a trail boss whose last herd was decimated by stampedes and a riverboat pilot whose last trip ended abruptly on a hidden sandbar with a broken paddle wheel second-guessed their decisions in similar circumstances on subsequent drives and trips. Leaders, by the nature of their positions, receive much scrutiny because the stakes are high and the cost of failure can be ruinous. In education, for the most part, the stakes have not included life-and-death decisions or huge financial loss to unwary investors.

Yet, the accumulation of educator decisions that have contributed to years of school and student underperformance and failure are receiving increased scrutiny. Under this pressure, it is increasingly difficult for school and district leaders to maintain focus on the broad combination of factors that causes organization, staff, and student success instead of focusing exclusively on testing results. Annual test results draw attention to behaviors likely to have caused poor results but not necessarily to the behaviors and practices that will improve them.

Leaders need to look at the interactions among the SDF, CPC, and stakeholder engagement interactions at all levels in the organization. Leaders need to be aware of how stakeholders use their limited time at work, if teams have improved their use of time in planning and implementing strategies, and what levels of expertise have been established and need to be established to realize a higher performance-health level within parts and the entire organization. Leaders need to assess how well the improvement process is managed by the structures and people responsible for them.

This is much easier to say than to accomplish. Performance improvement requires courage and a loss of fear of failure. Leaders need confidence in themselves and their organizations to meet the needs of student learners. They acquire the confidence by observing the impact of training and experience in performance-improvement activities. Leaders should expect that clinical practice will provide opportunities to improve the decision-making quality throughout the organization and the quality of learning for more students.

Where the CPM is not practiced, it is far more difficult to develop courage, to overcome fear, and to reach successful staff and student performance levels.

CHAPTER FOURTEEN STRATEGIES

Strategy Fifty-One: Confirming Degrees of Performance-Health

Performance-improvement efforts begin and end with a commitment to discover the truth about current performance. Improvement is solidified by discovering new and improved strengths, needs, and opportunities. Confirmation begins by answering the following questions:

1. What is the current predominant state of our performance health; that is, "Chaotic and Unpredictable," "Inconsistent," "Consistent," or "Optimized"?
2. What characteristics illustrate that state of health?
3. Do other states exist at the same time in some parts of the organization?
4. What states exist, and what are the defining characteristics?
5. How has health improved as a result of most-recent improvement efforts?
6. What new behaviors need to be maintained to keep performance health at this level?

7. What behaviors need to be improved to move performance health to the next level?
8. How do we establish a broad commitment by all major stakeholders to improve performance?
9. How do we create a vision and understanding of what the next level of performance looks like?
10. What training and coaching are needed to establish the skills that are needed at the next level of performance?
11. Which new strengths, needs, and improvement opportunities need to be included within the next prescription and prognosis?
12. How do we organize practice of the new skills under conditions that improve individual and organizational capacities?

Strategy Fifty-Two: Avoiding "Traditional" Planning Failures

Each prescription must be examined to identify selection biases that might indicate inherent weakness. Determine if any of the following rationalizing statements were used to select a prescription that was not specific enough to the diagnosis.

1. It worked somewhere else;
2. It almost fits our problem, or, we can make it fit our problem;
3. It is less expensive;
4. It takes less time;
5. It takes less training;
6. It is easier to explain;
7. It fits nicely with other programs we have;
8. It is easier to implement;
9. We can generate more interest in it; and
10. It makes political sense.

15

DEVELOPMENT OF A NATIONAL NETWORK FOR PERFORMANCE IMPROVEMENT

The estimated cost of proposed reform efforts in failing schools goes well beyond what can reasonably be expected to be spent in the next few years. However, clinical practice in education offers a promise for success similar to that achieved in medicine for the benefit of individual patients and society as a whole. Through professional sharing and collaboration, expert resources on performance improvement will be developed to build this exciting field of endeavor without high costs.

At the beginning of the twenty-first century, every district and school is working to achieve the universal student proficiency expected by the public and government agencies. Schools that have achieved this lofty goal one or more times since 2002 understand it is a fragile and temporary status, easily reversed by enrollment of new, less-prepared students, a revision in the state test of proficiency, or a turnover of key leaders and staff. Even extended absences caused by illness of only a few students may be sufficient to cause a loss of proficiency in a student subgroup.

Having a vision of universal proficiency and installing programs and services needed to improve student achievement are only very early steps in a complicated journey. The journey may have begun with a display of confidence, but a history of disappointing results in many schools has drained the well of courage needed to continuously engage in the battle for higher achievement.

While some schools surpass adequate yearly progress (AYP) requirements and a few others are close to universal proficiency, too many continue to struggle with goals that have come to dominate the planning of instruction and the use of time in classrooms. The continuing failure of so many schools has prompted debate about how to intercede where student proficiency rates remain very low and how to fund interventions.

THE COST OF PERFORMANCE IMPROVEMENT

Experts cited by the *NY Times* have estimated that the cost for the turnaround of a single failing school is $3–6 million.[1] Using a midpoint estimate of $4.5 million as an average, the cost for turning around 1 percent of schools (approximately one thousand per year) would be $4.5 billion.[2] This one-year expenditure is more than the entire amount ($4.35 billion) proposed by the federal government for improving school performance starting in 2010. For five thousand schools, as suggested by Secretary of Education Arne Duncan,[3] the total would be $22.5 billion dollars, or $4.5 billion each year for five years.

In a report of a turnaround of a Los Angeles School District high school, the cost of the four-year effort was estimated at $15 million, surpassing the maximum of $6 million to be allowed by the Federal Department of Education for an individual school performance turnaround.[4] If only one-third of the same five thousand schools were high schools and needed similar support, it would require almost $25 billion (1665 schools times $15 million).

The possibility of finding the necessary number of new teachers, administrators, and private profit and nonprofit school operators needed to fulfill announced federal remedies within a reasonable time period is unlikely. To compound the problem, there is no consensus about which efforts and programs funded by that money will result in sustained improvement. And it is not likely that any new funding close to the amounts discussed would be made available.

Answers to the question of how to support the performance needs of underachieving districts and schools go well beyond the infusion of financial support. Policy and programs that do not increase the willingness of educators to be accountable for improved performance are unlikely to succeed. Current policy and funding directions do not yet generate sufficient commitment and capacity among administrators and teachers for improved student achievement.

Legislatures, district offices, and schools address failure like the physicians of a century ago, by treating the initial symptoms of failure as they present themselves, but they fail to discover and successfully treat the underlying causes. Policy can set the general direction and expectations for behavior and performance and can excite and provide promise of new and better results. However, policy does not sustain desired behavior nor does it cause people to persevere in new behaviors long enough to obtain desired results.

Policy battles are not the context in which the vast majority of educators work each day. While an externally driven set of expectations can establish and maintain a healthy anxiety about performance results, it does not provide the tools each educator needs to knowledgeably and confidently improve practice and results.

Like the doctors of the late–nineteenth century, educators are faced with the obligation of reorganizing thinking, experience, and protocols to bring clarity and greater precision to identifying problems and developing solutions. Educators need to look at their districts, schools, and students in new ways and use the protocols of clinical practice to establish a unity of purpose among stakeholders, a suitability of action, a sharing and analysis of results, and a modification to practice that is more likely to improve performance.

MOVING INTO THE PROMISING FUTURE OF CLINICAL PRACTICE

Like alchemists and snake-oil salesmen of the nineteenth century, educators, after the first decade of the twenty-first century, are spending too much time and resource trying to concoct a single best solution to performance woes. Today's physicians have a wide variety of technologies and investigative protocols to reveal views of potential problems before making a treatment choice. Education needs the benefits that come from the use of similar diagnostic techniques.

Clinical practice recognizes that there are no magic remedies. Physicians use all four dimensions of space and time to gather and use information about patient discomfort, disease, injury, and treatment. Similar information is available to educators in four dimensions (SDF, CPC, interactive behaviors reported in VSPI, occurring over time), which can provide more-comprehensive information needed for desired performance results.

Educators use the CPM to identify inherent strengths and critical needs, develop available potential improvement opportunities and potential solutions, and implement selected interventions through comprehensive discovery, solution scenario, implementation, and assessment and revision processes. This process produces fundamental changes in the ways leaders and teaching staff members think and behave. These changes are grounded not only in the science of subject matter and the instructional strategies and support services that every student needs, but also in the art of understanding organization and individual behavior and decision making.

The need for more data is evident, but student performance data alone are isolated and devoid of the context in which students learn. Educators, administrators, and teaching personnel need to apply an understanding of curriculum, instructional techniques, student background and abilities, testing requirements, and expectations for student performance, as well as the school's history, culture, leadership behavior, resource distribution, and other variables that make up the context in which learning activities are shaped, to produce better results.

The clinical practice model is a powerful approach that excites, energizes, and guides actions that produce positive outcomes. The CPM can be implemented by a few people in every district and school and performance will improve, but the promise of long-term effectiveness increases as the use of clinical practice increases among a greater number of participants.

In medicine, the increase in knowledge and its application to patient care has been called the "magnificent obsession," and it has driven physicians to find appropriate treatment, relieve pain and suffering, and improve the overall quality of life, resulting in a longer life span. The use of the clinical practice model to solve problems in education should become a similar obsession for educator diagnosticians to establish more-productive adult and student learning environments.

Sharing an understanding of what works among colleagues and with those in training helps educators expand the application of their craft to solve learning problems uniquely and comprehensively. Eventually, positive effects achieved through clinical practice will establish a better foundation for improved outcomes. The baseline of educational expectation and performance will be raised just as the baseline of public health and food and drug safety has been raised.

PRECLINICAL AND CLINICAL EXPERIENCE

Educators pursuing performance improvement through clinical practice have an obligation to record and share what has proven to be effective. Not only is it important to recruit, hire, and supervise individuals with the ability and desire to educate students, it is also important to structure and provide opportunities for individuals to learn and practice preclinical and clinical skills that make them effective participants in performance-improvement processes.

Just as the physician enters medical school with a strong background in biology, chemistry, and related sciences, an educator enters clinical practice with substantial background and skills. Preclinical experiences include analyzing data, identifying needs and implementing plans to meet them, managing the behaviors of individual students, and small class-size groups, and developing effective instructional strategies. Clinical experiences include team membership, leading teams, communicating effectively with stakeholders about team work, and supervising and coaching others to improve their performance.

Educators that have experienced both success and failure in solving school and student performance problems help others become clinicians. A wider implementation of the clinical practice model promotes understanding of school and district performance health, accommodates internal and external stakeholder participation, and supports the development of a research base that improves practice.

The CPM provides the basic concepts that help educators practice protocols and processes of performance improvement, and once internalized personally and organizationally, it guides future efforts to improve performance. However, the introduction of the model only begins the process of new learning and its application to problem solving.

There is a need for the implementation of a performance-improvement curriculum for employees and related stakeholders—students, parents, and community members—who are invited to participate in performance-improvement activities. A significant part of the effort to utilize the CPM is the need for ongoing training of participants in the preclinical and clinical skills needed to understand and utilize the CPM. (See Strategy Fifty-Three at the end of the chapter.)

Just as hospitals serve as centers of both treatment of patients and training of medical professionals, districts and schools need to serve as centers of both educating students and training educational diagnosticians. This training must focus on preclinical *and* clinical skill and experience. This book has been designed to introduce current leaders to clinical-practice concepts, protocols, and strategies, so that they in turn can prepare all administrative and teaching personnel to become effective diagnosticians.

ALL DISTRICTS, SCHOOLS, AND STUDENTS WILL SUCCEED

Clinical practice is different from most other improvement efforts. It is not a product; it is a process. The CPM harnesses all of the performance-improvement activities in a district and school, and aligns and directs expertise, resources, energy, and time in directions that promote improved performance health and higher levels of success. The same clinical protocols and processes can be practiced in every district and school, but the diagnoses, prescriptions, and prognoses will differ depending on circumstance, resource, and other local conditions.

The clinical practice model provides knowledge and tools needed to encourage, support, and realize healing of performance weaknesses and to make healthy grade level, subject, school, and district practices from the inside out. With rapidly changing circumstances, attention and resources are often diverted from performance areas that are in the process of healing before a new state of performance health is confirmed. Following clinical-practice protocols ensures that strategies implemented to address identified needs are not ended before the full power of the remedy is realized.

To address today's problems, attention should be given to the district and school organ systems (CPC) that provide for measures of performance health and progress through vital-sign performance indicators (VSPI). While the diagnostic process may start with a concern limited to one SDF and one CPC, over time more-complex performance issues and problems that involve additional SDF and CPC will be investigated. The prescriptions devised and the interventions deployed will involve multiple SDF and CPC, and if these prescriptions are correct, healthful practice will spread among district and schools causing healing to occur more deeply and rapidly.

Even though many schools and districts have been unable to overcome chaotic and inconsistent performance health and reverse the negative trends in student achievement, the diligent application of clinical practice reverses those trends and creates an upward spiral of success. The use of the CPM makes advancements in both commitment and capacity orderly, aligned, and useful to stakeholders who take time to analyze results and share them with colleagues.

For educators, there is no lack of suggestions, recommendations, programs, and publications that describe how to improve performance at any level of the district or school. These materials and resources are readily available for purchase, and many have won a degree of acceptance after some success. They exist as thousands of examples of how to improve performance in small areas of district and school functioning.

However, these many potential solutions to learning problems are made available without consideration as to how each of them or any group of them impact one another, other programs, services, and performance functions. The clinical practice model provides context in which each of these smaller pieces can be assessed and compared with what is currently used, and compared and contrasted with one another to determine their "real" impact.

Clinical practice makes performance-improvement success possible in every district and school. Ultimately, the CPM makes it possible to view the organization and all of its stakeholders, as well as their attitudes, behaviors, and expectations, in ways only partially seen before. Used with patience, persistence, unselfishness, and some risk taking, educators and students will benefit by using the CPM.

THE EDUCATIONAL EQUIVALENT OF THE MERCK MANUAL

The publication of the first *Merck Manual* in 1899[5] marked the elevation of the practice of medicine from an inexact art to a modern application of art through ever-improving science. This compilation of empirical wisdom focused and organized the process by which disease was identified and treated.[6]

The modern processes of diagnosis and prescription supported by the Merck Manual improved the quality of professional practice and continue to be used in the identification of new diseases, the development of new and improved remedies, and the consideration of preventive health strategies.

Medical arts and science have provided the model and rich tradition of inquiry and clinical practice that has moved human health to previously unimagined strength. Clinical physicians understand that study and discussion of their experiences and those of their colleagues sharpen their skills at diagnosis, prescription, and prognosis.

It is appropriate to elevate the art and science of planning and performance improvement in education to increase student achievement in a similar way. By raising the standards of professional practice; developing processes by which weaknesses, strengths, and needs of districts, schools, and students are clearly identified; and applying only the remedies that are most likely to demonstrate effectiveness and efficacy, school and district personnel will establish the supports for improved student achievement.

A process for the identification, prioritization, prescription, implementation, prognosis, and monitoring of predictably successful interventions for specific performance maladies will encourage educators to address the demands for higher levels of accountability. Gradually, the wealth of information produced by researchers and practitioners will accumulate and be made available in a manual and online to support educators in their very important performance-improvement tasks and raise student achievement levels.

There is a confidence and a trust that emanates from the art and science of medicine that education does not enjoy. The suspicion, failures, mistakes, and errors that emerge in medicine have not diminished the basic trust the public has in the clinical process. It appears that mistakes are more readily forgiven if they form the basis of continued learning and practice. This trust allows patients, families, and the general public to be willing to allow the use of experimental drugs, surgeries, implants, and devices in efforts to treat disorders that have remained unresponsive to other interventions.

Adverse outcomes are perceived to be the exception in medicine, and the potential for positive outcomes outweighs perceived risk. In education, positive outcomes are perceived to be the exception, isolated among rich and

powerful communities where risk is mitigated by resource. Successful practice should not be limited to wealthy communities. Every district and school
should benefit from experiences, successful and otherwise, of every other district and school, something not possible except through processes that clinical
practice supports.

Such activity will produce a broad range of improved practice extending from
epidemiology (i.e., the discovery, examination, and prevention of the causes of
student failure), to individual care and facilitation of student learning, and to
preventive practice that prepares students and adults for new behaviors that
raise performance quality. (See Strategy Fifty-Four to see how the library of
performance-improvement practices in education can be established.)

AN INVITATION

All who are involved in improving educational opportunity and student outcomes should share with colleagues their experience, diagnoses, prescriptions,
prognoses, VSPI, and other important information. Their intent should be to
make available the experiences and findings of all applications of the clinical
practice model. Together, a new clinical database can be built to serve as the
education equivalent of the *Merck Manual*.

Implementation of the CPM will be felt throughout education: from college
and university training of teachers and administrators, to reporting systems and
processes, and to communities and governments. The manifesto of educators
beyond the first decade of the twenty-first century must be to accept both the
responsibility and accountability for thinking, planning, and behaving differently
to improve performance and increase student achievement. Success of our students and our country's future depends on it.

CHAPTER 15 STRATEGIES

Strategy Fifty-Three: Assessing Preclinical Expertise

Consider your district or school as a treatment or training center for education,
equivalent to the role of the teaching hospital in health care. Experienced leaders are trained in and continually practice the processes and protocols of the
CPM. The next "class" of leaders must be recruited and trained in the preclinical skills needed to prepare them for clinical practice. Stakeholders considered
for leadership experience in the CPM should have demonstrable skills in each
of these preclinical areas:

1. data analysis, including generation, organization, and reporting skills;
2. team work;
3. problem solving;
4. decision making;
5. planning;
6. effective communication;
7. resource prioritization;
8. management of student behavior;
9. goal setting, assessment, and reporting; and
10. leadership of others, both formal and informal.

Leaders of districts and schools have an obligation to select and train others in the development of preclinical and clinical skills. Leaders and future leaders need to be given opportunities to learn and practice skills needed to become educational diagnosticians.

How can the above ten areas of expertise and experience be incorporated into the professional and personal development processes?

Strategy Fifty-Four: Recording and Sharing the Results of Clinical Work

Following is a template to record and share clinical work among professionals. The template can be made more detailed, but reports should include at least the information that is requested here.

- Definition of Vital-Sign Performance Indicator (VSPI):
- Graphic Display of VSPI: (See chapters 4 and 5 for examples of graphic VSPI.)
- Scale:
- Key:

  1. District or School First Measurement
  2. District or School Second Measurement
  3. District or School Third Measurement

     Similar District or School
     Highest Performing Districts and Schools

- Primary Symptoms:
- Related Symptoms:
- Primary Syndrome:
- Primary Related Critical Performance Categories (CPC):

- Secondary Related Critical Performance Categories (CPC):
- Primary Related School and District Functions (SDF):
- Secondary Related School and District Functions (SDF):
- Potential Interaction with other VSPI:
- Potential Diagnosis:
- Potential Prescriptions:
- Prognoses:
- Revisions Implemented:
- Outcomes:
- Observations:
- Implications for Future Efforts:

NOTES

INTRODUCTION

1. Harris Poll #61, August 8, 2006, available at www.harrisinteractive.com.
2. Fauci, Braunwald, et al., eds., *Harrison's Principles of Internal Medicine*, 17th edition (New York: McGraw-Hill Medical Publishers, 2008).
3. Harrison, Adams, et al. eds., *Harrison's Principles of Internal Medicine*, 5th edition (New York: McGraw-Hill Medical Publishers, 1966).
4. Voltaire is the pen name of Francois-Marie Arouet (1694–1778), French author, humanist, rationalist, and satirist.
5. Editors of *Merck's Manual of Materia Medica*, Merck & Company, Inc.; and Merck Research Laboratories, publishers, 11th and 18th editions, 1966 and 2006 respectively.
6. Swift, Jonathan, "A Modest Proposal for Preventing the Children of Poor People in Ireland from Being a Burden to Their Parents or Country, and for Making Them Beneficial to the Public," 1729.

CHAPTER 1

1. Groopman, Jerome, M.D., *How Doctors Think* (New York: Houghton-Mifflin Company, 2007).

CHAPTER 2

1. Lencioni, Patrick, *Silos, Politics and Turf Wars: A Leadership Fable about Destroying the Barriers That Turn Colleagues into Competitors* (San Francisco: Jossey-Bass, 2006).

2. Marzano, Waters, and McNulty, *School Leadership That Works* (Aurora, CO: ASCD and McREL, 2005); Marzano and Waters, *District Leadership that Works: Striking the Right Balance* (Bloomington IN: McREL and Solution Tree Press, 2009).

3. A use developed before the twelfth century, as reported in *Merriam-Webster's Deluxe Dictionary*, 1998.

CHAPTER 3

1. We, the authors, have developed inventories that collect self and 360-degree assessments for school leaders, school boards, teams, and stakeholders from the district, school, and community.

CHAPTER 4

1. Flynn, John, M.D., ed., *Oxford American Handbook of Clinical Medicine* (New York: Oxford University Press, 2007), 8.

2. Flynn, M.D., *Oxford*, 8.

3. Mann, Horace, *On the Art of Teaching* (Bedford, MA: Applewood Books, 1989). Horace Mann identified the background and behavior of teachers that would guide decision making to benefit student behavior and learning. The content of this book is taken from Horace Mann's Fourth Annual Report of the Board of Education for the State of Massachusetts in 1840. Mr. Mann was the state board president. In this report and book, Mr. Mann wrote about the qualifications essential to the important task of training children. He wrote that teachers should have

1. Knowledge of Studies

   a. A thorough and critical knowledge of the subjects to be taught is needed.
   b. The knowledge should be as familiar as the alphabet, so that it will rise up in the mind instantaneously.
   c. There is no equivalent for a mastership in the rudiments.
   d. The first intellectual qualification of a teacher is a critical thoroughness, both in rules and principles.

2. Aptness to Teach

   a. The ability to acquire and the ability to impart are wholly different talents.
   b. Aptness to teach is the power to perceive how well a student understands the subject and to know the next step.
   c. The mind of a teacher should migrate into the minds of pupils to discover what they know and feel and need.
   d. Intellectual truths naturally give pleasure.
   e. By leading pupils to discover these truths for themselves, the teacher gives them a natural reward with each new discovery.
   f. A systematic acquisition of a subject knits all parts of it together.
   g. Those who are apt to teach are acquainted with both common methods and unusual methods and know many modes as cases that may arise.

3. The Art of Managing a Classroom
   a. Judgment is demanded in the organization of classes so that no student shall either be slowed or hurried by being matched with an unequal partner.
   b. Lessons should be adjusted to the capacity of the scholar.
   c. The preservation of order in the classroom requires a balance between the too much and the too little.
   d. The operations of the school should be systematized so that everything that needs to be done can be done.
   e. All is lost, unless order pervades the school.
   f. Caution, wisdom, uprightness, and sometimes even intrepidity are necessary in the administration of punishment.
   g. A school should be governed with a steady hand.
   h. It is harmful to the children to alternate between extremes of discipline.

4. Molding Good Behavior

   a. The Effects of good behavior recur constantly.
   b. In the schoolroom, selfishness collides with social duty.

CHAPTER 8

1. Stapleman, J., "Standards-Based Accountability Systems," [policy brief] (Aurora, CO: Mid-continent Research for Education and Learning, April 2000), 6–7:

CHAPTER 9

1. Gawande, Atul, M.D., *The Checklist Manifesto: How to Get Things Right* (New York: Metropolitan Books, Henry Holt & Company, 2010).
2. Gawande, *The Checklist Manifesto.*
3. Gawande, *The Checklist Manifesto*, 48–49.
4. Gawande, *The Checklist Manifesto*, 51.
5. Gawande, *The Checklist Manifesto*, 58–59.

CHAPTER 12

1. There are a number of sources that provide historical information about the cattle drives and the ranges in manpower and circumstance. A compelling and historically accurate description can be found in the journal of a Texas cowboy from 1868:

Bailey, Jack, *A Texas Cowboy's Journal: Up the Trail to Kansas in 1868*, edited by David Dary (Norman, OK: The National Cowboy and Western Heritage Museum, in cooperation with the University of Oklahoma Press, 2006).

CHAPTER 13

1. Twain, Mark, *Life on the Mississippi*, Signet Classics (New York: Penguin Group, 2009), 72.

2. Twain, *Life on the Mississippi*, 47.

3. Twain, *Life on the Mississippi*, 73.

4. Fauci, Braunwald, et al., eds., *Harrison's Principles of Internal Medicine*, 17th edition (New York: McGraw-Hill Medical Publishers, 2008).

5. Christman, Michael, "High Tech Medicine: Small Miracles, Big Breakthroughs," reported by Jim Walsh, *Courier-Post*, March 2008.

6. McKeough, Tim, "Philips iPill: The Ingestible Electronic Drug-Delivery System," *Fast Company*, March 2009, 42.

7. McKeough, "Philips iPill," 42.

CHAPTER 14

1. Stein, Gertrude (1874–1946), U.S. author, *Everybody's Autobiography* (New York: Random House, 1937), chapter 4. Referring to Oakland, where Stein spent her childhood, sometimes she is quoted as saying, "There is no longer there."

2. Self-selection bias is a flaw in efficacy studies of educational programs and is a factor for the individuals as well as the schools and districts that participate in pilot programs. It tends to make pilot programs appear more effective than they would actually be across a broader population. Following is an excerpt from a report of the Fiscal Research Division, a staff agency of the North Carolina State Legislature, regarding fiscal issues in education, provided to the legislators on August 8, 2008, entitled "Ten Questions to Better Pilot Programs": "One of the most common design flaws of North Carolina's pilot programs is self-selection bias. That is, pilot programs are conducted only in places that have expressed a desire to participate in the program. The problem is that participants' decisions to participate may be correlated with traits that affect the study. For example, schools that choose to participate in a pilot program might have teachers with higher levels of motivation than schools that choose not to participate. As a result, it may appear that the pilot program is working, when the results are just a reflection of the quality of the participant schools' teachers. Such studies would fail to show that the intervention is actually causing the desired outcome."

3. Groopman, Jerome, M.D., *How Doctors Think* (New York: Houghton-Mifflin Company, 2007).

CHAPTER 15

1. Dillon S., "U.S. Effort to Reshape Schools Faces Challenges," *New York Times*, June 2, 2009, A15, online version.

2. U.S. Department of Education, "Digest of Education Statistics—2008" (Washington, D.C.: U.S. Department of Education, 2008).

3. *New York Times*, "School Is Turned Around, but Cost Gives Pause," June 25, 2010, A3, online version.

4. *New York Times*, "School Is Turned Around," A3.

5. *Merck's Manual of the Materia Medica*, translated from the German-language edition, 1899.

6. Beers, Mark H., M.D., editor-in-chief, *Merck Manual of Diagnosis and Therapy*, 18th edition (Whitehouse Station, N.J.: Merck Research Laboratories, 2006).

INDEX

LIST OF STRATEGIES BY CHAPTER

Chapter 2 Strategies
  Strategy One: Understanding Anatomy and "White Space"
  Strategy Two: Reorganize the Boxes
  Strategy Three: CPC Worksheet

Chapter 3 Strategies
  Strategy Four: Data Notebooks
  Strategy Five: Analyze Stakeholder Perceptions
  Strategy Six" Multiple Matrix Maps

Chapter 4 Strategies
  Strategy Seven: Comparing Vital Signs
  Strategy Eight: Creating VSPI
  Strategy Nine: Designing VSPI

Chapter 5 Strategies
  Strategy Ten: Develop a VSPI Cluster
  Strategy Eleven: Critical Issue Priority Worksheets

Chapter 6 Strategies
  Strategy Twelve: Pre-diagnostic Assessment
  Strategy Thirteen: Level One of the Diagnostic Funnel
  Strategy Fourteen: Level Two of the Diagnostic Funnel

ABOUT THE AUTHORS

Dr. Bruce Hayes has been involved in the study and application of educational-reform strategies on five continents. He obtained his undergraduate degree at Union College, his masters from Colgate University, and his doctorate from the University of Pennsylvania. He has served as a teacher, coach, school administrator, and, for twenty years, a superintendent of schools.

He has also served as adjunct faculty at the University of Pennsylvania, Lehigh University, and Arcadia University, where he received the award for the student-selected outstanding professor. He has been a consultant to urban, rural, and suburban school districts, and he has worked with Native American communities. As a consultant, he has brought together for-profit and nonprofit organizations to redefine educational opportunity for students in the United States and in Africa. Dr. Hayes is the vice president of LeadershipEnergies, LLC.

Dr. Phil Esbrandt received his doctorate from Temple University and has served as a secondary school teacher, high school principal, and superintendent of schools. Additionally, he has extensive leadership experience in for-profit and nonprofit corporations, as well as in colleges and universities. In these positions, he has focused his attention and that of stakeholders on adult learning, personal and professional growth, attainment of better performance results, and higher student achievement. By reflecting, teaching, and writing about these leadership experiences, Dr. Esbrandt has identified many of the relationships that exist among employee performance, organizational structures and practices, and desired achievement results of students. Now, helping districts and schools learn about these relationships and applying them to improved organizational, employee, and student performance is his professional goal.

Presently, Dr. Esbrandt serves as the president and CEO of LeadershipEnergies, LLC. This firm focuses its efforts on the strategies and tools needed by districts and schools to meet performance goals under the rigorous requirements of state and federal legislation. Dr. Esbrandt and associates assist in identifying practices that need to be improved, develop plans and strategies that break down barriers that inhibit improvement, and design, implement, measure, track, and report successful changes. Designing and implementing productive teams in schools and school districts is a key component of performance improvement.

CPSIA information can be obtained at www.ICGtesting.com
Printed in the USA
BVOW060932101111

275747BV00005B/1/P

9 781610 485371